GEORGE SYLVESTER VIERECK / GERMAN-AMERICAN PROPAGANDIST

GEORGE

SYLVESTER IERECK

GERMAN-AMERICAN PROPAGANDIST

Niel M. Johnson

UNIVERSITY OF ILLINOIS PRESS
URBANA / CHICAGO / LONDON

From *My Flesh and Blood* by George Sylvester Viereck. Copyright renewed 1959 by George Sylvester Viereck. Reprinted by permission of LIVE-RIGHT Publishers, New York.

From *Spreading Germs of Hate* by George Sylvester Viereck. Copyright renewed 1957 by George Sylvester Viereck. Reprinted by permission of LIVERIGHT Publishers, New York.

From *The Strangest Friendship in History: Woodrow Wilson and Colonel House*, by George Sylvester Viereck. Copyright renewed 1960 by George Sylvester Viereck. Reprinted by permission of LIVERIGHT Publishers, New York.

From *The Official German Report*, by O. John Rogge. A. S. Barnes and Co., Inc., including publications of Thomas Yoseloff.

From *Glimpses of the Great* by George Sylvester Viereck. Gerald Duckworth and Co., Ltd., London.

From *The Nation* magazine, New York.

TO MY FAMILY / *V.G., Kris, and Dave*

CONTENTS

ACKNOWLEDGMENTS

$\mathcal{T}$ he results of this project, modest
as they may be, could be achieved only with the help of many
individuals. I am grateful for the cooperation of Elmer Gertz, a
onetime friend of Viereck and possessor of the largest single collection of material on him. The staff of the Special Collections
Department of the University of Iowa Library, headed by Frank
Paluka, performed similar service in making their important materials on Viereck readily available. When the Gertz papers were
shifted to the Library of Congress, Manuscript Historian Paul G.
Sifton smoothed the way for me to continue using them without
undue interruption. Brewster Porcella of the Acquisitions Division of the University of Iowa Library helped me overcome some
sticky problems in acquiring other essential documents, and Mrs.
Margot Spiro of the Anti-Defamation League provided me with
other items of information. Professor Marie Henault, biographer
of Peter Viereck, gave me additional data. On matters of interpretation or translation of documents I received welcome suggestions from a number of friends, including especially Frank
Fessler and George Schlenker.

I must acknowledge the special aid and encouragement I received from Peter Viereck and his family, who permitted me the
gracious hospitality of their summer home in 1967. These three
days of conversations deepened my understanding of the topic
and reinforced my own admiration for the theses that Professor
Viereck, son of George Sylvester, has set forth in his own poetry
and socio-political commentaries. Thanks also to Professor Ellis
W. Hawley of the University of Iowa, who edited some of the
material incorporated into this draft. Finally, I am indebted to

my wife, Verna Gail, for her encouragement and patience in the course of this project.

The end product is, of course, my responsibility alone. Hopefully, it will contribute to a better understanding of not only one individual, but of the world in which he lived, of key events, forces, and decisions that affected his generation and those which have followed. It was with this broader objective in mind that I embarked upon this project.

The reader is reminded that references to the Viereck collection at the University of Iowa will be identified in the footnotes as "Viereck MSS." Among other sources, especially useful were the Viereck papers in the Edward M. House Collection in the Yale University Library. The Oswald Garrison Villard Papers are located at the Harvard University Library. Viereck's scrapbook file is on deposit at the New York City Public Library. Citations to the Gertz MSS, as indicated earlier, allude to the collection at the Library of Congress.

GEORGE SYLVESTER VIERECK / GERMAN-AMERICAN PROPAGANDIST

In the modern era, Germany's prestige as a great power reached its apogee between the accession of Wilhelm II in 1890 and the plunge into war in August, 1914. The rise of the Hitler regime twenty years later, with its threat to world order and humane values, created an even more powerful state—but it could hardly lay claim to the kind of prestige that comes from practicing at least the elemental forms of domestic and international ethics. In both of these epochs George Sylvester Viereck emerged as America's most prominent defender and apologist for the cause and reputation of Germany.

The mirror of Viereck's career reflects the erratic course of pro-German nationalist sentiment in the United States during the first four decades of this century. In this same mirror we also catch revealing glimpses of other movements and issues, such as anti-puritanism in literature, dissent in wartime, ethnic and third-party politics, historical revisionism, Freudianism, and isolationism. Viereck's career was a complex one, involved as it was with both political and literary, domestic and foreign affairs. It is therefore not easy to offer a simplified thesis to sum up his career. Generally, it is contended that Viereck succeeded in producing effective propaganda for the cause of Germany but that the indifference or intractability of most German-Americans and the folly of German policies subverted his efforts; he also lost contact with political realities as a result of his own narcissistic and aesthetic values and fixations. It is implied, too, that these personality traits did not necessarily detract from his ability to gain the confidence of many great men of his time, and that his commentaries on these distinguished figures and their work offer fruitful insights into the spirit of the age. Yet these personal characteristics also help account for Viereck's stubborn defense of German fascism and his glossing-over of its immoral character.

More specifically, I will argue that Viereck displayed a dual loyalty, but that his primary commitment was to America, and that his interpretation of American interests ofttimes coincided with that of native isolationists. He went beyond most isolationists, however, in his eagerness to enhance the role of German-Americans in national political and social affairs and to defend the land of his forefathers against her detractors. The events of his career indicate that in spite of the ultimate failure of his causes, he rightfully earned a reputation as the most prominent, the most literate, and the most sophisticated of all of Germany's defenders in the United States during the period spanning two world wars.

A question that now suggests itself is whether or not pro-German nationalism had any important impact on American political policy or social standards. The answer is a qualified negative. By itself it was a negligible force in that English political ideals in America were never seriously threatened by German nationalist ideas or attitudes, but in combination with other forces—such as traditional isolationism and Irish-American Anglophobia—pro-Germanism played a noticeable role, especially in the isolationist movements preceding both wars and in the revisionism that followed World War I. In all of these movements, Viereck was to achieve national prominence as a spokesman for the German nationalist point of view in America. The main points of his message were that America had nothing to fear from the rise of German nationalism, that Germany had neither the aim nor the ability to conquer or dominate the United States, that Germany wished only to play a role in Europe commensurate with her intellectual and industrial preeminence on the Continent, that the American people should be educated to appreciate more the German heritage imparted by immigrants from the Fatherland, that German-Americans should be more prominently represented in domestic politics, and that American diplomatic policy should be less favorable to England and more friendly to the aspirations of German nationalists.

It is also worth noting that Viereck's pro-Germanism included a strong antipathy toward puritan moral codes in America. In fact, his devotion to aesthetic freedom and anti-puritanism in literature preceded his commitment to the German-American ethnic movement. In three books of poetry between 1904 and 1912 he assaulted traditional moral taboos with sensuous verse that reflected the influence of the "decadent" school of European poets.[1] Although some German-Americans, including George Sylvester's father Louis, promoted the idea of *persönliche Freiheit* or personal freedom and associated it with pro-Germanism, the relaxing of moral restraints on literary topics was not popular with such major groups as German-American Catholics and Lutherans. Thus Viereck's involvement in the prewar movement against traditional moral standards in literature was not specifically German-American in scope, but was part of a wider campaign that cut across ethnic boundaries.[2]

Finally, Viereck's aesthetic value system and his narcissistic qualities are stressed because they became evident early and remained operative throughout his career. At the age of thirteen he got his first poems published in local German-American newspapers.[3] Six years later, in 1904, he began publishing poems that emphasized pagan-mythological and erotic themes—in a style reminiscent of Algernon Swinburne and Oscar Wilde. Some critics depicted him as a *Wunderkind*, and his presumption that he was a genius became an indelible part of his self-image. He never quite outgrew this immature, inflated opinion of self. He conceded nothing to his critics and consistently practiced the art of self-justification. Also, like Swinburne and Wilde, he extolled art for art's sake and assumed that artistic or aesthetic values were

[1] G. S. Viereck, *Gedichte* (New York: Progressive Printing Co., 1904); G. S. Viereck, *Nineveh and Other Poems* (New York: Moffat, Yard and Co., 1907); G. S. Viereck, *The Candle and the Flame: Poems* (New York: Moffat, Yard and Co., 1912).

[2] See especially Henry F. May, *The End of American Innocence* (Chicago: Quadrangle Books, 1964) for a description of prewar anti-traditionalist movements. In this book May classifies Viereck among the prewar amoralists and aesthetes (pp. 199, 204).

[3] See G. S. Viereck, *My Flesh and Blood: A Lyric Autobiography with Indiscreet Annotations* (New York: H. Liveright, 1931), pp. 1, 202, 287.

superior to all others, including the moral.[4] Similarly, he praised Eros in his early poetry, accepting it as the primordial force that, along with art, gives ultimate meaning and pleasure to existence. He was to become a popularizer of Freudianism in the 1920's and a trusted acquaintance of the founder of psychoanalysis, until Freud ended the accord in 1933 because of his American apostle's decision to defend the Nazi revolution.[5] Although accepting the loss of Freud's friendship, Viereck retained his belief in Freudian pansexualism—employing it in two novels written in the last fifteen years of his life.[6]

[4] E. g., "There is no god save Beauty, and law / Save that of Numbers richly musical." From "A Poet's Creed," in Viereck, *Nineveh and Other Poems*.

[5] See letter, S. Freud to G. S. Viereck, April 16, 1933, in Ernst Freud, ed., *Letters of Sigmund Freud* (New York: McGraw-Hill, 1964), pp. 416–17.

[6] G. S. Viereck, *All Things Human* (London: Duckworth, 1950); G. S. Viereck, *Gloria: A Novel* (London: Duckworth, 1952).

George Sylvester Viereck was not alone in his admiration for the achievements of German *Kultur* prior to World War I. By the first decade of the twentieth century Germany had surpassed Great Britain in industrial output and had reached a position of world leadership in science and technology. There were some Americans, including influential writers Henry Adams and Admiral Alfred Mahan, who had misgivings about her search for empire, but one may surmise that many of those who distrusted Germany's foreign policy felt a grudging respect for her technological progress. German-Americans, in particular, expressed through their newspapers a sense of special pride in the accomplishments of the Second Reich, not only in its industry and science, but also in its progressive social legislation and its high level of scholarship. The German people, too, had become conscious of themselves as the foremost power on the continent of Europe, and their leaders had proclaimed Germany's right to "a place in the sun," which in effect meant that they wished to make Germany equal to Great Britain as a world power. Editors of German-language journals and papers in the United States, reaching an audience of nearly a million subscribers, generally accepted such German aspirations as legitimate and not necessarily detrimental to world peace; indeed, they tended to view the Kaiser as a leader who was instrumental in preserving the peace of Europe.[1]

[1] Foster Rhea Dulles, *America's Rise to World Power, 1898–1954* (New York: Harper and Bros., 1955), pp. 34, 61–62, 74; Fritz Fischer, *Germany's Aims in the First World War* (New York: W. W. Norton, 1967), pp. 7–8, 158–60; Carl Wittke, *The German-Language Press in*

It was in this setting, between 1908 and 1914, that Viereck commenced a noteworthy, if erratic, career as an "interpreter" of Germany to America. In a sense he was merely joining a number of other such "interpreters." But he was a distinctive figure among pro-German spokesmen in that he could claim kinship with Kaiser Wilhelm II and enjoy a reputation as the most prominent German-American poet of the prewar decade. To some literary critics he was a *Wunderkind*. He likewise distinguished himself by editing an outstanding literary journal and enlisting the aid of Theodore Roosevelt in fostering closer cultural relations between Germany and America. Furthermore, unlike the typical promoter of German-Americanism, he made little effort to work through ethnic societies. The only such group he belonged to in this prewar period was the German-American United Societies of New York, and he does not seem to have played an active role in its program. Instead he worked through his journalism and through his talents as an essayist, displaying a strong tendency toward egocentrism and individualism, qualities that help account for his evident reluctance to accept or work within the discipline or restraint of organizations.

Clearly, to understand Viereck and his career, one must be aware not only of the milieu in which he began his work as a propagandist but also of the peculiar experiences and influences that were to shape his values, personality, and behavior. In his decision to become an interpreter of Germany to America he was influenced strongly by the example of his father, the success of a book of impressions about Germany in 1909, the support of Hugo Muensterberg, and the interest of Theodore Roosevelt in enhancing cultural interchange between America and Germany.

Born on December 31, 1884, in Munich, Sylvester (as his friends were to call him) had a rather distinguished, if clouded, ancestry. His father Louis was reputed to be a son of Kaiser Wilhelm I, although another relative of the Hohenzollern family assumed legal paternity of the child born out of wedlock to Ed-

America (Lexington: University of Kentucky Press, 1957), pp. 237, 244; Carl Wittke, *German-Americans and the World War* (Columbus: Ohio State Archeological and Historical Society, 1936), p. 3.

wina Viereck, a leading German actress.[2] Apparently alienated in part by the uncertainties of his birth, Louis ignored his royal connections and worked as a publicist for the Social Democratic party for about a decade until leaving its ranks in the late 1880's. In 1896 he moved to the United States, where he settled the rest of the family a year later. Within the next decade Louis not only reconciled himself with the nationalistic and aristocratic tendencies of the German Empire but in fact became a publicist for German-American causes and an apologist for the political policies of the German government.[3]

Inspired by his earlier training as a political editor and publicist and encouraged by German-American friends in New York, the elder Viereck in 1907 launched a new monthly periodical called *Der Deutsche Vorkämpfer* (*German Pioneer*). The editors announced their intention to promote and lobby for the teaching of German in the schools, to oppose attempts by various groups to restrict immigration and thereby preserve Anglo-Saxon ethnic domination, to discourage the enactment of prohibition laws, and to help put an end to "puritanic" restrictions on personal freedom (*persönliche Freiheit*) such as the legal regulation of activities on the Sabbath.[4]

Although accepting a staff position on the journal, Sylvester remained in the background during the four-year life span of his father's magazine. Nevertheless, the experience prepared him for a similar effort of his own a few years later. In the meantime, he was riding the crest of national attention as a poet, a position he attained from publication of *Nineveh and Other Poems* in 1907. Critics like James Huneker, Clayton Hamilton, and Shaemas O'Sheel extolled Viereck as a *Wunderkind* and genius who not

---

[2] G. S. Viereck, *My Flesh and Blood: A Lyric Autobiography with Indiscreet Annotations* (New York: H. Liveright, 1931), pp. 3, 236–38; *Boston Herald*, April 26, 1931, p. D-1; Otis Notman, "Viereck, Hohenzollern?" *New York Times—Saturday Review of Books*, June 29, 1907, p. 413.

[3] Viereck, *My Flesh and Blood*, pp. 236–38; Guenther Roth, *The Social Democrats in Imperial Germany* (Totowa, N.J.: Bedminister Press, 1963), p. 178; Franz Mehring, *Geschichte der Deutschen Sozial-Demokratie* (Berlin: Dietz Verlag, 1960), pp. 635, 758.

[4] *Der Deutsche Vorkämpfer* I (January, 1907): 1.

only contributed some excellent poetry but also broke the hold of puritan moralism on American poetry.[5] But the acclaim was relatively short-lived. There were a few observers who noted the extreme subjectivism—even narcissistic preoccupation with self, the artificial posing, the gaudiness of the metaphors. The themes and style were reminiscent of Poe, Wilde, and Swinburne, all of whom inspired Viereck. Interestingly, he admitted less attachment to Nietzsche and Heine, whom he said were the only Germanic influences on his poetic development.[6]

Viereck wrote in the "romantic-decadent" style; its sophisticated amoralism was something new to America, and for a while it titillated. But it bore little or no relevance to the new industrial-urban age, and by 1912, when Viereck published another book of poems, he sensed his own poetic obsolescence. He announced his intention then of taking leave of poetry and becoming more involved in political events.[7]

As a poet, though, Viereck had formed some important alliances that would help him in his later career. One of these, for instance, was with Hugo Muensterberg, a famous Harvard psychologist and commentator on the American character who had been lured from Germany in the 1890's by William James. Muensterberg had praised young Viereck for his first published group of poems, *Gedichte*, in 1904.[8] After that they became mutual admirers. When Sylvester in late 1910 set up the machinery to publish a new German-language journal, Muensterberg contributed a letter for publication in which he said, "I have full confidence in Mr. Viereck as interpreter of German intentions and as stimulator of public interests."[9] Viereck undoubtedly val-

[5] Elmer Gertz, "The Stormy Petrel: Being the Life, Writings and Motives of George Sylvester Viereck," holograph MS, Ch. 10, pp. 8, 14, Gertz MSS; Clayton Hamilton, Review in *North American Review*, July 5, 1907, pp. 556–59; Viereck, *My Flesh and Blood*, pp. 3–4, 385–95.
[6] G. S. Viereck to George E. Woodberry, May 16, 1907, Woodberry MSS, Harvard University.
[7] G. S. Viereck, *The Candle and the Flame: Poems* (New York: Moffat, Yard and Co., 1912), p. xv.
[8] Gertz, "Stormy Petrel," Ch. 5, pp. 1–7; Ch. 10, p. 14, Gertz MSS; G. S. Viereck, *Roosevelt: A Study in Ambivalence* (New York: Jackson Press, 1919), pp. 18, 147.
[9] Reprinted in *Rundschau Zweier Welten* I (February, 1911): 62.

ued the support of a man of Muensterberg's stature, and later, at
the outset of World War I, he was to receive similar encouragement in setting up a pro-German journal.

Viereck first gained a reputation as a pundit on German affairs
through a book, *The Confessions of a Barbarian,* that recorded
his impressions of Germany after his initial return-trip there in
1908. In a brisk, colorful style he presented a favorable picture of
German society while proclaiming his own overriding emotional
attachment to the United States.[10] He also used the occasion to
speak to German audiences about America. Inspired by this success, he envisioned possibilities of a new era of American-German
cultural relations, and he wished to usher it in. He also saw the
need to enlist a prestigious figure in this plan, and he apparently
wished to aim high. Thus he decided to approach the man who
was probably the most popular figure in America—ex-President
Theodore Roosevelt.

Viereck first met Roosevelt, then President, at the National
Arts Club in New York in 1908; but his involvement with T.R.
(and thereby with politics) began in 1909, when U.S. ambassador
to Germany David J. Hill presented a copy of his *Confessions of
a Barbarian* and a letter to Roosevelt, who was then in Europe.
Upon Roosevelt's return, Viereck met with him and was pleased
to find that his host admired his verse, particularly *Nineveh.* After
becoming better acquainted with the Colonel, who was serving
as a consulting editor for *The Outlook* magazine, Viereck found
something probably equally satisfying: Roosevelt's apparent interest in maintaining and improving cultural relations between
the United States and Germany.[11]

Subsequent studies have shown that Roosevelt had mixed
feelings about Germany. He admired her for her material and intellectual achievements, but his democratic convictions, blended
as they were with belief in "power politics" in international affairs, prevented him from feeling favorable toward Germany's
autocratic system. Similarly, he liked the German Emperor and

[10] G. S. Viereck, *The Confessions of a Barbarian* (New York: Moffat,
Yard and Co., 1910).

[11] Viereck, *Roosevelt,* pp. 68, 75; G. S. Viereck to his parents, October
8, [1910], Viereck MSS.

thought him extremely capable, but he also decided after meeting the Emperor in 1910 that he was "vain as a peacock." Perhaps what Roosevelt liked most about Wilhelm II was the latter's ill-concealed esteem for the American Rough Rider. Along with these attitudes, Roosevelt could not deny England's special contribution to America's social and political institutions. The result was an ambiguous position, wherein he would speak well of Germany and its leader before those who were pro-German, and at the same time express reservations or suspicions concerning Germany's foreign policy when communicating with English sympathizers. For these reasons it comes as no surprise that he agreed with Viereck in conversations in 1910 that more cultural exchange with Germany would be of benefit to both nations.[12]

Obtaining Roosevelt's good will in 1910 was especially propitious, because late that year Louis Viereck decided to return to Germany and give up editorship of *Der Deutsche Vorkämpfer*. He said that his health was deteriorating and that he needed a more suitable climate. Obviously, however, he had made his peace with Wilhelmine Germany, and he was returning to the land of his first love. At the same time his journal was in reasonably healthy shape, having increased its circulation from over 5,000 copies in the spring of 1907 to nearly 11,000 at the end of 1910. In view of his father's desire to return to Germany, Sylvester proposed to continue the publication under another name and to issue it as a German-language edition of *Current Literature*, with the aim of enhancing the "culture exchange so ardently fostered by the German Emperor and Mr. Roosevelt." *Current Literature* demanded financial guarantees before approving the venture; thus Viereck turned for assistance to Roosevelt and to Count Bernstorff, German ambassador to the United States. Roosevelt offered to speak in favor of the project before a group of wealthy German-Americans, if a suitable occasion were provided.[13]

[12] Henry F. Pringle, *Theodore Roosevelt: A Biography* (New York: Blue Ribbon Books, 1931), pp. 22–23, 378–79, 517; Edward Wagenknecht, *The Seven Worlds of Theodore Roosevelt* (New York: Longmans, Green, 1958), pp. 241–42, 245–46, 278–80.

[13] *Der Deutsche Vorkämpfer* IV (December, 1910): 1; Karl Arndt and May Olson, *German-American Newspapers and Periodicals, 1732–*

Responding to Roosevelt's offer of support, Viereck arranged for the Colonel to speak at a fund-raising luncheon in the National Arts Club of New York. Among those who accepted invitations to attend were Hugo Muensterberg; Rudolf Franksen, the German consul-general in New York; Count Bernstorff; Edward Wheeler of *Current Literature*; a representative of the Moffat and Yard publishing firm; and a number of influential German-Americans, including Alfred Rau, a close friend of Viereck's. The event was held in early October, 1910. Conversing with Roosevelt at the banquet, Viereck told him there was something Napoleonic about his enormous dynamism. The Colonel, he said, "only half relished the compliment. The moralist in him condemned the Corsican."[14] According to Viereck, as Roosevelt spoke to the group he appeared "ruddy and blustering . . . in splendid form. . . . He held the attention of all from beginning to end, shouting across the table, if necessary, to bring back those who strayed from the fold." Referring to his recent European tour, the Colonel declared that of all the kings he had met, the Kaiser was the only one of them "whom I would treat as an intellectual equal if they were here at table." Moreover, the Kaiser, he explained, was the only one who could have carried his own ward if he were an American politician.[15]

Despite the cordiality of the meeting and the magnetic personality of the Colonel, most of the guests departed without pledging specific amounts to the project. But eventually Viereck was able to collect guarantees of $10,000, which enabled him to launch the new monthly journal, *Rundschau Zweier Welten* (*Review of Two Worlds*), with himself as editor-in-chief and publisher with the collaboration of the Current Literature Publishing Company. Sylvester's father was assigned as a contributing editor, resident in Berlin. The first issue was published in January, 1911. It followed the format of *Current Literature*, including sections offering a general survey of world events, science and

1955 (Heidelberg: Quelle and Meyer Publishers, 1961), p. 393; Viereck, *Roosevelt*, p. 75.

[14] Viereck, *Roosevelt*, p. 75; G. S. Viereck to his parents, October 8, [1910], Viereck MSS.

[15] Ibid.

technology, ethics and religion, literature and art, new poetry, and finance. In addition, it featured an *Austausch und Deutsche Bewegung* section dealing with cultural exchange and German-American affairs. Viereck told his readers that the journal was aimed primarily at serving the needs of Americans of German descent and of German citizens interested in American affairs, as well as "All those, whether of German extraction or not, who are especially interested in the genius and language of a great people whose leadership in so many realms of thought and action is today unchallenged throughout the world." He added that it would not be an organ of propaganda "except in the broad sense of giving each nation a better and more direct understanding of the other."[16]

The first issue was graced by a letter from Theodore Roosevelt, bestowing his blessing on the enterprise. He commended Viereck on his plans for an international magazine, which he noted was "intended to portray and develop both German and American culture." The Colonel explained, "I have, as you know, heartily believed in the culture exchange movement as being of peculiar importance to both countries. I feel that in America there is especial need of keeping alive a thorough knowledge of German; and I believe that your magazine will not only help in this direction, but will help in the converse way by interpreting American events to your readers beyond the ocean."[17]

The largest amount of space in each issue was given to commentaries on world events, where the magazine consistently took a pro-German stance on matters involving the European situation. Thus Louis Viereck, for instance, mirrored in most of his reports the German government's suspicions of British and French policies and intentions toward Germany's world role. Other articles were devoted to defending the Kaiser and the Crown Prince against criticism in English-language magazines. Another article claimed Germany and America had no conflicting interests—that, for example, both stood for the open-door policy in commerce. On the domestic scene, Viereck favored the New Nationalism of

[16] Viereck, *Roosevelt*, p. 79; *Rundschau* I (January, 1911): 3.
[17] *Rundschau* I (January, 1911): 4; Viereck, *Roosevelt*, pp. 81–82.

Theodore Roosevelt, including belief in regulation rather than the dissolution of trusts. A poll in 1912 also showed that the majority of his readers favored Roosevelt for president.[18]

Despite its prestigious beginnings, the *Rundschau Zweier Welten* lasted only a year and a half. In August, 1912, it merged with *The International*, an English-language literary journal that had come under Viereck's control by 1912. From a peak of over 11,000 in 1911, the *Rundschau's* circulation declined to about 8,000 in mid-1912. Already in the fall of 1911, a poll of readers showed that half of those responding preferred that the journal be published in English. Because of this, and because probably only a few subscribers were German residents, subsequent issues carried an occasional article in English. Viereck cited "practical and editorial reasons" in July, 1912, when he announced discontinuance of the journal and referred also to the financial strains incurred. He softened the blow of closing the *Rundschau* by pointing out that many of its objectives would be met in *The International*. He also made a final appeal in the *Rundschau* for the promotion of German and American friendship as the best guarantee of peace.[19]

To Viereck, the demise of his German-language journal signified two alarming trends: a spreading apathy among German-Americans concerning their ethnic inheritance, and a decline in both the quality and quantity of German-American journals. With the exception of one or two "scintillant writers," he asserted that German-American journalism "represented an investment in business, but not in genius." These journals, he claimed, failed not only as instruments of political influence, but fell equally short as interpreters of American ideals and of German culture. He implied that their readers were largely ignorant of and perhaps

[18] For examples, see L. Viereck, "Die Landung in Esbjerg," *Rundschau* I (January, 1912): 1–6; R. E., "As to the German Crown Prince," *Rundschau* II (April, 1912): 180; P. E. Werner, "The Unfriendly Attitude of the American Press toward Germany," *Rundschau* II (April, 1912): 224–25; *Rundschau* II (April, 1912): 171; *Rundschau* II (June, 1912): 293.

[19] Arndt and Olson, *German-American Newspapers*, p. 393; *Rundschau* II (July 1912): 338, 340–41.

indifferent to the modern cultural trends in either America or Germany.[20] Indeed, his impressions seem to be generally correct in that the German-language press was commonly concerned not with foreign affairs or literary matters, but with local problems and with the "threat" of prohibition and women's suffrage.[21] Obviously, Americanization was taking its toll—in spite of some contrary trends, such as the expansion of the National German-American Alliance and an appreciable growth in the number of pupils studying German in American schools.[22] It was going to take a crisis like the events of August, 1914, to restore temporarily the interest of German-Americans in supporting German-language publications.

Meanwhile, after promoting Roosevelt's losing cause in the campaign of 1912, Viereck turned away from political journalism and converted his *International* into primarily an avant garde literary journal. Its German-American character also faded as Viereck drew more and more upon writers such as Floyd Dell, Richard LeGallienne, Sara Teasdale, Blanche Wagstaff, and H. G. Wells. Among the Teuton contributors, who were in the minority in 1913 and 1914, were Muensterberg, Frederick F. Schrader, and Hermann Sudermann. In short, Viereck's journal lost much of its Germanic character, although it retained something of its "international" emphasis.

By 1913 Viereck no longer appeared to be interested in politics. But he had already adopted some of the attitudes and assumptions that would govern his future behavior as a partisan publicist or propagandist. Most notably, he assumed an aesthetic code of values that, when applied to politics, emphasized the role of charismatic personalities and cultural elites rather than of ideology, political structure, or moral theory. Applying his poetic temperament to politics, Viereck displayed indifference to the type of political system existing within a country, as long as it

[20] G. S. Viereck, "Review of Two Worlds," *International* VI (July, 1912): 43.

[21] Wittke, *German-Language Press*, p. 237.

[22] See John Hawgood, *The Tragedy of German-America* (New York: G. P. Putnam's Sons, 1940), p. 290; U.S., Congress, Senate, Subcommittee of the Committee on the Judiciary, *Hearings on National German-American Alliance*, 65th Cong., 2nd Sess., January 16, 1918, pp. 605, 655.

allowed freedom for the arts and other modes of self-expression and as long as it offered a basis for national pride. For example, in his *Confessions of a Barbarian* he defended Germany's political paternalism, its "state socialism," and its "inspired bureacracy" as curious but fruitful blendings of medieval and democratic institutions. He speculated that western civilization was in a transitional period, with authentic democracy probably lying at the end of the road. For himself, however, he admitted a preference for "some transfigured aristocracy," adding the suggestion that the greatest individual development was perhaps possible under a cultured tyrant. He had Kaiser Wilhelm II mainly in mind, but he implied that Roosevelt in some ways also fit this description.[23] In brief, he was interested in the personal dynamics of leadership but not in the mechanisms for distributing and controlling the exercise of political power.

Personal and literary reasons caused Viereck to venture to Europe for the third time in May, 1914. His main purpose was to visit his parents, who had taken up residence in Berlin three years earlier. He also hoped to write a book about English literature; thus he stopped in England for three days, interviewing several English authors, including H. G. Wells and George Bernard Shaw.[24] Although he was to become a notorious critic of British political policy, he had admitted his aesthetic debt to England (particularly to the poets Algernon Swinburne and Oscar Wilde) many years before, and he never was to repudiate this legacy.

During his two-month stay in Germany, he spent almost all of his time with his parents. He told a friend many years later that he recalled visiting several personal friends, but no government officials. He gave a copy of *Nineveh and Other Poems* to American Ambassador James Gerard. He recalled, too, that the possibility of war was not discussed in these conversations—that is, not until June 29. On that day he was with his father in Wildungen when they received word of the fateful assassination at Sarajevo. He related that he did not share his father's deep concern over the possible consequences of this act. Young Viereck

---

[23] Viereck, *Confessions of a Barbarian*, pp. 14–19, 33–39, 63.
[24] *New York Times*, May 17, 1914, III, 7:3; *International* 10 (April, 1917): 103

seemingly could not appreciate the potentialities of this event as a pretext for war.[25] With Europe sliding toward war, he embarked for home in mid-July and arrived in Boston near the end of the month.

[25] Gertz, "Stormy Petrel," Ch. 22, pp. 12–14.

*T*he outbreak of the war in
August, 1914, came as a surprise and shock to the German-
American community. By early 1914 many Europeans had sensed
that war was on the horizon, but in America the probability of a
general war had been ignored, especially in the German-language
press. The most important issue for the National German-
American Alliance on the eve of the war was the threat of legal-
ized nationwide prohibition. After the war started, the Alliance
continued its anti-prohibition drive—but it also turned its attention to Europe and, in the first week of August, 1914, instigated
or supported a variety of public demonstrations of German-
American support for the cause of Germany. The vast majority of
German-language newspapers in America also accepted Germany's claim that the war was caused by Russia's desire for more
territory, the French desire for revenge, and the British desire for
profits. They showed no disposition to challenge Germany's argument that the violation of Belgium's neutrality was an act of
self-preservation. And when English-language newspapers in New
York took a negative view of Germany's self-proclaimed innocence, the German-American United Societies of New York
complained publicly about the editorial tone of these papers.[1]

Yet this early polarization of editorial opinion was the excep-

[1] Laurence Lafore, *The Long Fuse: An Interpretation of the Origins
of World War I* (New York: J. B. Lippincott, 1965), pp. 186–89; Arthur
S. Link, *Wilson: The Struggle for Neutrality, 1914–1915* (Princeton:
Princeton University Press, 1960), p. 7; Wittke, *German-Language Press*,
p. 237; Clifton Child, *The German-Americans in Politics, 1914–1917*
(Madison: University of Wisconsin Press, 1939), pp. 16, 25; Wittke,
German-Americans and the World War, pp. 7, 17.

tion rather than the rule. In line with President Wilson's appeal for neutrality in "thought as well as action," the majority (242) of American newspapers polled (367) in the fall of 1914 declared themselves impartial in their sympathies toward the warring powers. Virtually no one was advocating American intervention on either side. Apparently only a minority of Americans felt strongly about the issues of the war, and isolationism and parochialism seemed especially widespread in farm, labor, and business groups. Nonetheless, the foregoing poll showed that 105 editors admitted a pro-Ally orientation, greatly exceeding the twenty who reported a pro-German position. One may surmise that the majority of Americans were unconsciously, if not overtly, sympathetic to England's cause—perhaps a consequence of America's dominant Anglo-Saxon cultural heritage.[2]

Predictably, George Sylvester Viereck did not fit into this majority. Instead, his reaction paralleled that of the bulk of German-language newspaper editors who believed that Germany had been goaded into the war. Having already established himself as a friend of German nationalism, Viereck decided that he should defend Germany's reputation in America and at the same time support the traditional policy of strict American neutrality and nonintervention in European affairs. Indeed, he was destined to set the pace in disseminating American-made, pro-German propaganda. Accordingly, one may trace the successes and failures of pro-Germanism in the United States by following the vicissitudes of Viereck's career in this interval.

At the outset of the conflict one of Germany's problems was improving her image in the American mind. Although Americans tended to be suspicious of the policies and power of both England and Germany, the former had taken steps after 1900 to insure friendly relations with the United States, whereas the German Empire had not yet offset the distrust aroused by its previous "power plays" in Samoa, Venezuela, and the Philippines. Prior to 1914, in fact, the United States had not played an important

[2] "American Sympathies in the War," *Literary Digest*, November 14, 1914, pp. 939–41, 974–78; Link, *Wilson: Struggle for Neutrality*, pp. 25–27; Harold D. Lasswell, *Propaganda Technique in the World War* (New York: Alfred Knopf, 1927), 187.

part in Germany's *Weltpolitik* calculations, except insofar as this country offered an economic challenge to Europe. Germany's main interests lay elsewhere, primarily in her hopes to achieve dominance in Central Europe, mid-Africa, and Asia Minor.[3] Consequently, as Count Johann Bernstorff, German ambassador to the United States, was to observe later, "no one in Germany had thought it possible that the Union [United States] would have to be reckoned with as a factor, much less a decisive factor, in a European war." He recalled that this feeling had persisted through the early phases of the war, resulting (he claimed) in his inability to obtain from his government adequate funds to use in influencing American public opinion. Bernstorff was in Germany when the war began, and he did not arrive in Washington until August 23. He then undertook to publicize Germany's point of view on the war and to arrange for the purchase in America of supplies for the German war effort.[4] In the meantime, Viereck had already launched a weekly magazine to promote sympathy for the policies of the Fatherland.

Arriving in Boston in the last week of July, 1914, Viereck spent three days visiting with long-time friend and admirer Hugo Muensterberg of Harvard. From there he returned to New York, where, on the night of August 3, he met with three other friends, Hans Hayo Hinrichs, Alfred Rau, and Franz Borgemeister, discussing with them the critical events in Europe and the state of public opinion in America. About the time they were conferring, German troops were advancing over the border into Belgium. Meanwhile, virtually the entire New York press of some seventeen newspapers had shown partiality for the position of the Entente. To the four German-Americans, it appeared that Germany's "bad press" was due mainly to the fact that American newspapers depended largely upon English sources for European news and commentary. To help redress this imbalance of news and opinion, they decided to establish a weekly journal which

[3] Fritz Fischer, *Germany's Aims in the First World War* (New York: W. W. Norton, 1967), pp. 28–29.
[4] Count Bernstorff, *My Three Years in America* (New York: Charles Scribner's Sons, 1920), p. 38, 50.

would present Germany's point of view concerning the crisis in Europe. In a defiant mood they decided to label it *The Fatherland.*[5]

Subsequently Hinrichs, Borgemeister, and Frederick F. Schrader (editor of the *Dramatic Mirror*) agreed to assume the responsibilities of publishing the journal, with Viereck, Schrader, and Louis Sherman of the *New York Globe* serving as editors. The first issue appeared on August 10, 1914. On its masthead it carried the slogan, "Fair Play for Germany and Austria." On its third page, it stated the following objectives:

1) To place the German side of this unhappy quarrel fairly and squarely before the American people. . . . The fact that the German people are engaged in a desperate struggle for existence against Cossack aggression is absolutely ignored [by the American press].

2) To review, week by week, the actual events of the war, so far as they can by authoritatively ascertained.

3) To review, week by week, the attitude of the American press, to combat, as far as lies in our power, the misstatements and prejudices of the Slavophile and the German-hater, to point out discrepancies and to protest against injustice towards a race that has rightfully earned the sympathy and admiration instead of the jealousy of the so-called civilized world for its industry, its art, its philosophy and its humanity.[6]

In another policy statement, the founders of *The Fatherland* decided that the magazine would not pay for articles used, and that any profits would go to German and Austrian war relief funds.[7]

Originally, the four founders had pledged to contribute fifty dollars each to subsidize printing of the first issue. This pledge did not have to be carried out, since the first issue was printed on

[5] G. S. Viereck, *Roosevelt: A Study in Ambivalence* (New York: Jackson Press, 1919), p. 100; G. S. Viereck, *Spreading Germs of Hate* (New York: H. Liveright, 1930), pp. 49–50; *The Fatherland*, August 11, 1915, p. 10; Elmer Gertz, "Stormy Petrel," Ch. 22, pp. 24–25; Horace C. Petersen, *Propaganda for War: The Campaign against American Neutrality, 1914–1917* (Norman: University of Oklahoma Press, 1939), pp. 159, 161.

[6] *The Fatherland*, August 10, 1914, p. 3.

[7] Cited in *New York Times*, August 11, 1914, p. 4:3.

the credit of the *International* and brisk sales brought in more than enough revenue to cover the cost. The intention at first was also to have an editorial staff of volunteers, but as sales began to rise, modest salaries were approved. Within a few weeks, weekly circulation reached a peak of over 100,000 copies, and in 1915 it leveled off at about 75,000, the largest circulation of any pro-German propaganda journal. Presumably this latter figure remained fairly constant until America entered the war in 1917. Viereck's work on the journal soon became his chief source of income. At its outset, *The Fatherland* was received with favor by most of the American press. It was welcomed to the ranks even by the *Louisville Courier-Journal*, whose publisher, "Marse Henry" Watterson, would three years later label Viereck "a venom-bloated toad of treason." To those who were suspicious of its motives, *The Fatherland's* editors claimed that they were presenting Germany's side of the quarrel "not because they owe allegiance to the Kaiser, but because they believe that any other course would be a base betrayal of their American citizenship."[8]

Because of *The Fatherland's* pressing demands upon his time, Viereck found little time to devote to the *International*. It continued without his close attention, maintaining a circulation of about 4,000 copies and meeting expenses, partly because it used the same "business machinery" as *The Fatherland*. After a survey by the *Philadelphia Ledger* showed that there were no monthly periodicals in the country presenting the German side of the conflict, Viereck also decided to use his literary journal as another vehicle for pro-German publicity. By May, 1915, he was able to report that the *International's* circulation had increased as a result of its pro-German orientation. He was also sending complimentary copies of it to more than 200 newspapers and was planning to send copies to congressmen.[9]

In both journals Viereck tried to defend *Deutschtum* (Germanism) as compatible with the spirit of Americanism. An early,

[8] Gertz, "Stormy Petrel," Ch. 22, pp. 26, 28; *The Fatherland*, August 31, 1914, p. 12.
[9] G. S. Viereck to Heinrich Albert, undated, as quoted in U.S., Congress, Senate, Subcommittee on the Judiciary, *Hearings on Brewing and Liquor Interests and German and Bolshevik Propaganda*, 66th Cong., 1st Sess., 1919, Sen. Doc. 62, III, p. 1422.

vivid example was a polemical poem entitled "William II, Prince of Peace." Lyric England had now become "serpent" England to this cousin of the Kaiser.[10] And in reference to the latter, one stanza declared:

> But thy great task will not be done
> Until thou vanquish utterly
> The Norman sister of the Hun,
> – England, the Serpent of the Sea.

Viereck concluded the panegyric with a dubious sentiment:

> Against the fell Barbarian horde
> Thy people stand, a living wall;
> Now fight for God's peace with thy sword,
> For if thou fail, a world shall fall!

Other, less jingoistic contributions to the *International* were offered by writers like Herbert Sanborn, a notable Germanophile and philosophy professor at Vanderbilt University, and by George Bernard Shaw, the Anglo-Irish playwright. The latter asserted in one article that England's cause was compromised by the fact that she was tied to autocratic Russia through her "entente" with France.[11]

The pro-German stance taken by Viereck and the *International* motivated one of its editors, Richard LeGallienne, to resign in the fall of 1914. In response, Viereck conceded that he, like LeGallienne, owed much to England as a land of letters. In this respect, he said, he owed as much to England as to Germany. But he also argued, "If in this present crisis I am heart and soul with Germany, my attitude is not influenced merely by my German antecedents and by my cultural obligations to Germany, but by my conception of my duty as an American citizen. I am of the opinion that the defeat of Germany and her brave ally—Austria-Hungary, would be a calamity to the United States."[12] He implied that if Britain successfully squelched Germany's efforts to be-

[10] *International*, September, 1914, p. 267.
[11] Ibid., pp. 277–81; *International*, October, 1914, p. 318.
[12] *International*, November, 1914, p. 332.

come a great sea power, she would then reassert herself in the waters of the western hemisphere and, along with Japan, would consolidate her power in the Far East. Hence America had less to fear from German militarism, confined as it was to the European continent, than she had to fear from developments that would heighten the Japanese threat to the Philippines. Besides being highly speculative, these views of course overlooked the fact that America had accommodated herself to British predominance on the oceans, that a German victory on land might soon be translated into German naval supremacy, and that most Americans could be expected to feel somewhat uneasy about the possibilities that a new and aggressive naval power would displace the English on the high seas.

Early in 1915 Viereck met Aleister Crowley, an Anglo-Irish poet and practitioner of "black magic" (among other blasphemies). Impressed with the sincerity of his opposition to British imperialism, he hired Crowley as a contributor to both journals. Later, after America's entry into the war, Crowley became chief editor of the *International*. Although some new and promising writers, such as Faith Baldwin, contributed to the magazine, its general quality continued to decline. Finally, in April, 1918, after concluding that his "multifarious activities" made it impossible for him to give the journal the attention it needed, Viereck transferred control of the journal to Lindley M. Keasby, a former professor of political science at the University of Texas who had presumably been dismissed for his pro-German attitudes. The journal folded soon thereafter.[13]

Meanwhile, *The Fatherland*, although banned from the mails in Canada, continued to circulate unrestricted in the United States. The only exception was one issue banned in 1918 because of an impudent character sketch of Wilson reprinted from another magazine. Having demonstrated early its serviceability as a public organ of propaganda for the German point of view, in the fall of 1914 it became part of a larger effort by the German

[13] John Symonds, *The Great Beast: The Life of Aleister Crowley* (London: Rider and Co., 1951), pp. 127–29, 140; *International*, April, 1918, p. 97; *New York Times*, September 25, 1914, p. 4:2.

Foreign Office to disseminate propaganda and promote sympathy for Germany among Americans. It was a program to which Viereck willingly lent his support.

According to Bernstorff, in his memoirs of the war years, there had been no systematic plan at the outset for establishing a propaganda organization in the United States. It simply grew out of other activities, particularly those of Dr. Bernhard Dernburg, a former colonial secretary of the Reich who came to America to seek donations for the German Red Cross, and of Dr. Heinrich Albert, a former minister of the interior and now representative of the Central Purchasing Company, a German agency that intended to purchase strategic materials in the United States. Although Dernburg did actually collect some monies for the Red Cross, his chief assignment was to raise loans in the United States backed by imperial treasury notes and apply the proceeds to pay for Albert's purchases. These attempts to raise money were frustrated in part by Wilson's order prohibiting foreign governments from floating loans in America. Of the $150 million in treasury notes allotted to Dernburg, only $5 million were subsequently used as collateral. Yet, according to American agents, between August, 1914, and February, 1917, the German government did manage, by one means or another, to raise and spend at least $35 million in America.[14]

As the efforts to raise large sums in America floundered, Dernburg contemplated returning to Germany. But, according to Bernstorff, he was dissuaded by England's control of the seas— meaning apparently that he wished to avoid the embarrassment of being intercepted and possibly searched by the British navy. He therefore began writing articles defending Germany's position and offered them to American newspapers, many of which made use of them. Encouraged by this experience, he then set up a press bureau in New York and began to expand its operations. In September he and Albert were joined by Karl Fuehr and Karl Meck-

[14] Viereck, *Spreading Germs of Hate*, pp. 166–67; *New York Times*, March 12, 1918, p. 9:4; Link, *Wilson: Struggle for Neutrality*, p. 31; Bernstorff, *My Three Years in America*, pp. 36, 38–41; *Congressional Record*, 66th Cong., 1st Sess., 1919, LVIII, Pt. 2, p. 1134.

lenburg, both from the German embassy in Tokyo, which had been closed by the Japanese government. Fuehr was particularly knowledgeable on American affairs. Other assistants included Anton Meyer-Gerhardt, also from the German Colonial Office, and Captain Ewald Hecker of the German Red Cross.

In line with their major duty, these agents under the leadership of Dernburg soon established contacts with known German sympathizers in this country, including Viereck. Others on their list included Professor Muensterberg, Dr. Hanns Heinz Ewers (a German alien whom Viereck described as "exotic poet, novelist and globe-trotter"), William Bayard Hale (a Hearst correspondent and confidant of President Wilson prior to the war), and officials of German steamship companies idled by the British blockade. A meeting of these persons was held in New York, probably in late September, 1914, to establish a unified propaganda organization in America. According to Viereck's subsequent account, Muensterberg and Ewers urged the inclusion of *The Fatherland* within the proposed organization. Prince Hatzfeld of the German embassy objected to this proposal, but Dernburg was finally able to persuade the participants that it should be adopted. Viereck's first act of assistance was to secure office space for Dernburg and Fuehr at 1123 Broadway, adjacent to his own offices as editor of *The Fatherland*. Albert took up quarters in the offices of the Hamburg-American Steamship Line.

Subsequent meetings of this "propaganda cabinet," as Viereck was to call it, took place at 1123 Broadway. The president of the Hamburg-American line and his publicity agent, along with Meyer-Gerhardt, soon dropped out of these deliberations, and neither Muensterberg nor Ewers ever became active. The former, according to Viereck, preferred to "play a lone hand in purely intellectual circles," while Ewers was "too colorful to fit into any organization." But the others remained, and Dernburg continued in charge until June, 1915, when he returned to Germany in the wake of public indignation over the sinking of the *Lusitania*. Following his departure Fuehr and Albert shared leadership of the operation. As Viereck described it, Fuehr actually directed the propaganda program, while Albert administered the complicated financial affairs of the operation and assisted in arranging several shipments of rubber and cotton to Germany through neutral channels.[15]

In a book published ten years after the war, Viereck stated that the objectives of this propaganda setup were threefold: "to strengthen and replenish Germany; to weaken and embarrass Germany's foes; and to keep America out of the War by spreading the truth as the Germans saw it." He also claimed that the German ambassador "abhorred sabotage and other illicit acts," and that Fuehr "eschewed all conspiracies." He further asserted that the group was engaged in "propaganda, not crime," and that the German representative on the cabinet never asked the American members to participate in any activity detrimental to the United States.[16] These contentions can be accepted with qualifications— the main one being that these men were to be accused in 1915 of having knowledge of plans to interrupt production of armaments under consignment to the Allies. It would be fair to acknowledge that none of them were to be charged or indicted with committing any crime during the period of neutrality.

As its first major project, the propaganda cabinet set up the German Information Service. Matthew B. Claussen, publicity agent of the Hamburg-American Line, served as its first official director; its real head, Dernburg (a foreign national), remained in the background. In December, 1914, William Bayard Hale succeeded Claussen. In its operations the bureau prepared a daily compilation of pro-German news items and editorials and distributed them free to 500–800 American newspapers. Viereck claimed that much of this material seeped into the press, especially in small-town papers, and alleged that more direct contacts were made with various sympathetic or uncommitted newspaper editors and correspondents. An investigation by American agents late in the war disclosed that between August, 1914, and June, 1915, the German government spent $786,000 on this service to the press.

[15] Bernstorff, *My Three Years in America*, pp. 38, 40–41; Link, *Wilson: Struggle for Neutrality*, p. 31; Viereck, *Spreading Germs of Hate*, pp. 51–54; 59–60; *Congressional Record*, 66th Cong., 1st Sess., 1919, LVIII, Pt. 2, p. 1134.

[16] Viereck, *Spreading Germs of Hate*, p. 55.

Furthermore, the bureau collaborated with Viereck in the preparation and distribution of large quantities of pamphlets, magazine articles, and books. Sometimes, Viereck recollected, it would buy thousands of copies of magazines with pro-German articles and have them distributed to the public through business houses, the American Truth Society, or other channels. It distributed official German publications as well, including 25,000 copies of the *German White Book*, and it sold for token prices large numbers of pamphlets, including those by pacifists and pro-Irish writers. One on munitions shipments, entitled *The War Business in the United States*, was a compilation of articles written by Viereck himself and based mainly on information that Franz von Papen, Germany's military attaché in Washington, had obtained from informers in factories and insurance circles. In other activities, the organization purchased a controlling interest in the *New York Evening Mail*, but the disclosure of this move to the public in August, 1915, offset its value. Viereck asserted later that he had wanted pro-German control of an important newspaper in each of thirty leading cities, and although the cost would have been high, such a move would have kept the United States out of the war. This statement was probably a conscious exaggeration, but it illustrated his conviction that the manipulation of public opinion was one of the most powerful of political weapons.

Besides these publishing activities, the propaganda cabinet helped establish and support the American Truth Society and the University League. The former, headed by Jeremiah O'Leary, concentrated on attacking England for her policy toward Ireland and the colonies. Although pro-Irish in its orientation, it, along with other groups such as the Friends of Freedom for India, obtained support from Dernburg's organization because it tended to arouse antipathy toward an enemy of Germany. The University League, established by Dr. Edmund von Mach, Max R. Hein, and others, solicited the aid of university professors sympathetic to Germany. Through the league's efforts, several academicians were induced to write pro-German articles for *The Fatherland* and *International* and to provide material for pamphlets. Von Mach, who had received his Ph.D. from Harvard and was one of

Viereck's close friends, contributed frequently to *The Father-land*. Next to Viereck, he became the most prolific and provocative pro-German propagandist in World War I.[17]

Finally, one should note Viereck's involvement in a public debate with one of his English counterparts. Backed up by his propagandist colleagues in the audience, in January, 1915, Viereck met Cecil Chesterton, editor of London's *New Witness*, in a public forum in New York. The topic: "Whether the cause of Germany or that of the Allies is just." Viereck emphasized such points as British control of most of the news coming from Europe, the military necessity of the German occupation of Belgium, the lower per capita cost of the armed forces in Germany, the superior German industrial efficiency and welfare programs, and Germany's "democracy" (meritocracy) versus England's alleged "feudalism." Germany, he said, was fighting above all for freedom of the seas, something that all non-English nations favored. The reporter for the *New Republic* called the discussion "cantankerous and unilluminating." He also accused Viereck of suffering somewhat from a "confusion of nationality, for he referred with equal eloquence to 'our Jefferson' and 'our Bismarck.' "[18]

It would be safe to say that England had the best of it in the battle for American public opinion. From the beginning, many Americans were appalled by Germany's invasion of small, defenseless, and neutral Belgium and by subsequent reports of German atrocities in that country. German propaganda, including denials of the atrocity stories, could offset only a part of the negative reaction that German military strategy evoked. England faced no such difficulties. She effectively spread her point of view across the United States without setting up a counterpart of the German Information Service, although a similar bureau was established after America entered the war. Neither did she need to subsidize periodicals or newspapers to publicize her policies. Her

---

[17] *Congressional Record*, 66th Cong., 1st Sess., 1919, LVIII, Pt. 2, pp. 1136–40; Viereck, *Spreading Germs of Hate*, pp. 80–84, 86, 89, 91, 94–95; *New York Times*, July 31, 1918, p. 7:3.

[18] See G. S. Viereck, *The Viereck-Chesterton Debate* (New York: Fatherland Corp., 1915), pp. 10–20; "Chesterton-Viereck," *New Republic*, January 23, 1915, pp. 7–8.

burden was lighter in that many American newspapers favored a British victory from the beginning and made no secret of it. Yet England, too, began in September, 1914, to generate a flow of propaganda materials. From his headquarters at Wellington House in London, Sir Gilbert Parker, chief of England's American Ministry of Information, bombarded American institutions and leaders with pro-Ally literature and sent speakers to the United States to further the cause. In the more remote areas of the country not served by pro-English metropolitan journals, he distributed to about 360 newspapers a weekly English organ offering review and comment on the affairs of the war. According to historian Horace Peterson, by 1917 Parker had fifty-four employees in his section, whereas Dernburg never had more than a dozen men working for him.[19]

The evidence above makes it clear that the British operation was more extensive and effective than the German. But in 1915 Britain's success on the propaganda front owed more to events over which she had no direct control. Her cause was to benefit greatly from the stand on the war taken by the popular Theodore Roosevelt and from the grisly results of German torpedoes striking the passenger-laden *Lusitania*.

The effort to improve Germany's image in America would undoubtedly have been helped if the pro-German propagandists had been able to enlist ex-President Roosevelt on their side. They tried to do so, but were unsuccessful. Convinced of Roosevelt's respect for Germany, Viereck had written the ex-President on August 8, 1914, asking him to contribute a statement to *The Fatherland*. Roosevelt refused, declaring he wished to avoid saying anything that would tend to "exaggerate and inflame the war spirit on either side and to be impartial; I simply do not know the facts. It is a melancholy thing to see such a war."[20]

[19] James D. Squires, *British Propaganda at Home and in the United States from 1914 to 1917* (Cambridge: Harvard University Press, 1935), p. 62; Peterson, *Propaganda for War*, pp. 16–21, 136; Gilbert Parker, "The United States and the War," *Harper's Magazine* CXXXVI (March, 1918): 521–31.
[20] G. S. Viereck, *Roosevelt*, p. 100; Wagenknecht, *Seven Worlds*, p. 278.

Roosevelt remained publicly noncommittal until November, 1914, when he used the columns of the *New York Times* to reproach Germany for her "breach of international morality" and the Hague Conventions in her violation of Belgian neutrality. He also criticized her methods of warfare, specifically her reported bombardment of defenseless towns. Yet he still expressed a feeling of admiration for the enthusiastic patriotism of the German people, which he implicitly compared with the "spiritless and selfish" type of neutrality that he perceived in President Wilson's policy. In fact, he implied a contradiction: that the United States should have intervened to uphold the Hague Conventions, and yet, that this country should not declare itself in favor of one side or the other in respect to the major combatants.[21] Following this statement, he continued to vacillate in his attitude toward the warring powers. On December 22 he refused to sign an Anglo-American appeal, replying in part that "England is not my motherland any more than Germany is my fatherland." He sent a copy of the letter to Hugo Muensterberg to prove his intention of playing fair.[22] On one issue he was consistent: he persistently sympathized with Belgium and her plight.

In the meantime, by his own account, Viereck was successful in arranging and attending a meeting at Oyster Bay between Bernhard Dernburg and Roosevelt. But Dernburg failed to convince Roosevelt that he should speak out in Germany's defense, and a subsequent exchange of letters had the same result. Viereck himself met with the Colonel once more, apparently at the latter's invitation in February, 1915, after Sylvester had written him an "impetuous" letter. At this meeting, Roosevelt said that Germany was "a nation without a sense of international morality," to which Viereck replied by cataloging the sins of England in foreign affairs. Late that same month, Viereck wrote to Roosevelt again, telling him that he himself was the only German-American friend the Colonel still had, and that the latter's defense of Belgium's right to neutrality, without condemning England's past record of violating the rights of neutrals, smacked of one-sidedness.

[21] *Theodore Roosevelt,* "The International Posse Comitatus," *New York Times,* November 8, 1914, V, pp. 1, 10.
[22] Wagenknecht, *Seven Worlds,* p. 279.

Roosevelt, he implied, had been only a "fair-weather" friend of Germany. Roosevelt responded by having his secretary inform Viereck that the "objectionable tone" of his letter made an answer inappropriate, but the latter persisted with still another letter, to which the Colonel replied that it was "unutterably silly" for anyone to regard it as "fair-weather friendship to feel good-will toward a nation and yet to condemn that nation when it is guilty of iniquity." He recommended that Viereck return to Germany where his "loyalty" and "heart" lay.[23] Another bitter exchange occurred in early April, after which their correspondence ceased, except for a letter from Viereck in June, 1916, which received no answer. A year later Roosevelt commented to a friend that Viereck was "conducting a campaign of treason against this country."[24]

One can see in retrospect that Roosevelt tried sincerely to be impartial in the early months of the war, and that he hoped to keep the good will of his German-American friends, Muensterberg in particular, although he made no secret of his sympathy for Belgium—a victim of German aggression. The event that clearly made him an enemy of Germany's cause, as it did for many other Americans, was the opening of unrestricted submarine warfare by Germany in early 1915 and the consequent sinking of the *Lusitania* passenger liner.

In early May, 1915, shortly before the *Lusitania* set sail from New York, Viereck wrote an editorial pertaining to the sinking of the *Gulflight*, which reportedly was carrying contraband material through the war zone. He said the *Gulflight* had "paid the penalty of her foolhardiness," and "before long, a large passenger ship like the *Lusitania*, carrying implements of murder to Great Britain, will meet with a similar fate."[25] The issue carrying this statement had hardly hit the streets when word was flashed that

[23] Viereck, *Roosevelt*, pp. 105, 107, 110, 113, 117–18, 120. Also see Elting Morison, ed., *The Letters of Theodore Roosevelt* (Cambridge: Harvard University Press, 1954), Vol. VIII, pp. 910–11.

[24] Viereck, *Roosevelt*, pp. 129–36; Theodore Roosevelt to Ralph Ensley, July 5, 1917, in Morison *Letters of Theodore Roosevelt*, VIII, p. 1207.

[25] *The Fatherland*, May 12, 1915, p. 10; Viereck, *Spreading Germs of Hate*, p. 64; *New York Times*, May 9, 1915, II, p. 4:2.

the *Lusitania* had been sunk. Reacting with a statement to the press, Viereck declared:

> Now that my prophecy has come true, I can only repeat what I have said editorially. Much as I regret the staggering loss of life, the facts absolutely justify the action of the Germans if the Lusitania was, indeed, torpedoed by a German submarine. Legally and morally there is no basis for any protest on the part of the United States. The Lusitania was a British ship. British ships have been instructed by the admiralty to ram submarines and to take active measures against the enemy. Hence every British ship must be considered in light of a warship.[26]

He continued with the argument that the ammunition on board the *Lusitania* would have killed more German soldiers than the number of passengers lost. He pointed out, too, that passenger liners had been warned by the German embassy to avoid the war zone and criticized the secretary of state for not warning all Americans of the peril involved. Germany, he said, "means business." She "does not bluff," and the "terrific lesson" of this incident should convince the State Department to issue a formal notice admonishing all Americans to shun ships flying the flags of belligerent nations and all ships carrying "tools of destruction." Having just completed a canvass of German-American publications on their attitudes toward the President's war policies, Viereck concluded that his sentiments paralleled those of almost every other German-American editor.[27]

In the wake of the *Lusitania* tragedy, the British ambassador complained to the American State Department that Viereck had "guilty foreknowledge" of the sinking. In response, Viereck accused the British government of "encouraging recruiting on American soil" and claimed that he had nothing to do with the *Lusitania*. Indeed, no evidence was ever produced to support the ambassador's charge. But suspicions lingered, particularly when, at Dernburg's suggestion, he published the ship's manifest showing that it carried tons of rifle cartridges and that it was officially designated as an auxiliary cruiser. Moreover, Dernburg himself, a man who was regarded now as the "Kaiser's official mouthpiece

[26] *New York Times*, May 9, 1915, II, p. 4:2.
[27] Ibid.

in the United States," defended the sinking in a public lecture in Cleveland, creating such a furor that the Administration soon forced his return to Germany. From a later perspective, Viereck would view the *Lusitania* incident as the first major setback to pro-German propaganda in the United States.[28]

As the pro-Germans might have feared, the sinking of the ship provided British and other Allied propagandists with a field day. Many Americans heretofore skeptical of anti-German propaganda were now ready to believe that Germany was uniquely guilty of inhumanity and *Schrecklichkeit* (terror) in the way that it conducted war. Theodore Roosevelt called it "murder on the high seas" and demanded that the United States seize all interned German ships and embargo all trade with Germany.[29] President Wilson responded to the challenge by sending Germany a series of notes that reaffirmed the government's position that Americans had the right to travel on unarmed passenger ships of any nation on the high seas and that Germany would be held to "strict accountability" for violating these rights.

In contrast, German-American leaders continued to argue that England was primarily responsible for the disaster. Viereck himself tried to embarrass the Administration by conducting a poll of German-American newspapers, the results of which, he said, showed that the President had alienated about 90 percent of the German-Americans who had voted for him in 1912. Nevertheless, in late July Wilson sent a third note, insisting that Germany respect the inviolability of unarmed passenger ships. The crisis dissipated in August, after the German government, following the sinking of the *Arabic* (which produced a few more American casualties), agreed to order its submarine commanders to give warning and to assure the safety of passengers before sinking any passenger ships.[30]

[28] *New York World*, August 15, 1915, p. 2; Viereck, *Spreading Germs of Hate*, pp. 64, 66, 68; *New York Times*, May 9, 1915, p. 4:2.

[29] Henry F. Pringle. *Theodore Roosevelt: A Biography* (New York: Blue Ribbon Books, 1931), p. 583.

[30] Peterson, *Propaganda for War*, pp. 125, 133; Child, *German-Americans in Politics*, pp. 67–75; Wittke, *German-Americans and the World War*, pp. 71–78; *The Fatherland*, June 23, 1915, pp. 6–7; Dulles, *America's Rise to World Power*, pp. 94–95.

In commemorating the first anniversary of their journal in August, 1915, the staff of *The Fatherland* chose to ignore the adverse effects of the *Lusitania* tragedy on American opinion toward Germany. The journal, Viereck said, was now regarded throughout the world "as the mouthpiece of the Teutonic element of the United States in the vernacular of the country." Reiterating its primary aim of "interpreting the nations to each other," he said it must also "teach the Germanic element and the Anglo-Saxon element to be friends, but without sacrifice of our dignity."[31] And it was attracting able contributors. In its first year, there had appeared articles by such American and German notables as Frank Harris, Professor Muensterberg, Professor John W. Burgess, Edmund von Mach, Ernst Haeckel, and Rudolph Eucken.

While the propaganda cabinet was publicly congratulating itself in the anniversary issue of *The Fatherland*, behind the scenes it undoubtedly was filled with dismay and apprehension. Only a few days earlier, on July 24, a briefcase full of plans and information about the pro-German propaganda organization had fallen into the hands of American Secret Service agents as the result of a moment of absentmindedness by Dr. Heinrich Albert.

The events leading up to this incident had begun in early 1915, when the secretary of the treasury, at the behest of President Wilson, had set up a ten-man counterespionage unit within the Secret Service to shadow various officials of the German embassy and other suspected German agents. In New York, William H. Houghton had been assigned to keep Viereck under surveillance, and on Saturday, July 24, he followed him to 45 Broadway, the headquarters of the Hamburg-American Steamship Line. Anticipating that Viereck might emerge with someone else worth watching, he called fellow-agent Frank Burke, who then joined him there. At three o'clock Viereck and Albert emerged from the building and boarded a Sixth Avenue elevated train at the Rector Street Station. The two agents followed closely. At the Twenty-third Street station Viereck left the train, followed by Houghton,

[31] *The Fatherland*, August 11, 1915, pp. 5, 13; *New York Times*, August 7, 1915, p. 3:6.

while Burke remained in the seat behind Albert. A few minutes later Albert placed his briefcase between himself and the window and became absorbed in a book.

When his train pulled into the Fiftieth Street station, Albert was late awakening to the fact. Shouting to the conductor to wait while he got off, he moved rapidly for the door, got to the platform, and then remembered the briefcase. In that instant, Burke grabbed it and left through the door at the front end of the car. Albert returned quickly to his seat, but was too late. He rushed back onto the platform and then went to the bottom of the steps. Burke attempted to slip by him, but Albert spotted the bag and gave chase. Burke then jumped on a Sixth Avenue trolley and told the conductor that the man coming toward the trolley and shaking his fists was "crazy—stark raving mad." The conductor told the motorman to speed up, and Albert was left empty-handed.

On Monday evening, July 26, an ad appeared in the *New York Evening Telegram*, asking for the return of the bag and offering a reward of twenty dollars. This, of course, was to no avail. By that time the contents of the briefcase had been translated and made available to President Wilson and Secretary of the Treasury William McAdoo. After extracting a promise of secrecy as to the source, McAdoo leaked the entire contents to Frank I. Cobb, editor of the *New York World*.[32] On August 15, readers of the *World* were confronted by a headline telling "How Germany Has Worked in U.S. to Shape Opinion, Block the Allies and Get Munitions for Herself, Told in Secret Agents' Letters." Under it also was a portrait of Viereck and portions of some correspondence between him and Albert. For the next several days the *World* published its exposé in installments, with appropriate commentary on the evidence it reproduced.

The *World* described Viereck's career as "interesting and at times erratic, his verse reflecting a high degree of weird emotionalism that has made him popular in certain cults of the metrop-

---

[32] William G. McAdoo, *Crowded Years: The Reminiscences of Wm. G. McAdoo* (Boston: Houghton Mifflin, 1931), pp. 323–27; Ernest Wittenberg, "The Thrifty Spy on the Sixth Avenue El," *American Heritage* XVII (December, 1965): pp. 60–64, 100–101; Viereck, *Spreading Germs of Hate*, pp. 69–70.

olis." One of his treasures, the newspaper added, was a framed violet from the grave of Oscar Wilde, "which he proudly exhibits to all visitors to his interesting apartments." However, Viereck's political activities were of the greatest interest to the World. On several occasions, it claimed, he had made trips to Washington, D.C., to offer data and encouragement to Senator Hitchcock of Nebraska, who was sponsoring a bill to prohibit exports of war materials to the belligerents. Furthermore, two letters were published which indicated that Viereck's work was being subsidized and perhaps controlled by the German government. In a letter to Albert dated June 29, 1915, for example, Viereck discussed the best means of transferring cash to him without arousing inquiry and suspicion. Referring to a payment for June, he noted that $1,750 was owed him, of which he had received only $250. He could see no reason, he said, why this payment could not be made "through Mr. Meyer, just like the other payments." If there were any objection to this, he could be remunerated through Ely Simpson, his personal friend and lawyer. Albert, in a reply dated July 1, 1915, acknowledged his intention to reimburse Viereck, but also asked for an auditing of The Fatherland's financial condition prior to guarantees of further advances. In the future, he asserted, he must exercise control over the journal's financial management and "must have an understanding regarding the course of politics which you will pursue, which we have not asked heretofore." "Perhaps," he continued, "you will be so kind as to talk the matter over, on the basis of this letter, with Mr. Fuehr."[33]

Both Viereck and Albert subsequently defended themselves in public statements. On August 17, Viereck denied that he had sold control of The Fatherland, despite the implications in the published letters. He noted also that he had established the journal before Albert or Dernburg had arrived in the country and without having met either of them. He had launched it because Germany deserved the means of presenting her views in America. His only intentions, he concluded, were to give Germany "fair play," to "properly represent and protect the interests of the

[33] New York World, August 15, 1915, p. 1.

United States as a neutral nation and to be the mouthpiece in the English language of American citizens of German descent."[34] On August 20, Dr. Albert declared in his defense that wrong deductions were being drawn from the *World's* exposure. He claimed that no agent or representative of the German government had any control over or any voice in the affairs of *The Fatherland.* Calling Viereck's letter to him "entirely legitimate and unobjectionable," he explained that the implied purchase of control had never been carried out "for the reasons that Mr. Viereck refused to subscribe to the conditions set forth in the letter." More explicitly, he said he had told Viereck: "We were not in sympathy with his attacks upon the Administration, and especially upon the President, and that we would lend no substantial support to the publication, notwithstanding any claim to which it might otherwise be entitled because of its pro-German attitude, unless we could have a sufficient control over its editorial policy to prevent such attacks."[35] It is doubtful that Albert's explanation was very convincing or consoling to the American public. Over a decade later Viereck noted in reference to Albert's case, "The propagandist who is compelled to explain or to defend himself is already lost."[36]

Additional evidence bearing on Viereck's ties with the German government would not come to light until later, notably in the investigations of wartime propaganda conducted by the Overman committee. This would show that his assertions in 1915 were only partially correct. He had begun receiving subsidies from Albert and Dernburg in June, 1915, after arguing that they should help pay for the new features he was adding to *The Fatherland.* From a letter he had written to Fuehr on July 7, 1915, it is also clear that he had been amenable to Albert's gaining control of the journal through the purchase of stock, the payments for which would be disguised as subscription receipts so that Viereck would not appear, in his words, as "Germany's subsidized agent in the eyes of men like Dr. Hale and Mr. Myer." Apparently this trans-

[34] *New York World,* August 17, 1915, p. 4.
[35] *New York Times,* August 20, 1915, p. 7.
[36] Viereck, *Spreading Germs of Hate,* p. 74.

action had been underway when Albert's briefcase was stolen. The $250 mentioned in Viereck's letter of June 29 was probably not for subscriptions, as he claimed, but for subsidizing the new features, and the additional $1,500 was apparently to be the first payment on the purchase of stock in the Fatherland Corporation. Perhaps Viereck saw in this scheme a convenient source of additional income, and he may have felt that he could take the money and retain his independence. But his conduct was clearly questionable, and the fact that the scheme fell through and that he remained in control of a self-supporting journal was due not to his opposition to it, but to the *World*'s exposé.[37]

Along with the letters implying German control and financing of *The Fatherland*, the *World* also published documents bearing on Viereck's other publishing plans and activities. One letter to Albert, for example, suggested new schemes that should be implemented, among them a recommendation that "neutral publishers like Funk and Wagnalls publish books for us during the war," a proposal for building a "strong publishing house which will be a centre of German culture and of books bearing on the commercial relationship between Germany and the United States," and a plan to have Crowell and Company handle the book, *Secrets of German Progress*, by Frank Koester. The latter company, Viereck noted, had ties to 25,000 American booksellers. In addition, it was apparent from the Albert papers that a large portion of the estimated $2 million per week that Germany was spending on secret operations in the United States was going for the publication of a multitude of pamphlets and books by the Fatherland Corporation. In July, 1918, Viereck would admit that he had received funds for this purpose on a regular basis from Dr. Dumba, the Austro-Hungarian ambassador in the United States, and on an irregular basis from Ambassador Bernstorff and Karl Fuehr.[38]

Finally, there were other documents in Albert's briefcase which indicated that German agents had more sinister and dan-

---

[37] Cited in *Hearings on German and Bolshevik Propaganda*, pp. 1425–27, 1430; *New York World*, August 17, 1915, p. 4:1.

[38] *New York World*, August 15, 1915, p. 1:7–8, August 17, 1915, p. 4:2–4; *New York Times*, July 26, 1918, p. 20.

gerous plans than mere propaganda. These documents did not implicate Viereck, but it is likely that he had knowledge of the plans. They included a proposal to obtain control of at least one major munitions plant through a dummy purchaser and then buy up basic ammunition ingredients that otherwise might be used in manufacturing orders for England. They also included suggestions to bribe labor leaders and foment strikes in munitions plants, to buy up the American supply of chlorine gas, and to purchase the Wright Company's aircraft engine patents—all schemes that Viereck would later refer to as "harebrained," and "half-hatched." From a postwar perspective, he likened the theft of Albert's papers to the loss of the first battle of the Marne. The propaganda cabinet was unable to repair the damage. This episode, he said, shifted attention away from British publicists and fastened the badge of propaganda upon the Germans. In the public's mind, "German propaganda became German conspiracy."[39]

The reaction of the Administration to these disclosures was mild, perhaps even lenient. No civil or criminal action was taken against any of the participants. The later recall of Austro-Hungary's ambassador Dumba and of Germany's military and naval attachés, Captains Franz von Papen and Karl Boy-ed, was occasioned by other disclosures showing that these individuals were plotting to sabotage ammunition production and disrupt transportation of war material. No other major participants in the Albert exposé, including Viereck and Albert, were either arrested or forced by the government to leave the country. Albert and Fuehr did not return to Germany until the severance of diplomatic relations in early 1917. Viereck himself was able to remain unmolested for about two years after the affair.

Of course, this is not to say that there were no calls for prosecution. The New York Times on August 17, 1915, published a lengthy legal opinion on the issue by Maurice Leon, a noted lawyer. He cited a federal statute enacted on March 4, 1909, which empowered the government to punish any citizen of the United States who directly or indirectly commenced or carried on any

[39] See New York World, August 15, 1915, pp. 1–2; August 16, 1915, pp. 1–2; August 17, 1915, pp. 1–4; Viereck, Spreading Germs of Hate, pp. 71, 73–74.

verbal or written intercourse with a foreign government, or any of its agents or officers, with the intent of "defeating the measures of the U.S. Government." Leon recommended imprisonment of those implicated in the Albert incident, which to him was a "conspiracy."[40] On August 19, however, Attorney General Gregory informed the President that in the opinion of the Justice Department the government had neither the evidence nor the jurisdiction to justify criminal prosecution. Nor was there anything in the episode that might violate the neutrality laws. Apparently, the New York Times observed, there would be no action against "those who have been active in furthering the German cause in this country."[41] It may be surmised that the Administration felt the public disclosure of the German plots would appreciably frustrate any further activities along these lines. Henceforth, the American public could be expected to be highly suspicious of the credibility of pro-German propaganda. Perhaps, too, the fact that British representatives and pro-Allied groups were active in seeking favorable publicity and legislation for their cause made it expedient for the Administration to avoid compromising its strict stand on neutrality by bringing charges against pro-German propagandists.

At any rate, the government did not prosecute; editorial opinion on the matter, at least in the small sampling collected by the New York Times, seemed to approve that decision. Predictably, there were comments about the ineptitude of German espionage, and there was evidence of subdued anger about this kind of "insult" to the United States. One editor proposed a housecleaning of America's diplomatic corps because of evidence that the State Department had overlooked forged passports by German aliens and had displayed inefficiency in other ways, while another called for legal action against the propagandists and agents involved in the plot. But most of them felt that exposure itself would correct the situation and prevent its recurrence.[42]

The World's exposé and renewed vigilance by the Secret Service did apparently forestall any attempt by German agents

[40] New York Times, August 17, 1915, p. 2.
[41] New York Times, August 20, 1915, p. 2.
[42] New York Times, August 17, 1915, p. 2.

to carry out the plans mentioned in the papers purloined from Albert. However, the episode did not appreciably affect the editorial policy or tone of *The Fatherland*. It remained unabashedly pro-German and anti-Entente (Britain, France, Russia) in its sentiments. And Viereck himself remained unrepentant. His attitude was reflected in a letter to Franz von Papen, written on December 4, 1915, and uncovered in early January, 1916, by British agents at Falmouth who stopped and searched the ship on which von Papen was a passenger. "While I am thoroughly ashamed of my country at present," Viereck wrote, "I nevertheless intend to stay here and fight for justice and fair play."[43] His "shame" apparently referred in part to the State Department's decision to expel von Papen from the country. The latter wrote in reply that he had filed an "impolite protest with the American Ambassador" concerning the seizure of his papers and other possessions, "but," he added, "what can you do against the principle that 'might is right?' " He also expressed his conviction that the United States and Germany would not come to blows, "as we have to go together after the war—for the common sake of [the] social development of our peoples." He concluded with a word of encouragement for Viereck: "I know you will continue to fight for the improvement of final understanding—and that you will do so unerringly and undisturbed by the clamoring American press, which pretends that you make German policy instead of American. The Americans of German extraction will combine to fight for what they think is right—for the sake of their adopted country first."[44]

The interception of von Papen offers additional evidence of the country's problem in steering a neutral course. Because of the submarine threat and the British blockade, America's ability to assure the safety and inviolability of her citizens or ships in the war zone around the British Isles was severely limited. This fact was demonstrated again in early 1916 when Viereck's mother, who was returning to Berlin (via the *Nieuw Amsterdam*) after a trip to the United States, was searched three times and stripped of her belongings twice by order of British authorities. Both she and

[43] *New York Times*, February 8, 1916, p. 1:5.
[44] Franz von Papen to G. S. Viereck, January 6, 1916, Viereck MSS.

her husband were American citizens, although they had been re-
siding in Berlin, where Louis was serving as a correspondent for
The Fatherland. In a statement made public on March 1, 1916,
Sylvester said that his mother had been visiting relatives in San
Francisco over the Christmas holidays. He asserted that she was
not a spy since the only papers she had on her were several copies
of *The Fatherland,* and although the British authorities had been
courteous, she was emotionally distressed by the search. After the
war, Viereck would note that because his father and mother were
living in Germany, his fight for that nation was in defense not
merely of the Fatherland, but of his "father's land."[45] In the
meantime, the issue of neutral rights and the sentiment for a trade
embargo were to agitate the political scene throughout 1915 and
1916.

Undaunted by the public exposure of their ties to German
propaganda agencies, Viereck and *The Fatherland* joined with
other German-American editors in 1915 in demanding a more
conciliatory American policy toward Germany and a firmer position against British interference with neutral shipping. They
particularly wanted an embargo on the munitions trade with
Britain and her Allies. Since President Wilson continued to reject
such advice, he became a prime target for almost all the German-
American newspapers and journals.

That such tactics could backfire was apparent to several observers. For example, on November 18, 1915, the editor of the
New York Evening Post pointed out that the open organization
of the German-American vote, or that of any other foreign-born
element, to oppose the President would be the surest way of reelecting him. It was a great mistake, he warned, to suppose "that
German-Americans can successfully unite to punish the President
of the United States for doing what nine-tenths of his fellow-
countrymen heartily approve." But such warnings seemed lost on
Viereck. He continued to insist that the Administration be "more
neutral" by being less sympathetic to the Allies. For instance, on
December 24, 1915, he wired a statement to Secretary of State

[45] *New York Times,* March 1, 1916, p. 4:7; Viereck, *My Flesh and
Blood,* p. 276.

Lansing, asking him to intern three members of the French Army Aviation Corps who had recently debarked at New York. Although American-born, he claimed these flyers were troops belonging to a belligerent nation and therefore, under Article II of the Hague Conventions of 1907, they should be interned "as far as possible, at a distance from the theatre of war." A neutral power like the United States, he added, had no choice in the matter—"unless we regard international conventions as 'scraps of paper.'" There is no record that the State Department took the complaint seriously.[46]

Suspicious as the German-American groups were of Wilson, they were even more disdainful and derogatory toward Theodore Roosevelt and his candidacy for the Republican presidential nomination in 1916. Prior to 1915 Roosevelt had been in good standing with the German-American ethnic community. But as we have seen, he turned unequivocally against Germany in the spring of 1915. Later he broadened his attack to include a denunciation of the German-American National Alliance as a disloyal organization that was retarding assimilation of the German-Americans into American society. Accordingly, attacks on Roosevelt became common in the German-American press, while only Hugo Muensterberg and a few other German-American leaders would venture a good word for him. Muensterberg contended that Roosevelt was really German at heart and would have vigorously enforced American rights against English interference if he had been president.[47]

Early in June, 1916, the leaders of the National German-American Alliance declared that they would not endorse any particular nominee for the presidency, but would oppose three possible candidates—Wilson, Elihu Root, and Theodore Roosevelt, "the Wild Man of Oyster Bay." Since Wilson's renomination was virtually certain, their main concern was to influence the delegates to the Republican party convention. Consequently, representatives of a group of German-American societies and

[46] Wittke, *German-Americans in the World War*, pp. 64, 83; *New York Evening Post*, November 18, 1915, p. 8; *New York Times*, December 25, 1915, p. 3:4.
[47] Wittke, *German-Americans in the World War*, p. 92.

German-language newspapers held a conference in Chicago, which Viereck apparently did not attend, and then sent a committee to the chairman of the Republican National Committee to inform him that neither Roosevelt nor Root could expect to get many votes from German-Americans. There is no evidence that they recommended any other particular candidates.

Prior to the Republican convention there was scarcely a comment in the German-American newspapers about the possible nomination of Charles Evans Hughes, associate justice of the Supreme Court. Little was known of his position on the war issues, but he was not considered a "German hater," and the *New York Staats-Zeitung* felt he could be trusted to enforce strict American neutrality. He also was supposed to be a liberal and was free of taint from the party split in 1912. Mainly because of these traits, he proved to be the Republican party's most acceptable candidate, and was the one finally nominated. At the close of the convention, Viereck publicly credited the German-American press with a dominant role in defeating the candidacy of Theodore Roosevelt. Viereck alleged that Roosevelt was unpopular among German-Americans, not because he was anti-German but because he was "not pro-American," and because he was "more pro-English than anything else." He disparaged Roosevelt for his "one-sidedness" in condemning Germany for the violation of Belgium's neutrality and the *Lusitania* incident while remaining silent in regard to England's naval blockade.[48] The irony, of course, is that Viereck was following the same technique of one-sidedness, albeit for the other side.

While deprecating Roosevelt, Viereck announced his readiness to support Hughes, provided he would "pledge himself to hold England to the letter of international law." But at the same time Viereck admitted that Wilson would get some German-American votes if he continued his current pressure on England. In an unusual turn of events, favorable references to the President began to appear in *The Fatherland* in June, 1916. Noting Wil-

[48] Ibid., pp. 88, 91, 93; Peterson, *Propaganda for War*, p. 274; *New York Times*, June 7, 1916, p. 7:1. Viereck's "one-sidedness" was especially blatant in his *Songs of Armageddon and Other Poems* (New York: M. Kennerly, 1916).

son's speech at Charlotte, North Carolina, Viereck commented that the President "for the first time in his life discovered America" and had pointed out correctly that "the most singular fact about this great nation which we represent is that it is made up of all the nations of the world," and that its function therefore was not to judge, but to mediate between the different national groups. He also had guarded praise for Wilson's speech of May 27 at a banquet of the League to Enforce Peace, in which the President criticized England for violating American rights on the sea. Three months later, he stated his agreement with several points made by Wilson in his acceptance speech.[49] As the electioneering gained momentum, *The Fatherland* reflected an air of uncertainty about which candidate to promote, especially since Hughes had refused to repudiate the support of Theodore Roosevelt. In this mood of indecision, it published little about the campaign in the fall of 1916.

According to Viereck's subsequent account, it was during the campaign that he and other German-American spokesmen, including Victor Ridder of the *Staats-Zeitung*, met in New York with Senator Stone, chairman of the Committee on Foreign Relations. There, in a long discussion period, Stone solicited their support in reelecting Wilson. At one point he asked, "What would you do if we were to declare war against Germany?" Viereck replied, "We would do our duty as American citizens. We would shoulder a gun and fight." "You wouldn't and you shouldn't," Stone said. "No one would expect you to fight against your kinsmen." Viereck then remarked, "Senator, we Americans of German descent are true to our oath of allegiance. We would do our duty. But, after it was all over, we would punish the rascals who got us into this mess."[50]

This meeting had been arranged by American journalist J. J. Dickinson, alias Josiah Wingate, who was employed by *The Fatherland* as an "informer" in Washington. (He later claimed to have been spying for the government.) It was through Wingate

---

[49] Ibid.; *The Fatherland*, June 7, 1916, p. 282; September 13, 1916, pp. 90–91; November 1, 1916, pp. 202–3; November 8, 1916, p. 218.
[50] Child, *German-Americans in Politics*, p. 147; Viereck, *Spreading Germs of Hate*, p. 242.

that contacts with key Administration and congressional leaders were established and confidential reports secured. According to Viereck, there was even an arrangement under which he would be invited to talk to the President about the possibility of participating in peace negotiations that might be initiated with the belligerents. This was rejected, Viereck said, because he was still suspicious of Wilson's policies.[51]

While Viereck vacillated in his views of the candidates, Wilson's stature among many American noninterventionists and strict neutralists was strengthened by a series of events that developed into a "hard line" toward England. To be more specific, after the "Sussex pledge" of April, 1916, had again committed the Germans to refrain from sinking unarmed merchant and passenger ships on the high seas, relations between the United States and Germany began improving. At the same time, American feelings toward England soured as the latter's naval authorities continued to stop and board American ships, seizing and inspecting the mail as well as other cargo. President Wilson, responding to accumulated American ire, sent notes to England and France, calling their seizure of mail "lawless," and demanding that they respect America's rights as a neutral nation. The English government remained unmoved, and a few weeks later it courted even more disfavor by announcing a "black list" of American firms doing business with Germany. Again Wilson issued a formal protest. In October, moreover, when a German submarine that had recently docked in America sank several Allied ships near the coast of the United States, the President remained silent—to the chagrin of the British, who were highly angered by the episode. All of these actions presumably helped to convince some wavering German-Americans that their President was genuinely interested in maintaining strict neutrality and that there was truth in his campaign slogan, "He kept us out of war." One may surmise that such was the case, although the German-language press continued its editorial opposition to Wilson.[52]

[51] Viereck, *Spreading Germs of Hate*, p. 245; *New York Times*, December 14, 1918, p. 1:1.

[52] Ray Stannard Baker, *Woodrow Wilson: Life and Letters, Facing War, 1915–1917* (Garden City, N.Y.: Doubleday, Doran and Co., 1937),

Indeed, the results of the presidential election of 1916 indicated that the German-American vote, if such an entity existed, "disappeared on election day." As pointed out by the *New York Times*, except for Cincinnati, a traditional Republican stronghold, the major centers of German-American population, including Milwaukee and St. Louis, had voted for Wilson. The *Times* concluded that either there was no "hyphen" vote or that it was cancelled by the "anti-hyphen" ballot. Implicit, too, was the assumption that the German-American press did not necessarily speak for or reflect the views of its readers.[53]

Viereck conceded that the hyphen vote had been split; he surmised that many Americans of German descent had concluded that Wilson, from the tenor of his actions since early 1916, was at least for the time being on the proper track toward impartiality and peace. Viereck himself seemed to feel this way. His newfound affection for Wilson reached its apotheosis on January 22, 1917, when the President went before the Senate to discuss his ideas for a "peace without victory" and a concert of nations to insure the peace. In Viereck's opinion, this speech was "the splendid bloom of constructive American statesmanship." Wilson's "winged sentences can never be made unspoken," he exulted. "The heart of mankind will never forget them." Unfortunately, he seems to have temporarily forgotten German war aims when he added that Germany had gone to war for the same principles, and although she had won many victories, she "was willing to accept the verdict of a drawn game."[54] But a stalemate was hardly Germany's desire. In about a week she would declare unrestricted submarine warfare, in a desperate gamble to force the Allies to their knees; one of the casualties would be the pro-German propaganda program in the United States.

The hopes of Americans for peace, based upon Wilson's formula of "peace without victory," were soon dashed, for when

pp. 196, 214, 220, 312–16, 330–31; Child, *German-Americans in Politics*, pp. 135, 152; Wittke, *German-Language Press*, pp. 254–56.

[53] *New York Times*, November 9, 1916, p. 6:3.

[54] *The Fatherland*, November 22, 1916, pp. 250–51; December 6, 1916, p. 282; January 31, 1917, p. 419; Child, *German-Americans in Politics*, pp. 149–50.

Germany proclaimed unrestricted submarine warfare on January 31, 1917, she began a course of action fated to end in conflict with the United States. The first result was the breaking of diplomatic relations. On February 14, Fuehr, Albert, Mecklenberg, and the other German aliens remaining in Dernburg's original propaganda organization departed the country, along with other members of Germany's diplomatic corps. According to a later American intelligence report, Germany had exported thirty-one agents to the United States between August, 1914, and February, 1917, and during the same period had managed to raise and expend at least $35 million for propaganda, espionage, and sabotage.[55]

Obviously, Viereck's pro-German "Americanism" was becoming less and less tenable in the face of renewed German militancy and of growing American disgust with the Kaiser's policies. Responding to the changing climate of opinion, Viereck retitled his journal *The New World* in mid-February, and then two weeks later changed it again to *Viereck's: The American Weekly*. For the masthead he adopted a new slogan, attributed to Carl Schurz: "My Country, Right or Wrong; If Right to Be Kept Right, If Wrong, to Be Set Right." These changes, he said, would help avoid "misunderstanding . . . and unnecessary provocation." Moreover, he now intended to be not only the mouthpiece of German-Americans, but of "all Americans who believe in maintaining the Declaration of Independence and who, remembering the advice of George Washington, abhor an entangling alliance with the ancient enemy of the United States." In line with this objective, he reproduced a message from William Jennings Bryan, admonishing American citizens to write their congressmen imploring them to keep America out of the war. He added, however, that "between America and Germany, or between America and any other land, we are for America always." As a further concession he accepted the necessity of Wilson's forceful reply to Germany's declaration of unrestricted submarine warfare, and he asserted that if Congress declared war, "it will be our duty as

[55] *Hearings on German and Bolshevik Propaganda*, p. 1685; *Congressional Record*, 66th Cong., 1st Sess., 1919, LVIII, Pt. 2, p. 1134.

Americans to accept the accomplished fact in a spirit of loyalty and devotion to the Government."[56]

Although not willing to admit it directly, Viereck faced his worst enemy in Germany's inept foreign policy. This fact was demonstrated in late February when the Zimmerman telegram (perhaps the Foreign Office's greatest blunder) was intercepted and decoded by British agents and then published in the American press. Viereck quickly responded with a statement issued to the Hearst newspapers. The telegram, he declared, was "obviously faked." It was simply unbelievable that the German foreign secretary or any other "Realpolitiker of the Wilhelmstrasse" could have been responsible for such a preposterous scheme or so negligent in its transmission. The note was "unquestionably a brazen forgery planted by British agents to stampede us into an alliance and to justify violations of the Monroe Doctrine by Great Britain." The entire story, he continued, read "like a dime novel concocted by our guest, Sir Gilbert Parker, Great Britain's chief propagandist, in cooperation with E. Phillips Oppenheim." And while the American people were "willing to be thrilled," they would refuse, he predicted, "to be humbugged."[57]

One can imagine Viereck's subsequent disgruntlement when Zimmerman admitted to William Bayard Hale, Hearst correspondent in Berlin and a past contributor to *The Fatherland*, that the telegram was genuine. In a public statement, Viereck felt compelled to declare: "If the German Government allies itself with our foes, then, no matter how deep our attachment to the German people may be, no matter how earnestly we may be convinced of the justice of the German cause on the original issue, we have reached the parting of the ways. We are Americans before we are pro-Germans."[58] He then repeated many of the old arguments about his suspicion of British-based reports, the presence of a "war party" headed by a "former President," and the efforts of the munitions lobby to arm England and compromise

[56] *New World*, February 14, 1917, pp. 1, 3, 26.
[57] *New York Times*, March 2, 1917, p. 3:4.
[58] *Viereck's*, March 14, 1917, p. 90; *New York Times*, March 4, 1917, I, p. 2:6.

American neutrality. Despite his repudiation of the Zimmerman proposal, he denied that it represented a "plot." "From the point of view of statesmanship," he explained, "we can hardly blame the German Government if it seeks to protect itself in case we add our strength to the coalition against her." In a curious twist of logic, he claimed that the telegram offered even more reason for America to stay out of the war. "Sane patriotism," he concluded, "would dictate to remain aloof from the quarrels of Europe and to keep our powder dry."[59]

A few years later Viereck would meet Zimmerman and ask him why he had not foresworn himself "like a diplomat and a gentleman." Zimmerman replied to the effect that the Allies "had the goods on him" and it would have been futile to deny it.[60] The Zimmerman debacle, followed as it was by the sinking of several American ships, virtually ended pro-German propaganda in the United States. By late March there was little doubt that the majority of Americans saw no solution except war—unless Germany reversed her submarine policy and renounced any further "plots" against American security.

Nonetheless, until America's declaration of war in early April, 1917, Viereck persisted in his assertions that war was wanted only by Wall Street and the Morgan interests. In his journal he maintained a tone of hostility toward the Allies while at the same time taking a less laudatory attitude than usual toward Germany. Circulation figures are not available to judge the reaction of his readers, but it may be surmised that sales of his journal declined appreciably during this period. Perhaps it was in response to this kind of trend that the editor was motivated in the May 2, 1917, issue to publish a map showing that the journal had subscribers in every state and was the type of publication that deserved even more support from its readers under the new set of circumstances.[61]

The events of February and March, 1917, thus brought an effective end to the remnants of Germany's "propaganda cab-

<hr/>

[59] Ibid.
[60] G. S. Viereck, *The Strangest Friendship in History: Woodrow Wilson and Colonel House* (New York: H. Liveright, 1932), p. 190.
[61] See *Viereck's*, April 4, 1917, p. 132; May 2, 1917, p. 219.

inet" in America. Being pro-German was now tantamount to being anti-American. Viereck's journal survived this reversal of fortunes, but it labored under a new name and in a strained atmosphere. Viereck could no longer function effectively as a pro-German publicist, although he continued for several months to defend the German people and culture against their many detractors. A turning point in Viereck's career had arrived, and at this juncture it would seem appropriate to assess briefly his value to the German cause in the United States and to note the Administration's appraisal of his role.

With respect to the first point, his value to Germany, it should be noted that Ambassador Bernstorff, in a coded message to Berlin on October 27, 1916, had asserted that he would be "glad to be free from *The Fatherland*, which had shown itself to be of little value." He had been considering at that time the possibility of establishing a weekly or monthly paper more amenable to his purposes, but he had also noted that it was "particularly difficult in a hostile country to find suitable persons for help of this sort [i.e., editing or managing pro-German journals or newspapers]." And to this, he continued, "as well as the *Lusitania* case we may attribute the shipwreck of the German propaganda initiated by Herr Dernburg."[62] According to Viereck, Bernstorff did not attend meetings of the propaganda cabinet, but individual members did confer with him in Washington and in a New York hotel. In his memoirs of his American experience, published in 1920, Bernstorff declared that Viereck rendered "very valuable services" to the German cause through his weekly journal. Yet he qualified this assertion by explaining that, because of *The Fatherland's* reputation as a partisan journal, "it naturally could not exert so deep an influence as the local daily papers, which carried on the English propaganda without allowing it to become too conspicuous."[63]

These reactions leave little doubt that *The Fatherland* had been discredited, in the eyes of the ambassador, by the exposé in 1915 and by certain inadequacies in its editorial policy and orien-

[62] *New York Times*, December 8, 1918, p. 3:5.
[63] Viereck, *Spreading Germs of Hate*, p. 54; Bernstorff, *My Three Years in America*, pp. 52–53.

tation. In regard to the latter, it is worth noting that his adverse comment came during the 1916 presidential campaign when he disagreed with *The Fatherland*'s anti-Wilson position, a coincidence that may explain his chagrin. Still, it seems to have been wishful thinking for him to believe that a new or different journal could have made any substantial difference in American opinion toward Germany.

With respect to the second point, the Administration's appraisal of Viereck, we have the postwar testimony of Colonel House. According to him, the Administration was aware of Viereck's activities and "looked upon him as the ablest exponent of the German cause," a "man of consequence," but also one who was "misinformed, prejudiced, unfair." House added that there were no definite plans on what to do with Viereck or other pro-German American citizens in the event of war. He said, "It was a matter of awaiting what would happen."[64] House's remarks serve to confirm my contention that Viereck was an exceedingly capable propagandist whose effectiveness was, nevertheless, curtailed by circumstances beyond his control—such as Germany's unpopular submarine warfare.

Viereck's role may also be measured against the overall effectiveness of the cause for which he worked. Historical judgments of the efficacy of pro-German propaganda in the United States have varied, but most observers rate it as less effective than the British. One historian has concluded that publicists for the German cause "were far too open about their activity; far too obvious in their appeals; far too negligent of tact and finesse in spreading their message."[65] According to another observer somewhat sympathetic to the problems of the Central Powers, the German propaganda organization in America was "makeshift," made up of a "chance-medley of individuals . . . unacquainted with the American situation," and it was not taken seriously by the German government. He concludes that Germany's most successful investment was *The Fatherland*, but that neither it nor its smaller counterparts, *Fair Play* and *The Independent*, could achieve much against the generally pro-Ally sympathies of

---

[64] Gertz, "Stormy Petrel," Ch. 32, p. 21.
[65] Squires, *British Propaganda*, p. 45.

the American press.[66] A third well-known student of propaganda, Harold Lasswell, observes that Germany's focus on preserving and spreading her *Kultur*, especially when it was accompanied by military overtones, did not gain the kind of support obtained by the humanitarian appeals of the Allies.[67] In the opinion of historian Arthur S. Link, German propaganda in the United States was, with few exceptions, "shrewed and intelligent." The latter also believes that propaganda did not play a decisive role in the forming of American attitudes toward the war. More important was the character of overt events that could not be concealed or explained away by propaganda.[68]

In my judgment, the pro-German propaganda cabinet performed reasonably well. In particular, *The Fatherland* had a respectable reputation and a fairly wide circulation. The tone of many of its articles was somewhat pedantic, and on occasion perhaps overbearing, but Viereck's fluent and persuasive touch was also in evidence. In itself, the journal presented forceful arguments for the principles of "fair play," justice, and sympathy toward Germany. And apparently the propaganda cabinet was at least moderately successful in disseminating publicity for Germany through the organization's press bureau. The only major blotch on its record was the loss and public exposure of Albert's papers.

The failure of German propaganda must, therefore, be traced to something other than the inadequacies of the publicists themselves. It seems clear that they failed mainly because Germany adopted inept policies and because most Americans felt a closer cultural and political affinity to England than to Germany. Beginning with her violation of Belgium's neutrality, Germany committed a series of strategic blunders that simply could not be coped with by her propagandists. Such actions seemed merely to reinforce the assumption of many Americans that Germany had yet to learn the Anglo-Saxon concept of "fair play." There appeared to be little appreciation of the fact that both sides had annexationist claims on the other that precluded the probability

[66] Peterson, *Propaganda for War*, pp. 136–37.
[67] Lasswell, *Propaganda Technique*, pp. 196, 198.
[68] Link, *Wilson: Struggle for Neutrality*, p. 36.

of a fair and negotiable peace settlement. It was only after the Zimmermann telegram that Viereck himself publicly admitted the folly of German policy, but by then it was clear that the German government cared little about its image in the United States. In short, Viereck had failed in his objective of keeping America friendly to Germany, but his efforts have shed light on the causes of that failure and they have revealed some important facets of pro-Germanism in America during a critical period of history.

Obviously, by their decision to resume unrestricted submarine warfare, Germany's leaders felt they could afford to lose American neutrality. German policymakers, influenced heavily by military advisors, did in fact ignore warnings by a few lesser figures (like Count Bernstorff and Bernhard Dernburg) against underestimating America's ability to develop quickly a massive military machine. The Kaiser reportedly said in January, 1917, that the probability of America being drawn into the war against Germany was a matter of indifference to him. German leaders calculated that before America could effectively intervene, England would be defeated by German submarines; even if the United States did enter the war before Britain's defeat, German submarines would prevent the transfer of American troops to the continent.[1]

There is no evidence that German leaders expected Americans of German descent to help the cause of the Central Powers by attempting to disrupt the American war effort. Pro-Ally propagandists had made efforts in 1915 and 1916 to picture the National German-American Alliance as a collaborator with the German government and an agency of pan-Germanism, but these reports lacked documentation and credibility, and they seemed to have little public impact. Still, there were many Americans ready to believe the worst about the loyalty of German-American societies. Soon after the United States broke diplomatic relations with Germany in early February, 1917, the leaders of the Alliance hastened to pledge publicly that in the event of war with Ger-

[1] Fritz Fischer, *Germany's Aims in the First World War* (New York: W. W. Norton, 1967), p. 305.

many "we will fight no less loyally than the German-Americans fought under Lincoln in the Civil War for the preservation of the Union."[2]

Chagrined as many German-Americans were by Germany's actions in February and March, 1917, most of them still hoped that America could somehow avoid an open military confrontation with Germany. It galled German-American societies and newspaper editors to observe that American intervention would aid the cause of their long-time villains, Great Britain and her allies. They called on all American citizens to support their government in case of war, but at the same time they continued to promote policies of appeasement and neutrality. They also implied that the Allies would collapse before American involvement could alter the course of the war.

For a while after April 6, when war was officially declared by Congress, a considerable portion of the German-language press continued to blame Wall Street and England for sustaining the war. These editors also emphasized German military victories in the spring of 1917. But an adjustment to the prevailing climate of opinion became noticeable in the summer of 1917, and by the fall of that year nearly all German-language papers were offering full support to the American war effort. Carl Wittke notes, "By the analogy of a man loving his mother and yet owing first allegiance to his wife, the German-American group generally explained their new attitude toward the war."[3]

Most of these editors probably responded to genuine feelings of patriotism, but their attitude may also have been affected by passage of the Trading-with-the-Enemy Act in October, 1917, which in effect forced foreign language publications to prove their loyalty or face the threat of censorship. In fact, there was virtually no foundation for the fears of some Americans that fellow citizens of German descent were poor loyalty risks. Through their support of war loans and their service in the military forces, as well as in other ways, German-Americans after April, 1917, demonstrated that they were loyal Americans. Sylvester Viereck

[2] Child, *German-Americans in Politics*, pp. 97–103, 158, 160–61.
[3] Wittke, *German-Americans and the World War*, pp. 122, 127, 129–31, 162, 173–74.

proved to be no exception; he conformed to this generalization, but his support of the American cause did not come without a conflict in emotions and a period of adjustment and reorientation. Indeed, there were a few Americans who remained unconvinced that he had been "purified" of his Teutonic sympathies; their actions were to make life unpleasant for him in 1918 and 1919.

When the course of events finally culminated in Wilson's war speech of April 2, 1917, and the congressional declaration of a state of war on April 6, *Viereck's* magazine, as it was now called, rose to the occasion with a new motto: "America First and America Only." Viereck was not happy with the decision to wage war on his beloved Germany, but his protest was muted. "We shall only register a dissenting opinion," he said, "and then prepare ourselves to serve our country to the best of our ability, hoping that the course of events will justify its decision."[4] On April 7 he wrote a letter to President Wilson proclaiming his loyalty to the American cause.[5] He asked his readers to follow his lead in standing behind the government, even though "our heart goes out to Germany. . . ." He agreed to the advisability of a powerful army and navy for U.S. defense, but he added that America must cease fighting once its ends were achieved. Baring perhaps for the first time in his journal an attitude of despair, he explained, "We regard war as a relic of barbarism, but we realize that civilization is bankrupt." He advised German-Americans not to ask for special favors, but to "calmly insist upon our constitutional rights. Let us exercise free speech, but tempered with moderation." He concluded that German sympathizers should not behave like the old pro-English Tories.[6]

Although the climate of opinion began to change perceptibly, as evidenced by passage of the Espionage Act in June, 1917, Viereck did not at first find it necessary to reverse completely the policies and tone of his magazine. For several months—in fact

[4] *Viereck's*, April 11, 1917, p. 162.
[5] U.S., Congress, Senate, Subcommittee on the Judiciary, *Hearings on Brewing and Liquor Interests and German and Bolshevik Propaganda*, 66th Cong., 1st Sess., 1919, Sen. Doc. 62, III, p. 1698.
[6] *Viereck's*, April 11, 1917, pp. 162–64.

until about March, 1918—Viereck was able to express opinions
which did not conform with the official dictum that the primary
motive for the war was to make the world safe for democracy. On
several occasions in this period he stressed the dubious motives
of industrialists and of businessmen who were becoming rich
from the war.[7] He also periodically revealed his continued distrust
of the aims of America's allies. On the other hand, he remained
consistent in his support of and loyalty to President Wilson—a
policy that undoubtedly helped protect him from the weapons
of suppression provided by the Espionage Act and later, in May,
1918, by the Sedition Act. There perhaps was one exception to
this policy, in that he mildly reproached Wilson for his Flag Day
speech in June, 1917, which excoriated Germany, her ambitions,
and her sympathizers. He particularly noted the contrast between
this speech and the one on January 22, and he concluded with the
hope that the President's newly aroused belligerence represented
only a temporary deviation from the principles elucidated in the
"peace without victory" speech.[8] As a further example of his prudence, he refrained from defending Germany's war aims, but he
still did not adopt a tone critical of Germany—that is, not until
the spring of 1918, when he finally found it expedient to use an
article by James W. Gerard criticizing Germany's monarchical
system as inherently inimical to peace because it lacked democratic control over its war-making power.[9] Not until the final
weeks of the war does one find him using the terms "war lords"
and "military clique" in referring to the German government.[10]

The most indicative of Viereck's divided emotions about the
war, and perhaps the most risky of all his editorial campaigns,
was his attempt to induce Congress to protect Americans of German descent from the "horror of fratricide" that would result
from their deployment on the European front. He implied, too,
that these soldiers would not be the most efficient fighters on the
German front. He suggested alternative use of these soldiers in

[7] See esp. "The Millionaires War Is Making," *Viereck's*, July 25,
1917, pp. 422–27.
[8] *Viereck's*, June 27, 1917, pp. 350–51.
[9] *Viereck's*, May 15, 1918, pp. 236–37.
[10] *Viereck's*, November, 1918, p. 68; December, 1918, p. 99.

other theaters of war or in noncombatant duties. He did not ask for a draft exemption for them, claiming that he concurred in the idea of universal conscription.[11] He himself was barely over draft-eligible age. Perhaps surprisingly, his campaign received varying degrees of public support from a number of noteworthy people, including the president of Stanford University and nine congressmen. Indeed, Congressman Britten presented a resolution to this effect, but it received little support and was defeated.[12] One of the negative responses Viereck's proposal received was from Senator John Sharp Williams, who wrote Viereck in July, 1917, that his proposal was an audacious and contemptuous gesture. Williams said he did not believe Viereck represented the German-Americans, and concluded by citing the Kaiser's statement, "I know what a German is; I know what an American is, but I don't know what a German-American is."[13] After the war, Viereck admitted that this tactic was doomed to fail and that the "ordeal was inescapable."[14] Moreover, while raising questions about conscription, he was careful not to defend German-American or other critics of the war who were counselling disobedience of laws enacted to prosecute the war.

Although his efforts to alter the conscription law were unavailing, Viereck soon found some practical causes that would demonstrate his loyalty toward America without negating his affection for Germany. On May 2, 1917, he announced the formation of two services that his office would begin performing. First, he set up an Agricultural and Industrial Labor Relief Bureau, with the approval of the U.S. Department of Agriculture, for the primary purpose of locating farm employment for aliens who were no longer welcome as workers in business or industry, especially in munitions plants. The plan also met with the approval of the Departments of Labor and Justice and various state officials.[15] By the end of the war Viereck claimed to have helped place 5,000 to 6,000 aliens on farms and in businesses where they

[11] *Viereck's*, June 20, 1917, p. 334.
[12] *Viereck's*, July 4, 1917, pp. 359–62; July 11, 1917, pp. 379–82.
[13] John S. Williams to G. S. Viereck, July 9, 1917, Viereck MSS.
[14] Viereck, *Spreading Germs of Hate*, p. 243.
[15] *Viereck's*, May 2, 1917, p. 1; May 9, 1917, p. 235; June 13, 1917, p. 319.

could be free of suspicion and harassment.[16] His second venture, launched at the same time, was a Legal Information Bureau; it consisted of a panel of attorneys who answered questions regarding the rights and duties of citizens and aliens under wartime conditions. Selected questions and answers were published periodically in Viereck's weekly journal.[17]

Recognizing that the spirit of the times called for more positive demonstrations of loyalty to the government, in October, 1917, Viereck joined with several other German-American spokesmen in urging Americans of German descent to support the Liberty Bond campaign. As evidence of his concern about English domination of the seas, he called at the same time for America to build the greatest navy in the world. He also asked for a cessation of the "press campaign" against loyal Americans of German origin.[18] While offering support to America's preparations for war, Viereck could not completely suppress his lingering sympathy for the German nation.

For example, in August, 1917, he claimed to be in company with La Follette, Hearst, and Hillquit in demanding a "peace with honor, a peace without victory."[19] Holding to these aims, in January, 1918, Viereck joined most organs of public opinion in endorsing Wilson's newly announced Fourteen Points as a basis for peace. Nevertheless, as the St. Paul Pioneer Press observed, Viereck's interpretation gave the impression that those points generally considered favorable to Germany (freedom of the seas in peace and war, abolition of secret diplomacy, no trade war after the war, and reduction of armaments) were mandatory with the President, while the remaining proposals were open to negotiation.[20] Viereck followed up, however, with unqualified praise of Wilson's February 12 speech as an "olive branch to the Central Powers" and a commendable attempt by the President to establish international relations upon a new, moral plane.[21]

[16] Viereck, Roosevelt, p. 28; Viereck, Spreading Germs of Hate, p. 167.
[17] Viereck's, May 2, 1917, p. 215; May 30, 1917, p. 283.
[18] New York Times, October 22, 1917, p. 22:3.
[19] Viereck's, August 8, 1917, p. 12.
[20] Noted in Viereck's, February 13, 1918, p. 35.
[21] Viereck's, February 20, 1918, pp. 42–43; February 27, 1918, p. 62.

Viereck's overt support of the President after the declaration of war no doubt tended to mollify postal authorities and Department of Justice agents who had his journal under surveillance. But this rapport was interrupted in February, 1918, when Viereck reprinted a fictional dialogue from *Metropolitan* magazine in which President Wilson was depicted as a hypocrite for denying self-determination to this country's colonies and to certain Latin American states. After a discussion with postal authorities who questioned the propriety of publishing it, Viereck agreed to withdraw the issue from circulation and thus evaded possible legal action.[22] In a subsequent number he conceded that German-Americans must remain above suspicion and "avoid whatever would add to the present commotion." His journal became virtually silent on the role played by England and France in the common effort to defeat Germany. Through spring and summer of 1918 he devoted considerable space to publicizing Liberty Bond drives, and he reproduced some articles furnished by the Committee on Public Information. Beginning in April, 1918, at about the time American troops were first being committed to battle in appreciable numbers, his editorials took a decidedly critical tone toward some of the policies of the Central Powers. He also reiterated that "duty and the voice of his children" demanded of the German-American that he "unreservedly devote himself to the task of winning the war for America."[23]

Yet there were at least a few Americans who would not believe that Viereck was genuinely pro-American. They could not forget his pro-German associations and proclivities of the previous three years, nor would they overlook his qualified support of the country's wartime policy after April, 1917. Moreover, their growing hatred of Germany motivated them to search for suitable and convenient objects on which to vent their hostility. Thus Viereck became the target of threatening letters. He also claimed his literary works were boycotted by distributors. His publisher, Moffat, Yard and Company, returned the plates of his works—five

[22] *Viereck's*, February 27, 1918, pp. 59–60; *New York Times*, March 12, 1918, p. 9:4; Viereck, *Spreading Germs of Hate*, p. 167.
[23] *Viereck's*, March 13, 1918, p. 94; April 17, 1918, p. 192.

heavy boxes of them. Some unknown crank in Texas sent him a million-dollar check signed "William Hohenzollern" every day for two years.[24]

Viereck's attempts to be pro-American without being pro-Allied or anti-German came under scrutiny by his own poetic compatriots. The verdict of some of these patriot-poets was that he had not succeeded in proving his loyalty to America or in dispelling the impression that he was still an enemy of the Allied powers that were fighting Germany. Edward Wheeler, Viereck's old colleague on *Current Opinion* and president of the Poetry Society of America, wrote Viereck on April 10, 1918, that forty members of the society had requested his resignation and suggested that he comply. He also sent him a compilation of articles Viereck had written or published which cast doubt on his loyalty. Viereck refused to resign and denounced the charges as unfair. There was another exchange of letters in May; Wheeler asked for a quiet resignation, saying that the society's executive committee did not wish to take action to expel him. He also told Viereck that he had noted his recent efforts in his weekly journal to aid the American cause, but he said he failed to see any condemnation of Germany and her aims.

Viereck's reply was that to resign under the circumstances would be an "impeachment" of his patriotism, and that poetry "cannot abase itself by being handmaiden to intolerance." Not surprisingly, he condemned what he considered to be political intrusion into a nonpolitical organization. At the end of May, Wheeler informed him that the executive committee in two consecutive meetings had adopted a resolution to request Viereck to resign because of the "objection of many members to his continued membership."[25] Viereck remained adamant. Finally, on September 28, the society's executive committee passed a resolution expelling Viereck, but the action was not publicized among the society's members. Shaemas O'Sheel, who had been ostracized by the group in 1917, learned about it, however, and wrote an open letter to all members excoriating the leaders of the society. He also helped make a shambles of the November meeting

[24] Viereck, *My Flesh and Blood*, pp. 303–4.
[25] Quoted in *Viereck's*, July 10, 1918, pp. 363–65.

during which the fifty members present (of 350 on the rolls) voted to support the expulsion ruling.[26]

Although a ballot by the full membership had not been taken, it seems likely that the majority of the society's members felt at the time that the expulsion action was justified. At least, there was no loud outcry against the move. Yet support for the decision was not unanimous. Conrad Aiken resigned in protest over the "childish and shameful manner" of Viereck's expulsion. Other members offered to resign, according to Viereck, but he told them to stay and "fight autocracy from within."[27] Edwin Markham, honorary president of the organization, was the only officer who vocally opposed the resolution. His argument was that disloyalty was an issue for the courts, not for a "society that has other and more difficult problems to settle, problems that concern rhymes, meters and fresh phrases."[28] Among the ironic aspects of the episode, Viereck noted that he had been instrumental in the founding of the society, that he had nominated Wheeler as president and had later suggested that a poet be selected as an honorary president—his choice for the role being Edwin Markham.[29]

By the time the Poetry Society decided to remove Viereck from its rolls, it already had a precedent it could follow. The mounting American casualties in Europe after April, 1918, and Viereck's inability to utter more than mild censure of the enemy who was killing Americans aroused the wrath of many members and the leaders of the Authors League of America. The secretary of the league notified Viereck on July 6 of the charges against him and the action pending. One of the six specific counts of the accusation scored Viereck for "his repeated charges that our war is the 'Wall Street War.'" Theodore Roosevelt, honorary vice-president of the group, "cordially indorsed" the pending expulsion action. Viereck responded that the charges were "preposterous" and claimed that garbled quotations from his articles had been interspersed with "scurrilous misinterpretations and

<hr>

[26] *Viereck's*, January, 1919, p. 135.

[27] *Viereck's*, March, 1919, pp. 20–21.

[28] Florence Hamilton, "The Man with the Hoe: The Poet and the Problem; the Intellectual Biography of Edwin Markham" (unpublished MS, ca. 1938), pp. 219, 256, Markham MSS, Library of Congress.

[29] *Viereck's*, March, 1919, pp. 20–21; August 7, 1918, p. 423.

malicious insinuations." He then defended the continuation of his journal as an obligation he owed his readers and his country. He explained that "having roused my followers to a high pitch of pro-Germanism it was my duty to help them to readjust themselves to new conditions," a process that he called "education in constructive Americanism." Having set forth his defense, Viereck submitted his resignation to the league on July 24; but, unlike the Poetry Society, the Authors League wished to take the initiative; it refused to accept his resignation, publicly expelling him, instead, on July 26. Viereck claimed that his interest in this group had been minimal, and that he had attended no more than two of its meetings while he was a member.[30]

Another problem that plagued Sylvester Viereck in the spring of 1918 was the declining circulation of his journal. Apparently the weekly magazine and his other publishing interests returned ample profits, at least through 1917. He reported a net income of nearly $130,000 for the Fatherland Corporation in the year ending November 30, 1917. He claimed to have 50,000 subscribers at that time, and he asserted that the corporation's sole financial backing came from its readers and its 1,200 stockholders, of which the "vast majority" were American citizens. He declared that whatever German affiliations his corporation had had before April, 1917, had been "radically eliminated." In February, 1918, Viereck advertised the offering of $10,000 worth of stock to improve and enlarge the corporation's facilities for printing and selling books.[31] This move may have been a publicity gambit to assure his readers of his own confidence in the future of his journal. Defections among his readers had apparently begun by the beginning of 1918, and this trend became a deluge in the spring of 1918. The Sedition Act in May no doubt caused many readers to terminate their subscriptions as a prudent gesture. Viereck mildly criticized the bill, but later he praised Attorney General Thomas Gregory as "sane and conscientious" in his administration of the law.[32]

[30] *Viereck's*, August 7, 1918, pp. 430–31; *New York Times*, July 26, 1918, p. 20:2.
[31] *Viereck's*, February 13, 1918, pp. 16–27; May 8, 1918, p. 223.
[32] *Viereck's*, June 12, 1918, p. 315; October, 1918, p. 44.

Public sentiment for a sedition law had arisen largely in response to fears about the loyalty of radical labor groups, especially the extremist Industrial Workers of the World. These apprehensions were heightened by the success of the Bolshevik Revolution in November, 1917. In early 1918 several states passed laws providing heavy punishment for anyone using "disloyal, profane, scurrilous, contemptuous, or abusive language" (as the Montana statute put it) in regard to the American form of government, the flag, the Constitution, or military personnel and their uniforms. The federal statute passed in May carried the same provision and outlawed the publication of any material intended to bring these institutions "into contempt, scorn, contumely, or disrepute." Violations of these terms carried heavy punishments. As one historian has noted, "It is clear that dissent of nearly every imaginable form was to be silenced or punished under this bill."[33]

Presumably, many readers of *Viereck's* magazine concluded that justifiable criticism of the Administration or objective treatment of the Central Powers would be suppressed, and that the journal could no longer serve a useful purpose. Others probably felt that Viereck's previous affiliations and his lack of enthusiasm for the Allies might make him a target of the law, and they in turn would be embarrassed and perhaps even harassed as subscribers to a "seditious" journal. Such fears proved groundless as Viereck successfully strived to abide by the law, but in this process his magazine became more bland and colorless.

Meanwhile, shortly after passage of the Sedition Act Viereck moved the offices of his journal and library from 1123 Broadway to 202 East 42nd Street in New York, probably as an economy measure. In July he admitted that the journal had been "hard hit" and that an increase in circulation was imperative. The downward trend continued nevertheless, and in August he converted the magazine to a monthly periodical, mainly for reasons of economy.[34] He confessed in January, 1919, that his prior pleas had produced only $2,500 in stock subscriptions and donations,

[33] Horace C. Peterson and Gilbert C. Fite, *Opponents of War, 1917–1918* (Madison: University of Wisconsin Press, 1957), pp. 167, 213–16.
[34] *Viereck's*, May 15, 1918, p. 244; July 24, 1918, p. 401; August 14, 1918, p. 437.

and virtually nothing in subscriptions. It is apparent that the journal was operating at a loss by early 1918. Viereck claimed in 1919 that the publication had run a $30,000 deficit in the course of the war and its aftermath.[35] In spite of such setbacks, a government investigator in late 1918 estimated Viereck's wealth (presumably net worth) at $80,000 to $100,000.[36]

Part of the renewed hostility toward Viereck was aroused by the Justice Department which, in mid-1918, reopened its investigation of Viereck's propaganda activities in behalf of Germany's cause. Viereck was interrogated in July by agents of the department. His testimony, as released to the press, indicated that he had received about $100,000 from German and Austrian sources for expenses connected with his German propaganda activities. According to the press account of the testimony, Viereck admitted receiving $250 per week for a considerable period from Ambassador Dumba. In addition, he "now and then" received $1,000 from Ambassador Bernstorff. He received other large sums from Karl Fuehr. The testimony also indicated that Viereck had published about 750,000 pamphlets in the first five months of the war at a cost of $25,000.[37] Viereck did not publicly deny the truth of these statements, either then or after the war. However, in 1922, when being interrogated in a trial involving a libel suit by Chicago Mayor William Hale Thompson against the *Chicago Tribune*, he swore that Dr. Dernburg informed him that any funds placed at his disposal for publicity purposes were taken from contributions by wealthy Americans of German descent who wanted an "anti-toxin" for British propaganda.[38] Moreover, at the latter trial, May Binion, his secretary up to mid-April, 1917, testified that he had received a total sum of about $140,000 in the two years preceding America's entry into the war.[39] Viereck conceded that Miss Binion's figure might be correct, but he explained that it paid for approximately seventy-five different pamphlets in

[35] *Viereck's*, January, 1919, p. 160; August, 1919, p. 186.
[36] *Hearings on German and Bolshevik Propaganda*, p. 1424.
[37] *New York Times*, July 16, 1918, p. 1:2; July 26, 1918, p. 20:1.
[38] *American Monthly*, March, 1922, p. 16.
[39] *New York Times*, February 11, 1922, p. 28:4.

millions of copies. He also admitted that he had destroyed much of his correspondence—including letters from German officials—after the diplomatic break, and likened this act to closing out a chapter or burning love letters before being married.[40]

No indictment resulted from the Justice Department's investigation. The grievances against Viereck appeared to be based essentially on his activities prior to passage of the Espionage and Sedition Acts, and their provisions could not legally be made retroactive. Moreover, one may conclude that his conduct since April, 1917, had met at least the minimum demands of these laws, and that his lack of love for the Allies or of hatred for Germany could not be prosecuted as a legal offense. He also had been prudent and loyal enough to urge his readers to comply with these laws. Although legal grounds for prosecution were lacking, public opinion was inflamed and was not so easily to be assuaged, as events in the sweltering summer months of 1918 were to demonstrate.

In June, 1918, following the birth of their second son—George Sylvester II—the Viereck family took up a temporary abode in the New York suburb of Mt. Vernon, moving into the home of Mrs. Viereck's father, Max Hein. Presumably, the move was made to escape the molesting letters and other harassment previously noted. His anonymity did not last long, however, and Viereck's tenure there was short-lived. In early August a letter was published in the local paper that derided him for his published work about "American barbarians" and his admiration of the Kaiser. The letter ended with a thinly veiled call for vigilante action. Threats against the Vierecks became more blatant, and on August 8—near midnight—they spotted a group of khaki-clad men outside their home. They hurriedly called for police protection, but the group dispersed.[41] The next evening a carload of vigilantes aimed to escort Viereck out of town, but they left when told he was not home. They had failed to recognize the bespectacled, innocuous-looking figure on the porch as the man they were seeking. The trouble soon subsided when it became known that

[40] *American Monthly*, March, 1922, pp. 16–17, 21.
[41] *New York Times*, August 8, 1918, p. 11; August 9, 1918, p. 13.

Viereck was no longer living in Mt. Vernon.[42] He had found it expedient to take up residence in a hotel in New York; from there he periodically visited his wife by stealth—at night. After the war, he said this experience added romance and spice to his life.[43]

The armistice did not end Viereck's notoriety. About six weeks before the war ended, a Senate judiciary subcommittee began investigating the brewing and liquor interests and their connections with unpatriotic groups in America. This inquiry was inspired by widespread antagonism toward German-American societies that was reinforced by the well-founded suspicion that many of these groups depended heavily on contributions from brewing companies for financial support. The investigation was soon broadened to include an examination of pro-German and pro-Bolshevik propaganda. The committee's chairman was Senator Lee Overman. Although not called on to testify, Viereck was mentioned often in the testimony offered by A. Bruce Bielaski, chief of the recently formed Justice Department Bureau of Investigation, and by Captain George B. Lester, an Army staff member of the Military Intelligence Division.[44] Much of what they said about him had been publicized before, in 1915 and in July, 1918, but this renewed evidence of Viereck's complicity in German-sponsored propaganda hardly served to improve his public image or to relieve his strained relations with diverse literary organizations and personages.

Indeed, the end of the war did not bring immediate peace on the home front. Many Americans had developed a hatred of Germany and her sympathizers that was slow to subside, and in some cases this hostility even found expression in renewed acts of intimidation toward suspected disloyalists. But Viereck was not about to repent or ask forgiveness from his accusers and critics. He felt he had no apologies to make for his conduct. He had supported and advocated an American victory, but he had failed to praise the Allied powers or harshly and repeatedly to criticize Germany. These failures were held up before him. In response,

[42] *New York Times*, August 10, 1918, p. 14; Viereck, *Roosevelt*, p. 27; *New York Times*, August 11, 1918, p. 9.

[43] Viereck, *My Flesh and Blood*, p. 302.

[44] *Hearings on German and Bolshevik Propaganda*, p. 1390ff., 1685ff.

on the day the armistice was signed, Viereck penned a poem dedicated to his wife—a poem of indignant self-justification and dubious "Americanism." He called it "The Winners"; it was not published until 1919.[45]

> Never on the winning side,
> Always on the right—
> Vanquished, this shall be our pride
> In the World's despite.
>
> Let the oily Pharisees
> Purse their lips and rant,
> Calm we face the Destinies:
> Better "can't" than Cant.
>
> Bravely drain, then fling away,
> Break, the cup of sorrow!
> Courage! He who lost the day
> May have won the morrow.

While venting the bitter side of his feelings in private verse, Viereck in his journal expressed optimism and jubilance over the surrender of Germany and the promise of peace based on the Fourteen Points. Alleging that Germany could have held out for another year militarily, he asserted that she gave way to Wilson's "moral bombardment." He claimed that the German people were basically moral, and that their refusal to make an honorable peace in the spring of 1917, when they should have done so (in his opinion), could be blamed on the Junkers and the "militarist clique" which did not place faith in the people. The German people in turn had lost faith in the government, in Viereck's view. He recognized in November, 1918, the probability of territorial losses by Germany, including loss of its colonies and the conversion of Danzig into a free city to allow the Poles access to the sea. He said that the forfeiture of her colonies would be unimportant because of anticipated provisions for freedom of trade and freedom of the seas. Moreover, in the principle of self-determination he saw a boon for Germany in that she would thus be able to achieve racial homogeneity and unity. He acknowledged the justice of Germany paying war damages, but he also

[45] Viereck, *Roosevelt*, p. 5.

expected that unjustified reparations would be demanded of her. If the Fourteen Points were applied fairly and in good faith, one could expect a new era of good will to dawn upon the world, he concluded.[46] Within six months Viereck no longer entertained such hopes and, in fact, became a cynic devoted to thwarting or upsetting the peace terms finally imposed upon the land of his fathers. There were many other Americans who shared this postwar disillusionment, but there were few Americans in the immediate aftermath of the war who wished to identify themselves with the notorious George Sylvester Viereck.

Following the armistice and his expulsion from the Poetry Society, Viereck prepared a long essay, *Roosevelt: A Study in Ambivalence*, in which he attempted to vindicate his own role in the war and in which he analyzed his changing relationship with Theodore Roosevelt. He used the Freudian theory of ambivalence to explain his view of the deterioration of his friendship with Roosevelt. He published this work in 1919 under the auspices of his own Jackson Press (a subsidiary of the Fatherland Corporation). He noted in his opening statement that because of the ostracism pronounced upon him by various literary bodies, this book would not be reviewed in the American press.[47] He proceeded to disclaim that this stigma could be properly attributed to his pro-Germanism, his egotism, his mixing of poetry and politics, his acceptance of money for promoting Germany's point of view, or his support of Irish independence. Rather, he claimed, it was his "Americanism" that had gotten him into trouble with an "invisible government" of superpatriots and with others whom he had offended. It was, for instance, his attacks on American insurance companies for their generous loans to the Allies that got him on their blacklist. He alleged that other groups and indi-

[46] *Viereck's*, December, 1918, pp. 99–100.
[47] Viereck, *Roosevelt*, p. 11. Viereck reported that *Publisher's Weekly* —under pressure from Putnam's publishing house and other advertisers— refused to repeat its first advertisement for the book. The *New Republic*, allegedly fearing the loss of some of its advertisers, also refused to accept an advertisement for the book, according to Viereck (see Viereck, *Roosevelt*, p. 12, and *American Monthly*, December, 1924, p. 317).

viduals had less-than-worthy motives, too, for blackballing him. Alluding to other arguments against him, he denied that he was either a racist, a nationalist, or a monarchist.[48]

Viereck was most vulnerable on the charge of being a paid propagandist for Germany. On this issue he contended that any political movement requires funds. In his fight against the so-called "greatest combination of political power and finance ever aggregated in one camp," he admitted turning "for assistance to those whose interest it was to help me." He added, "Is a reformer insincere because he accepts campaign contributions?" His efforts, he reiterated, were aimed at keeping America aloof from foreign entanglements. It was also his contention that German propaganda was a "direct descendant of British Propaganda." The one was made necessary by the other. He noted that some Americans considered it a patriotic duty to combat so-called British domination in American life. As for cost, he guessed that ten times more money was spent by pro-British propagandists than by pro-German groups. He admitted to printing and distributing millions of pamphlets but added, "all I have in the world would have hardly sufficed to pay the printer's bill for one week." He attributed the failure of German propaganda in the end to the "inept declaration of unrestricted submarine warfare by the German Government and to the preposterous Zimmerman note." In other words, as he noted, German propaganda was defeated not in Washington, but in Berlin.[49]

It may be said in Viereck's favor that on one point he had a valid complaint: many of the judgments against him on patriotic grounds were extended to cover his literary work. Those writers and poets who expelled him from their associations perhaps overextended themselves when they made ideological conformity with their version of Americanism a test of membership, in place of literary achievement. Harriet Monroe, who in the interval had succeeded Wheeler as president of the Poetry Society of America,

[48] Viereck, *Roosevelt*, pp. 1–50 passim. Actually, there were reviews or commentaries in various newspapers, but none of the nationally recognized journals of opinion or literary organs bothered to review it. These editorial comments may be found in *Viereck's*, September, 1919, p. 28, and January, 1920, p. 149.

[49] Viereck, *Roosevelt*, pp. 15–17.

more or less acknowledged this mistake in February, 1919, in the society's journal. She expressed regret over the fact that a society of poets—who are "nothing if not arch-individualists, jealous guardians of spiritual freedom"—became "more suppressive of one of its members than the United States government has been during a year and a half of war. . . ." Her point was that the punishment of extremists, when war or other violence made it expedient, should be left up to authorized agencies of law and order.[50] The same kind of view was expressed by George Bernard Shaw, who wrote Viereck on January 10, 1919:

> If the Authors' League or the Poetry Society or any other organization expels a member because of his political opinions, it thereby constitutes itself a political body and violates whatever literary charter it may have. Literature, art and science are free of frontiers; and those who exploit them politically are traitors to the greatest republic in the world: the Republic of Art and Science.[51]

One may well agree that art and politics should be kept separate. Yet one may decide for himself whether Viereck was justified in using such testimony for his own vindication as a practitioner of Americanism. In other words, his strenuous effort to defend his own Americanism had little relevance to Shaw's defense of the "Republic of Art and Science." Despite his denials, Viereck still seemed captive to concerns of nationalism—German and American. Underlying all his arguments was the expression of his own egotism—a condition which he defined in the Freudian sense as "the defensive measure erected by genius against its environment." More specifically, he pictured it as a virtue, for "without this protective armor, the man of genius would be not the captain of his soul but the helpless victim of mediocrity and of circumstance."[52] One may see in his use of Shaw's statement and other utterances of support by European literati that his principal concern in this essay was to defend his own ego by all expedient means—including impugning the motives of his detractors and parading before the reader all the glowing excerpts from reviews

[50] Harriet Monroe, "The Viereck Incident," *Poetry* XIII (February, 1919): 265–67.
[51] Viereck, *Roosevelt*, pp. 49–50.
[52] Ibid., p. 107.

of his previous works. A part of this ego-defense was to explain why Theodore Roosevelt became one of his most bitter detractors. The last ninety pages of his 144-page work were devoted to this purpose.

Viereck opened his analysis of Roosevelt by paying homage to Freud and psychoanalysis. It was Freud that "gave us the key to the soul"—the means of knowing and being ourselves. Yet Viereck acknowledged that psychoanalysis is a two-edged sword. He noted that by the depth of its probing it might "destroy those emotions and processes which cannot exist save in the haze of illusion." Perhaps under its scapel, "art withers and affection dies. It cannot give us the love that passes all understanding but it can give the understanding that passes all love." After this introduction Viereck turned to the phenomenon of contradictory feelings existing simultaneously within the heart. He recalled in Wilde's *The Ballad of Reading Gaol* the words, "Each man kills the thing he loves." The psychoanalyst, he said, inverts this to add, "Each man loves the thing he kills." He noted that the coexistence of contrary emotions like love and hate, the "plus and minus of emotion," had been given the name "ambivalence" by Bleuler, one of Freud's first associates. In an attempt to define the term, Viereck turned to the works of Freud—*Totem and Taboo* in particular, where the "sway of coexisting contrary tendencies" is explained in relation to hero worship, taboos of the dead, and other social phenomena.

Viereck decided that Roosevelt was a typical example of the bi-polarity described by psychoanalysis. "He was Sophist and Rough Rider, Simple Simon and Machiavelli, rolled into one." He was English at heart; yet he hated and patronized them, according to Viereck. Similarly, he loved the Germans, yet bitterly denounced them. In his contradictory nature he again bore resemblance to the Kaiser, whom Viereck had described before (in *Confessions of a Barbarian*) as both rationalist and mystic, Anglophile and Anglophobe. Like the Kaiser, Roosevelt could not be considered a hypocrite, Viereck concluded; thus he could be adequately explained only in terms of the ambivalence theory.

It was not too difficult for Viereck to point to instances of Roosevelt's moral preachments, for instance, about international ethics, and his actions—such as in Panama—which were not consistent with such principles. There were instances in which his self-centeredness was matched only by his selfless devotion to the national welfare. His attitude toward big business also seemed ambivalent. Having established these facts, Viereck traced the course of his relationship with the Colonel, dealing at some length with the circumstances surrounding their mutual estrangement after 1914. Viereck predictably attributed much of this conflict to an alleged deterioration in Roosevelt's physical and psychological condition during the war. He contrasted Roosevelt's prewar praise of German-American cultural interests with his wartime revulsion toward anything resembling pro-Germanism. Interestingly, he dwelt upon Roosevelt's "malevolent" antipathy toward Wilson and implied that much of Roosevelt's spleen was generated by "defeated ambition." He compared Roosevelt with Torquemada; something of grandeur survived in both, "albeit both were victims of some psychosis." Upon Roosevelt's death, Viereck confessed that much of his own repressed affection for the ex-President had welled up again, indicating his own ambivalence. He was willing to accept the deceased Roosevelt as a symbol with virtues outshining faults. Thus the book's ambivalent plot ended in a final tribute for the fallen hero.

In its structure and tone, Viereck's study of Roosevelt may be seen as a projection of the author's own emotional and moral dualities. Viereck did let Roosevelt speak his mind about him by reproducing unabridged correspondence between the two. But he did not provide for a rebuttal by the Colonel, which might well have followed the same technique of depicting Viereck's inconsistency. For instance, Roosevelt might have pointed out that the kind of Americanism espoused by Viereck was not the type demonstrated by the majority of German-Americans. He could have noted Viereck's statement in 1912 that Roosevelt's inconsistency should not be held against him because this "appellation, just, when applied to a shopkeeper, is inadequate to describe the orbit —unintelligible to mediocrity—of the eccentric planet of genius."[53] He may also have stressed that if his pro-British utterances

---

[53] G. S. Viereck, "Roosevelt," *International* V (April, 1912): 67.

made him less an American, then the same logic should apply to Viereck's pro-German activities. Perhaps Viereck did not change to the same degree that Roosevelt did as a result of the war, but he shared equally in many of the same extremes of manners and polemics, including common personal attacks on President Wilson, albeit for opposite reasons.

Yet the book was not without its psychological insights. The experiences of both author and subject tended to confirm one of Viereck's statements taken from Freud; namely, that "we do wrong to value our intelligence as an independent force and to overlook its dependence upon our emotional life. . . . Intellect can work reliably only when it is removed from the influence of powerful emotional incitements; otherwise it acts simply as an instrument at the beck and call of our will and brings about the results which the will demands. . . ."[54] Many years later, in a reflective moment, Viereck admitted as much. He then confessed, "I am not, I never was, concerned in the question of war guilt. Irrespective of the rights or wrongs of the case, something in me leaped instinctively to the defense of my race." Also at that time he recognized something of the father figure in Roosevelt. He said that he had been over-awed physically by Roosevelt in the same way as by his own father. He concluded that the alternating feelings of tenderness and hostility which he had experienced toward his father were reflected in his attitude toward Roosevelt.[55]

[54] Viereck, *Roosevelt*, p. 108.
[55] Viereck, *My Flesh and Blood*, pp. 263, 276.

Τhe end of the war did not
bring an end to Viereck's concern about the image of Germany
in America and her status in the world community. Although he
had originally been optimistic about a peace based on the Fourteen Points, when the final terms became known in the spring of
1919 he rose in fury against the treaty and against one of its authors, Woodrow Wilson. Animated by anger and wounded pride,
he lobbied and propagandized in opposition to the Wilsonians—
going so far as to support Harding in 1920 and Robert La Follette
in 1924. Not unexpectedly, he noisily trumpeted the causes of
revisionism and isolationism and urged German-Americans to be
more active in government and lobby for a pro-German foreign
policy. Concurrently, he encouraged the German people to revive
their national aspirations in Europe.

Viereck's crusade against the Versailles Treaty began in
March, 1919, when it first became publicized. He objected to a
League of Nations that did not guarantee freedom of the seas and
did not include Germany and Russia as members. The American
people, he said, might submit to a "Parliament of Man," but
should not "consent to take stock in a close corporation of the
powers of the Entente." He was also unhappy at the prospect of
Germany's losing Alsace-Lorraine to France or giving up some of
her territory to Poland. In these two cases he called for "self-
determination" by the people involved, expecting that in both
cases the majority of the population would elect to remain under
German rule.[1]

The "punitive" peace, in fact, helped turn Viereck into a

[1] *Viereck's*, March, 1919, p. 3; June, 1919, p. 102.

veritable gadfly or a carper—depending on one's sympathy for his role. It also brought him back into the public eye after several months of relative obscurity following his expulsion from the Poetry Society. On May 30, 1919, he attended a New York celebration marking the centennial of Walt Whitman's birth. There the toastmaster noticed him and asked if he had any remarks he would like to add. Viereck thereupon launched into a diatribe against Wilson, asserting that he had followed the President when he reflected the spirit of Whitman but had now repudiated him for accepting the spirit of Clemenceau. He added that the League of Nations was a "travesty on all the hopes of humanity," a device to crush the Russian nation and "our sister republic of Germany." These comments brought outcries of disapproval, and at least thirty of those in the audience left the room, muttering denunciations of Viereck as they departed. But the crowd seemed to be incensed more by his notoriety as an apologist for the Kaiser than by the position he had taken on the League.[2]

In the months that followed, the themes that Viereck had set forth at the Whitman celebration would be reiterated again and again. Psychologically, they seemed to reflect his frustration over the fact that his adopted "mate," America, had been party to a humiliating treaty forced upon his unadopted or natural "father," Germany. A villain was needed to explain this tragedy of betrayal, and for Viereck President Wilson logically filled that role.

In Viereck's rhetoric Wilson was the "tricky schoolmaster" who had deceitfully broken faith with Germany by not insisting on fulfillment of the Fourteen Points. Allegedly, he was a "deliberate malefactor" and the greatest betrayer since Judas. A climactic exchange of blows came in September, 1921, when Viereck sent the retired President the drafts of two articles by Edmund von Mach, implicating Wilson in the alleged misconduct of the Custodian of Alien Property and also charging him with misrepresenting the intentions of the Alien Property Custodian Act. Viereck offered Wilson a chance to answer the charges in his journal. Wilson replied immediately, through his secretary, that he did not care "to read anything by Dr. Edmund von Mach or to receive any communication from you." Viereck responded that the feel-

[2] *New York Times*, June 1, 1919, p. 17:1.

ing was "entirely mutual," that "nothing short of public duty" could induce him "to communicate with Mr. Wilson," but since the latter's actions "affected the honor of the United States no less than his own," he had hoped for a reply.[3] Again, one might note that this jab at the ex-President probably served a psychic as well as a strategic need for Viereck and von Mach. By featuring the exchange under the headline "Wilson Pleads Guilty!" they were in a sense projecting onto a scapegoat their own feelings of guilt for having once favored Wilson's Fourteen Points. Now, in view of Germany's humiliation and suffering from the treaty, they were eager to divorce themselves emphatically from it; one way to do this was to denounce the alleged author of the so-called "Devil's Pact of Versailles."

It might also be observed at this point that Viereck's position did not have the merit of consistency. In 1918 he had called for a peace based on complete fulfillment of the Fourteen Points, but he later expressed fears of German territory being annexed by Poland and of Alsace-Lorraine being returned to France.[4] Yet these two contingencies were clearly implied in those points calling for Polish access to the sea and "righting the wrong of 1871." Viereck was quick to see in the Fourteen Points the death knell of British domination of the seas and of secret agreements that might involve the United States in support of France or England. He was much slower in perceiving that they also entailed sacrifices from Germany. He was also unable, it seemed, to understand that the thwarting of hopes for a nonpunitive, conciliatory peace was due not to Wilson, but to the anti-German climate of opinion among the Allied peoples, particularly the French and English.

Neither was pro-Germanism popular in the United States in the early postwar period. This situation provided Viereck with an excuse to continue publishing his journal, which had been converted to a monthly in September, 1918. He felt that defeated Germany needed friends and "fair play" more than ever before. Severely weakened by the war, his journal barely managed to survive financial crises in 1919 and 1925; in the latter year he would complain particularly about his inability to obtain support from

[3] Quoted in *American Monthly*, November, 1921, p. 266.
[4] *Viereck's*, June, 1919, p. 101.

wealthy German-American businessmen.[5] German-Americans, it seemed, had either concluded that there was no further use for it, changed their opinion of Germany, or, like other citizens, wanted a return to "normalcy"—that is, to leave Europe to its decadent ways and resume as far as possible the prewar policy of isolationism. Its circulation probably ranged only between 5,000 and 10,000. Still, it provided a sounding board for legislators, historians, and public officials that shared Viereck's opinions, and it was recognized, along with *Issues of Today* (later the *Progressive Magazine*) published by the Steuben Society, as being representative of the most highly motivated and controversial segment of the German-American portion of the population.[6]

From the tone and content of his journal, one could surmise that Viereck hoped to reach not only the concerned minority of ethnic-minded German-Americans but also those anti-League isolationists who distrusted the intentions of Britain and France. He did not make a strong effort to cover the organizing activities of other ethnic groups. It is notable, too, that after 1920 the public press paid little attention to his efforts for promoting German-American political activity. But his views on foreign affairs found a large audience after 1922, when he began writing for the Hearst newspapers. Between 1922 and 1927 he served periodically as a special foreign correspondent for the Hearst chain's "March of Events" section, and about three dozen of his articles on European affairs were published in this period. Most of them dealt sympathetically with Germany and with the life and opinions of the exiled Wilhelm II. Viereck claimed that these articles reached a public of about ten million, but he also noted in retrospect that no important personages commented upon these writings. It is therefore difficult to estimate his influence, but it is logical to conclude that he contributed something appreciable to many Americans' disillusionment about World War I and to the more favorable image of Germany that emerged in the latter half of the 1920's.

[5] *American Monthly*, July, 1925, p. 157; G. S. Viereck to Charles Nagel, March 7, 1925, Nagel MSS, Yale University.
[6] Ralph F. Bischoff, *Nazi Conquest through German Culture* (Cambridge: Harvard University Press, 1942), p. 165.

It had become clear by 1920 that Viereck was intent on using his journalistic and lobbying talents to pursue an anti-Wilson, anti-League policy, to promote the participation of German-Americans in politics, and to enhance American-German foreign relations. The consequence was that he would support a motley crew of dissident politicians, isolationists, and revisionists—all of whom contributed in some way toward meeting one or more of these objectives. Most notable in the period 1920–22 was his unsuccessful attempt to persuade German-Americans to vote as a bloc and to demand a larger share of high offices in the government.

It has been said that politics makes strange bedfellows; judging from Viereck's experience in the 1920's, one could say this maxim also applies to propagandists or publicists. In support of those who looked on America's involvement in World War I as a mistake or those who opposed the Versailles Treaty, Viereck found it expedient to back the presidential aspirations of such disparate personalities as Harding, Debs, and La Follette.

Less unexpected was his decision to identify himself with new ethnic organizations dedicated to political as well as cultural objectives. But it should be noted that Viereck was not the type to subject himself to organizational discipline. He used these organizations more or less as tools for achieving his own particular aims. Even though he was at one time regional director in the German-American Citizens League, he rarely publicized himself in that capacity. It appears that he was more intent on projecting himself as a kind of father figure for all German-Americans who were properly conscious of their ancestry and of America's debt to German influence. In fact, various observers have accepted him as a leading spokesman of what might be called American Germandom.[7] He thus pretended at times—such as in the presidential campaign of 1920—to be the intellectual and political leader of the German-American electorate. Actually, most German-Americans, including the majority of German-language newspapers,

---

[7] Including Louis L. Gerson, *The Hyphenate in Recent American Politics and Diplomacy* (Lawrence: University of Kansas Press, 1964), p. 10; and Bischoff, *Nazi Conquest*, p. 165.

either ignored or disputed his claims to leadership. In fact, many of them objected to the idea of "hyphen politics,"[8] considering it an un-American attitude in spite of Viereck's contention that his approach was "America first, America only."

Viereck hoped to persuade American voters, members of Congress, and presidential candidates to reward capable German-Americans with high offices in recognition of the size of this ethnic element and the contributions it had made to American institutions. In pursuit of this goal he played the part of lobbyist and ethnic political agitator and spokesman. His objective was, in short, to enlarge German-American influence upon American political policy. He seemed to assume that this would result in American repudiation of the Versailles Treaty and the League of Nations, which (as we have seen) were his *bêtes noires*. Before the war his main targets were the prohibition movement and puritanic moral laws; in the 1920's he scarcely mentioned these issues. He was obsessed until about 1926 with foreign affairs, mainly because it was in this area that he felt so much personal frustration. In large part he pursued a "politics of anger"; his underlying intention was to register protest, especially after he found—by 1921 or 1922—that the German-American vote could not be organized or manipulated as he had hoped. Meanwhile, in a variety of ways he did what he could to avenge himself upon the war and upon those who were pro-Wilson.

In respect to German-American political influence, Viereck's call for ethnic unity went largely unheeded in the 1920's, but it did arouse controversy and receive publicity, especially in the presidential election of 1920. The vehicles he tried to use were the short-lived Committee of 96, the German-American Citizens League, and the Steuben Society of America (established in 1919). For these groups, the *American Monthly* (changed in October, 1920, from *Viereck's: The American Monthly*) became a publicity organ. These organizations tried to promote German-American political self-consciousness and to unify this element nationwide in the manner achieved by the first German-American National Alliance, which had been disbanded during the war. But they were unable to restore this sense of ethnic unity. The

[8] *Viereck's*, February, 1920, p. 181; March, 1920, p. 4.

Steuben Society, to be sure, did develop a modicum of influence, but its membership remained small and confined mainly to the "intellectual" German-American.[9]

Viereck's public involvement in postwar domestic politics began in early 1920 when he and Dr. Edmund von Mach established the Committee of 96, "to arouse all Americans, especially Americans of German descent, to a sense of their civic rights and civic duties," and "to solidify political opinion among Americans of German descent and to create voting units, irrespective of party affiliations in opposition to the Invisible Government." The organization was so named because its national committee was to be limited to two delegates from each state. Among its specific objectives were the revision of the Versailles Treaty, self-determination for European nations, cordial relations with all free nations (especially Germany), reproval of those who would make the United States a "colony of Great Britain," restoration of the "spirit of the Declaration of Independence and American Constitution," and the removal of the United States from all European quarrels and from any affiliations with "international cutthroats" (League of Nations). Viereck stated that the organization was to serve not as a political party but rather as a "balance wheel in each state and community." Its headquarters were located in the offices of the *American Monthly*.[10]

Already in 1919 the *American Monthly* had offered advice on techniques for organizing local political clubs or pressure groups. But it appears that the Committee of 96 had meager success in setting up local units, and a national committee was never organized as planned. The *American Monthly* mentioned only a few local or county units being organized. This fact contradicted the wishful conclusion of Edmund von Mach, who alleged, after a tour of major cities in the East and Midwest, that there was an urge among German-Americans to organize along political lines. One development accounting perhaps for the lack of success was the competition offered by other groups, such as the Committee

[9] *American Monthly*, September, 1922, p. 22; Bischoff, *Nazi Conquest*, pp. 169, 173.

[10] *Viereck's*, February, 1920, p. 181; March, 1920, p. 4; April, 1920, p. 46.

of 48, which appealed to dissident ethnic and political factions, and to the Steuben Society of America. Another seemingly negative influence was Viereck's own notoriety as a propagandist for the German Empire and as an outcast from the Poetry Society and the Authors League. For example, in July, 1920, the Committee of 48 told him he would be welcome at their convention, but that he should not make himself too conspicuous or try to exploit his notoriety. Undoubtedly, too, the majority of Americans of German descent were averse to the revival of "hyphenism" in the American melting pot. Finally, the Committee of 96 could find little clear-cut guidance from Viereck on what parties or nominees to support. Viereck was beset by a dilemma: he foresaw the unlikelihood that either of the national parties would nominate "suitable" candidates, yet he feared that the formation of a third-party movement might result in the election of a "Wilsonian" Democrat—the worst of all possible alternatives, in his view.[11]

Speaking at least indirectly for the Committee of 96, early in 1920 Viereck had noted his tentative preferences in respect to presidential and vice-presidential candidates. They were as follows: Republican—Senator Robert La Follette and Charles Nagel or Mayor William Hale Thompson of Chicago; Democrat—Senator James Reed (Missouri) and Samuel Untermyer or Charles P. Grace; Socialist—Eugene Debs and Daniel W. Hoan (Wisconsin); and Independent—William Randolph Hearst and Jane Addams or F. P. Walsh (Missouri). Nagel had been secretary of commerce and labor in Taft's cabinet, and Untermyer had a wide reputation as a liberal lawyer active in the Progressive movement. A policy common to virtually all of these individuals was their opposition to American participation in the Great War. By June, Viereck was telling his readers that if the two old parties failed to put forth acceptable candidates and if no independent movement "worth its salt" materialized, it would be advisable to vote for Debs in protest. "It is better to vote for this man in jail than to vote for the men who jailed him," he quipped. The situation was complicated, he noted, and it might be better to concentrate on

[11] *Viereck's,* May, 1920, p. 86; July, 1920, p. 133; September, 1920, p. 204.

electing suitable candidates for Congress. He then offered the curious advice, "Whenever we are in doubt, let us vote for the Socialist; a healthy sprinkling of radicals will be an antidote to jingoism." In July, he spoke of the possibility of electing Harding and at the same time piling up a large complimentary vote "for the most saintly character in our political history, the martyr of Atlanta, Eugene V. Debs."[12]

Viereck admitted that it was difficult to grow enthusiastic over Harding and conceded, "The best that can be said for him is that there is little to be said against him." Yet he felt that any candidate would be preferable to a Wilsonian. He remained skeptical of a third-party movement, although he said he would "hail" Borah or La Follette at the head of a new Progressive party if they showed an ability and inclination to break the Democratic hold on the Solid South. Viereck's endorsement of Harding became official in August, 1920, as a result of his agreement to a program adopted by the German-American Citizens League of Chicago. On August 16–17, Viereck and other members of the Committee of 96 attended a conference in Chicago, presided over by the League; the participants consisted of leaders of German-American groups in twenty-two states. The conferees agreed to support the candidacy of Senator Harding, mainly because of his opposition to the covenant of the League of Nations and to other Wilsonian foreign policies. They also called for the release of Debs from federal prison, for the withdrawal of French occupation forces from the Rhineland, for Irish independence, and for the withholding of aid to Poland.[13]

Viereck wrote to Harding shortly thereafter, outlining his position on the Versailles Treaty and relations with Germany and on the role of German-Americans in domestic politics. He claimed that the elements he represented had the advantage of firsthand knowledge of European conditions, and that they regarded it "not merely as our right, but as our duty, to demand a

---

[12] *Viereck's*, February, 1920, p. 167; June, 1920, p. 101; July, 1920, p. 133.
[13] *Viereck's*, July, 1920, p. 133; September, 1920, p. 199; *New York Times*, September 4, 1920, p. 1:1.

hearing and to be adequately represented in Congress and in the Administration." Harding refused to commit himself on this issue, but he did not disavow the support offered him by the German-American conference.[14]

Viereck soon became a prominent figure in the 1920 presidential campaign. The *New York Times*, in particular, accepted him as the unofficial spokesman of the German-American groups attempting to influence the election. The *Times* on September 5 reported that he was hoping to line up six million German-Americans in support of Harding. About two weeks later, the Democratic party's vice-presidential candidate, Franklin D. Roosevelt, charged that the Republican campaign managers were making every effort to obtain the "hyphenated vote" and were making special appeals to "the small but very dangerous element which was not loyal during the war." He added that Senator Harding was seeking the support of "un-American elements in the electorate" and that the support of Harding "by men like George Sylvester Viereck is an evidence of the object to be gained."[15]

Viereck retorted with a telegram to Roosevelt, pointing out that he had not been arrested during the war; he also implied that Roosevelt was a dupe of British propagandists as well as a man of less loyalty to America than Harding. He sent another telegram to the chairman of the Senate committee investigating campaign funds in which he swore that he neither sought nor received any money from the Republican party. Roosevelt deplored the injection of "hyphenism" in the campaign; Viereck exploited it. Predictably, Democratic presidential candidate James Cox took up the cudgel against Viereck; the latter again responded with telegraphic counterstrokes, duly reported in the press. The ostracism and the obscurity that had plagued Viereck in 1919 and the first half of 1920 were now over. He undoubtedly was most pleased with the publicity he and his cause were receiving. The grandiloquence and posturing in some of his phrases (e.g., "God help-

[14] *American Monthly*, October, 1920, p. 230; July, 1924, pp. 137–38.
[15] *New York Times*, September 5, 1920, p. 3:1, September 23, 1920, p. 4:2.

ing us, we can do no other") also indicated that he had returned to his old form.[16]

In his November congratulatory message to President-elect Harding, Viereck said he rejoiced "that six million Americans of German descent have cast their vote for you as I foretold in my messages to you and to Governor Cox." He added, nevertheless, that Harding would enter the White House a free man, under obligation to no group, ethnic or economic. Americans of German descent, he explained, held no promise from him and expected from him nothing but a "square deal." Yet a few weeks later he wrote an article on "What We Expect from Harding," in which he implied that Harding should appoint some German-Americans to important positions in his Administration. He said that if the German element was not recognized in this way, it would compel Americans of German descent hereafter to organize their political activities strictly along racial lines, either alone or in conjunction with other non–Anglo-Saxon elements, "in order to obtain, by political strategy, their just share of the government."[17] Other German-American spokesmen soon joined in a concerted effort toward this end.

On January 10–11, 1921, Viereck joined with about forty representatives of various German-American societies in a meeting convened by the German-American Citizens League of Chicago. At this meeting the German-American Citizens League of the United States was officially organized. In retrospect, Viereck asserted that many German-Americans were spurred to organize in reaction to feelings of persecution and treatment as an inferior class of citizen brought about by "Anglophile persecution and nativistic mob violence." These conditions, he alleged, brought forth the determination to compel recognition and respect for their civil rights. He said also that many German-Americans were eager to join with others in raising their voices against prohibition.[18]

[16] *New York Times*, September 25, 1920, p. 14:2; September 29, 1920, p. 1:1; September 30, 1920, p. 3:2; October 17, 1920, p. 3:1; October 18, 1920, p. 2:3; October 30, 1920, p. 1:3.
[17] *American Monthly*, December, 1920, p. 296; January, 1921, p. 325.
[18] *American Monthly*, August, 1921, pp. 175–76.

The League adopted fourteen resolutions which were subsequently endorsed by several German-American groups, although Viereck conceded that there was opposition to them by certain sections of the German-language press. In its first policy statement the League called upon the President-elect to consider the contribution that Americans of German descent had made to the country; although it would not ask him to select any man because he was of German extraction, it asked that Harding not discriminate against anyone for that reason. In other resolutions, the League called for an immediate, equitable peace with Germany and Austria, condemnation of the annexation without plebiscite of German-speaking populations by non-German states, the withdrawal of American occupation forces in Germany, the building of a large merchant-marine fleet protected by the largest navy and air force in the world, the restitution of alien property, the release of Debs and reevaluation of other convictions under the Espionage Act, a national referendum on the prohibition law, and sympathy for Irish independence. The League was divided into five national zones; Viereck was selected as chairman of the eastern zone. Ferdinand Walther was elected national chairman. According to the *New York Times*, Viereck played a dominant role in the conference. When interviewed at that time, Viereck specifically stated that Harding should appoint at least one German-American to his cabinet, as well as to other important positions.[19]

Viereck was appointed to a five-man committee that was assigned responsibility for presenting these resolutions to the President-elect. Other members included Walther and Dr. Geoffrey Arthur Lang, secretary of Protestant Friends of Irish Freedom. This committee, Viereck said, would not offer names for the cabinet unless these were requested by Harding. Nevertheless, when asked about possible candidates he offered the names of several German-Americans prominent in either national affairs or in German-American circles.[20] Later, some of these people complained to Viereck that use of their names in this connection had not been authorized. One of the most prominent, Charles

[19] *New York Times*, January 11, 1921, p. 2:1; January 12, 1921, p. 3:3; *American Monthly*, February, 1921, pp. 359–60.
[20] *New York Times*, January 12, 1921, p. 3:3.

Nagel, told the *St. Louis Star* that he did not believe in the "hyphen" approach.[21] American newspaper editors responded to Viereck's plan with derision and ridicule. Meanwhile, Viereck had already corresponded privately with Harding on the matter of cabinet appointments and other issues. Harding was courteous but noncommittal in his replies.[22] Nevertheless, Viereck and his associates pressed forward with their attempts to bring German-American influence into the high offices of government.

Granting a request received from Ferdinand Walther, Harding agreed to meet with the delegation on February 16 in St. Augustine, Florida, where he was planning to vacation. At about the same time, a German-language newspaper editor sent a telegram to Harding, telling him that Viereck was in no way representative of the bulk of German-Americans. Similar expressions were received from other Americans of German descent, and it must have become clear to Harding that this ethnic element was far from unified in its political sentiment. In fact, Viereck appeared to be a divisive influence on German-American affairs. But Harding received the delegation with cordiality, explaining to the press that he had been elected President "of the whole American people, and I shall see any American citizen with a mission who asks to see me." Still, some Republican party leaders were reported to have had misgivings about Harding's tacit recognition of Viereck as a representative of citizens of German extraction. The delegation presented to Harding the resolutions and a memorandum derived from the January conference. The committee reported it gained a favorable impression of the President-elect and interpreted his attitude to mean that a just and equitable peace with Germany was in the offing.[23]

It is not too surprising to find that Viereck was displeased by Harding's subsequent appointments and policies. The President showed little regard for the ethnic issue. No German-American was appointed to his cabinet or to any major position in the Ad-

---

[21] *American Monthly*, February, 1921, p. 379; July, 1924, p. 141.

[22] Cited in *American Monthly*, July, 1924, pp. 136–37, 139.

[23] *New York Times*, February 17, 1921, p. 17:6; Alexander Harvey, "German-American Unity and the President," *American Monthly*, July, 1924, pp. 140–41.

ministration. Publicly, Viereck said little about this course of events. Perhaps he realized that his intrusion would more likely harm than help the cause. He did become involved, in a minor way, in the promotion of a candidate for ambassador to Austria. Viereck joined with those who backed the candidacy of Bernard G. Heyn, a New York lawyer who had served with Viereck on the committee that visited Harding in February. Viereck wrote to Harding in November, 1921, after it had been rumored that Heyn would not be appointed, protesting that 25 percent of the population was still unrepresented in any important post in the diplomatic corps. Harding replied that there was no intended discrimination against citizens of German stock or origin, noting that some German-American groups supported one of two other candidates for the ambassadorship. Heyn subsequently withdrew from the fray. The only American of German origin subsequently appointed to an ambassadorship in Europe was Judge Theodore Brentano of New York, who served as envoy to Hungary. Alexander Harvey, describing this episode in the *American Monthly*, pointed to German-American "cliques in New York and Cincinnati" which he charged were hostile to Viereck and helped create in the President's mind the idea that German-Americans were hopelessly divided and could be ignored as a political force.[24]

The year 1921 was one of frustration on the political front for Viereck and other rabid German-Americans. Besides the foregoing rebuffs from the Harding Administration, the Senate in mid-1921 approved a treaty with Germany which Viereck called a "miserable makeshift" and a "backdoor to Versailles." He said he had not had the heart to oppose it because it was necessary to put an end to the uncertainty still existing in relations between the United States and Germany. He remained particularly perturbed over the lack of action on restoring alien property to its original owners.[25]

Searching for new avenues of influence, Viereck in late 1921 found another rostrum from which to publicize his causes by joining the All-American Committee for the Promotion of an Irish Republic. He soon became chairman of the Committee and

[24] Harvey, "German-American Unity," pp. 141–43.
[25] *American Monthly*, November, 1921, p. 266.

tried to use it in consolidating racial societies opposed to the dominance of Anglo-Saxon influences in American political life, but he achieved little success in this effort. He remained opposed to the idea of establishing a third party based on racial lines; such a plan had been proposed by his old friend and cohort Frederick F. Schrader, who was then editing *Issues of Today*.[26]

In another project that bore little result, he supported a campaign led by Edmund von Mach to petition Congress to raise its voice against the "horror of the Rhine," a euphemism alluding to France's use of black African soldiers in its occupation of Germany's demilitarized zone. Besides publicizing the petition, in early 1921 he sent every member of Congress a selection of documents reporting the alleged crimes and misdeeds of these "uncivilized" troops. A joint resolution was subsequently submitted in the House of Representatives, requesting the President to ask the French government to withdraw Negro troops from German soil immediately. The resolution was reported to the Foreign Affairs Committee, where it died for lack of support.[27]

The year 1922 witnessed further setbacks in Viereck's hopes for at least political unity among Americans of German descent. In April and May he saw fit to castigate the Ridder brothers, publishers of America's leading German-language newspaper, the *New York Staats-Zeitung*, for promoting the idea that editors of German-language newspapers were the most logical and suitable leaders of German-Americans. He also upbraided them and other "professional German-Americans," especially other German-language newspaper editors, for not taking a united and militant stand on issues affecting Germany.[28] As mentioned earlier, it was evident that Viereck's extremism appealed to only a small portion of German-American citizens. Finally, it should be noted that one of his goals, the freeing of Eugene Debs, had finally been achieved in the last days of 1921; but Viereck could feel only slight satisfaction since he considered it a tardy action on Har-

[26] *New York Times*, December 8, 1921, p. 1:3; February 21, 1922, p. 6:8.
[27] *American Monthly*, October, 1920, p. 241; January, 1921, passim; March, 1921, pp. 2–3; *Congressional Record*, 67th Cong., 1st Sess., 1921, LXI, Pt. 6, p. 5865.
[28] *American Monthly*, April, 1922, pp. 40–42; May, 1922, pp. 74–76.

ding's part.[29] Irritated by the indifference of the Republican party
and exasperated by Germany's humiliation at the hands of the
French, he was ready by 1924 to support a political maverick—a
third-party candidate who nonetheless carried a popular name:
Robert La Follette.

Robert Marion La Follette, the famed reformer from Wisconsin, had gained Viereck's eye as one of the few senators to
oppose America's entry into the war against Germany. He kept
up his opposition to foreign entanglements after the war was over
and helped defeat the Administration's efforts to put the United
States behind the Versailles Treaty and the League of Nations.
In the disillusionment with the war that came after 1918, La
Follette retained popularity with the voters in Wisconsin, many
of whom were of German descent. In 1922 a movement of dis-
sidents and liberals, representing mainly labor and farm groups,
got underway. Its founders espoused some semi-socialistic economic reforms at home and an isolationist-revisionist stance in
foreign affairs.[30] La Follette became a leader of this movement,
and efforts were underway by 1924 to have him run as an independent Progressive candidate for president.

Impressed by La Follette's disdain of England and France,
and by his insistence on American aloofness from foreign quarrels, Viereck came out strongly for the Senator's candidacy in the
June, 1924, issue of American Monthly. Viereck asserted that if
La Follette decided to enter the race, "the German-American
element, ever ready to battle for the principles of authentic Americanism, will be a solid phalanx behind him." Viereck added that
it was even more important to strengthen the Progressive bloc in
Congress, for the legislature was "the bulwark between the American people and the despotism of the Invisible Government." He
considered it unlikely that a president could be elected on a third-
party ticket, but he felt that the complexion of Congress could be
altered. "We liberals," he said, "cannot build overnight a nation-

[29] American Monthly, February, 1922, p. 362.
[30] For an account of this movement and its role in the campaign of
1924, see Kenneth C. MacKay, The Progressive Movement of 1924 (New
York: Columbia University Press, 1947).

wide machine strong enough to count in the presidential election. If we could, we might be in danger of becoming ourselves the slaves of the machine we had created." He labeled Coolidge a "weak" president and implied that he was subservient to the interests of "International Finance."[31]

Viereck wrote La Follette on July 11, 1924, offering him his services in the campaign. Robert La Follette, Jr., replied with a note of appreciation and added that he would be glad to get in touch with Viereck "from time to time as situations develop wherein I feel that you could be helpful."[32] In the July number of *American Monthly* Viereck noted readers' favorable responses to his decision to back La Follette, and he praised the Wisconsin standard-bearer for his opposition not only to the Versailles Treaty and the League of Nations but also to the World Court and the Dawes Report. A vote for La Follette, Viereck declared, meant a "vote against the witches cauldron from Wall Street out of which all the unclean demons plaguing the world have arisen."[33] In the next issue Viereck invited his readers to contribute to a "La Follette Publicity Fund" sponsored by the *American Monthly*, which he said would add 10 percent to the amount contributed by readers. He pointed with particular satisfaction to the foreign-policy plank of La Follette's Wisconsin platform, which stated: "We favor an active foreign policy to bring about a revision of the Versailles Treaty in accordance with the terms of the Armistice, and to promote firm treaty agreements with all nations to outlaw wars, abolish conscription, drastically reduce land, air, and naval armaments and guarantee public referendums on peace and war."[34]

In the same issue of his journal Viereck predicted that the six million votes of German-Americans which he had predicted for Harding, a prophecy that he said was verified by events, would this time swing into line for La Follette. The ticket, Viereck felt, was made even more attractive by the selection of Burton K.

[31] *American Monthly*, June, 1924, p. 97.
[32] Robert W. La Follette, Jr., to G. S. Viereck, July 17, 1924, Gertz MSS.
[33] *American Monthly*, July, 1924, p. 133.
[34] *American Monthly*, August, 1924, p. 187.

Wheeler as La Follette's running mate. He praised Wheeler's "courageous exposures of bi-partisan corruption" and his defense of free speech and assembly even in wartime. In his further endorsement of La Follette, Viereck lauded his speech before the Senate on June 6 as a "fight for the starving women and children of Germany." The Progressive party's candidate, he also noted, fought alone on the floor of the Senate for the German-relief bill proposed by Hamilton Fish.[35]

Among other particular activities in support of La Follette's campaign, Viereck spoke several times at rallies sponsored by the Steuben Society's National Campaign Committee for La Follette and Wheeler. He also performed translation work for this committee. In addition, he prepared a report on the probable status of the German-American vote in various states and sent it to the candidate early in August. To Arthur Garfield Hays, chairman of the La Follette-Wheeler Campaign Committee, he donated copies of the *American Monthly* containing articles pertinent to the campaign. The support of the Steuben Society is especially noteworthy. Viereck reproduced in the September issue of his journal the Society's resolutions adopted on August 12, endorsing the Progressive party's candidates. This Society was hopeful that La Follette could revise or repeal certain laws, such as the recently enacted immigration acts, which it felt discriminated against German-Americans.[36]

For Viereck and his associates the high point of the campaign came on September 21, when, as part of a Steuben Day celebration, La Follette and Frederick F. Schrader addressed some 20,000 people in Yankee Stadium. In his journal, Viereck claimed there was nothing "racial" about the affair, "nothing to suggest that our citizens of German origin expect either privileges or rewards in return for the solidarity they will manifest as supporters of the Progressive party when they go to the polls next November."[37] Viereck's intimation that there was a uniformity

[35] Ibid., pp. 165–66.
[36] Theodore H. Hoffman to G. S. Viereck, November 8, 1924; William H. R. Schultz to G. S. Viereck, December 4, 1924; Arthur G. Hays to G. S. Viereck, October 22, 1924, Gertz MSS; *American Monthly*, September, 1924, pp. 225–28.
[37] *American Monthly*, October, 1924, pp. 250–53, 255; Selig Adler,

of political opinion among German-Americans was backed up by Alexander Harvey, who wrote an article claiming that German-Americans had finally awakened to the fact that they must unite in the political sphere if they "hoped to impress an idea upon the American mind."[38] But these statements seemed to represent a "publicity ploy," rather than any realistic analysis of the situation. Only four months earlier, Viereck had pointed to the attacks made upon him by some German-American newspaper editors who took exception to the role he had adopted in the 1920 campaign and were again challenging his position in 1924.[39] These challenges had not abated, but it would, of course, have been impolitic for Viereck to express openly any doubts he had about his ability to arouse the typical American of German descent from his complacent acceptance of the conservative doctrines of the major parties.

On election eve Viereck received from the national manager of the La Follette headquarters a note of appreciation for his "splendid work" on behalf of the ticket. La Follette subsequently sent him a portrait carrying the inscription, "with assurances of my high appreciation of your work for human rights and the restoration of government to the people."[40]

The degree to which the electorate seemed satisfied with so-called "Coolidge prosperity" was evident in the fact that little more than half of the eligible voters went to the polls. Most disappointing for Viereck, of course, was the fact that La Follette managed to secure only 4.8 million votes out of the 29 million votes cast, with Coolidge receiving a sizeable majority (15.7 million). The next most galling fact was the defeat of Senator Magnus Johnson of Minnesota, whom Viereck had especially extolled.

Viereck did not receive the verdict in good grace. He wrote the defeated third-party candidate on November 5 that "against organized stupidity and organized plunder even the gods contend

---

The Isolationist Impulse: Its Twentieth-Century Reaction (London: Abelard-Schuman, Ltd., 1957), p. 163.

[38] *American Monthly*, November, 1924, pp. 283–85.
[39] *American Monthly*, July, 1924, p. 136.
[40] *American Monthly*, December, 1924, p. 336.

in vain." The election of Coolidge and Dawes, he continued, "upset one's faith in democracy." Nevertheless, "If Sodom and Gomorrah were worth saving for the sake of ten righteous men our country is worth saving for the millions who cast their vote for the Progressive cause." He concluded that he for one was proud to enlist under La Follette's banner "following the dauntless leadership that always lost the day and always won the morrow."[41] In an editorial he called the results a victory for Morgan and Wall Street, and he alleged that La Follette had been defeated by economic intimidation, skillful manipulation of public opinion, slander, legal trickery, and the unscrupulous use of money—all "superimposed upon national imbecility." He noted that most observers had expected at least six to eight states to swing to the Progressive column, but such calculations "ignored the fact that the average voter is a moron." For corroboration of the latter statement he alluded to army intelligence tests which showed that the average American's mental age was twelve.[42]

Of course, it was apparent that many German-Americans had not voted for La Follette. Yet Viereck maintained that, except for "weaker brothers and sisters" who fell by the wayside "here and there," the "German element in the United States, standing steadfast for authentic Americanism, constituted the backbone of the La Follette vote." The party, he noted, had been tagged with a socialist label which hurt its chances, but he still expressed admiration for Debs, Hillquit, and Berger. The main defectors among German-Americans, he averred, were the "silk stocking element" which had never been sympathetic to La Follette, as well as "political soreheads and notoriety hunters" who had succeeded in attracting attention to themselves by denouncing the Steuben Society and La Follette. He claimed, too, that the Republican campaign committee had seduced many German-American and Negro newspapers with lucrative advertising offers. As for the future of a third party, he said it would not be advisable for German-Americans to join such a movement if it were controlled by "intellectual snobs or Socialists." As a final straw of

[41] Quoted in *American Monthly*, December, 1924, p. 310.
[42] Ibid., p. 309.

hope, he told his readers, "Let us never forget that wherever six American voters foregather, one of the six is with us."[43]

On the occasion of La Follette's death a few months later, Viereck published a eulogy in which he attributed La Follette's poor showing in 1924 to mistakes made by his lieutenants. He alleged that "force was not always applied where it would have been most effective strategically." Without furnishing any particulars, he added, "The Senator's intimate advisors blundered or La Follette would have carried eight or ten states." The fallen fighter from Wisconsin was, he said, the greatest, the most sincere, and most courageous American statesman since Abraham Lincoln. He considered La Follette not a visionary, but a "practical leader whose only fault was that he saw too far into the future." He concluded that his "weakness as a politician and his greatness as a man was his inability to compromise."[44]

This work for La Follette in 1924 marked the end of Viereck's active involvement in presidential campaigns. By the time of the next election in 1928 his interest in political polemics and publicity had paled, and he was becoming increasingly involved in a variety of literary and other journalistic pursuits. Meanwhile, from 1923 to 1929 Viereck found another avenue by which he might influence government policy in his efforts to "right the wrong" of Versailles and to keep America out of alliances with any of Germany's wartime enemies. In this period he became a friend or acquaintance of various congressmen sympathetic to his views, and he encouraged and counseled them on foreign-policy matters. He likewise drew support from revisionist historians who were taking exception to the prevailing interpretation of World War I.

Viereck's attempts to influence the elections of 1920 and 1924 represented one aspect of a two-fold strategy. His other tactic was promoting and joining the "revisionists" who began to make their voices heard in the early 1920's in opposition to the conventional explanation for the causes of World War I and America's intervention. The ranks of the latter group held a motley assortment of individuals, ranging from liberals to re-

43 Ibid., pp. 310–12.
44 *American Monthly*, July, 1925, p. 133.

actionaries and from politicians and publicists to professors. It is perhaps no surprise that Viereck found in revisionism the ammunition suitable for making Germany respectable again in the eyes of Americans.

At the end of World War I the verdict among Americans and people of the Allied nations was almost unanimous: Germany bore the chief, if not sole, responsibility for starting the war, and Austria-Hungary was her guilty accomplice in arms. Yet already by November, 1918, the innocence of the Allies—Czarist Russia in particular—was being challenged by documents published by the revolutionary Bolshevik regime. These documents portrayed Russia and France working secretly and vigorously to strengthen their forces against the Triple Alliance. Then, after the terms of the punitive Versailles Treaty were presented to Germany in the spring of 1919, liberal writers and publications in America such as the *Nation, New Republic,* and *Dial* began to judge harshly a war settlement which seemed to ignore Wilson's principles of peace without annexations or indemnities.[45]

Even in England and France there soon appeared vocal critics of the peace treaty and its assignment of war guilt, and their testimony was especially damaging. Edmund D. Morel, an English liberal and member of Parliament who had been imprisoned during the war, gained considerable attention as a "revisionist"—that is, as one who attempted to revise the conventional interpretations of the war. But most English historians remained faithful to the orthodox view. According to Selig Adler, an American analyst of this phenomenon, French revisionists exerted an important influence on American public opinion. This challenge to the earlier consensus was encouraged by the English and French governments' failures to open their archives until after 1926, when the dissenting movement was well underway. But revisionism in a larger sense was a logical ingredient of the debunking, denunciatory age that followed a most disillusioning war.[46]

In America Sidney Fay was the first reputable historian to

[45] Selig Adler, "The War-Guilt Question and American Disillusionment, 1918–1928," *Journal of Modern History* XXIII (March, 1951): 4, 10.

[46] Ibid., pp. 2–10, 23–24.

begin a cautious revision of the prevailing interpretation. In an article in mid-1920 he showed that both the Kaiser and the Czar had been misled by their military advisers and that neither leader sought war. Later in the decade Fay completed an extensive study which put the major onus of immediate responsibility for launching the war on Austria and made Russia equally if not more responsible than Germany for making war inevitable by ordering hasty mobilization. Less cautious and more biased toward the German position was well-known historian Harry Elmer Barnes, who in the mid-1920's offered the judgment that Serbia, France, and Russia shared primary responsibility for the conflict. Among American politicians the most outspoken and persistent promoter of a reconstructed view was Oklahoma senator Robert Owen, who was indelibly impressed by evidence of Czarist culpability. Through the efforts of these and other rewriters of history, Germany again by 1929 "enjoyed a decent respect in the opinion of mankind," concludes Adler.[47]

During the first half of the 1920's Viereck found several legislators worthy of support; in addition to Senator Owen, they included Emmanuel Celler (New York), Hamilton Fish, Jr. (New York), Henrik Shipstead (Minnesota), William E. Borah (Idaho), and Hiram Johnson (California). Only a few of these individuals seemed to have an active interest in German affairs, and none of them appeared to share Viereck's extreme desire for a resurgence of German national power. Yet they were all sympathetic in some degree with the plight of postwar Germany and its attempts to restore a viable economy. More notably, all were opposed to American membership in the League of Nations or in any other organization that would entail American military or political obligations to Europe, and most of them were outspoken critics of British imperialism. Several also attacked the assignment of primary "war guilt" to Germany and attempted to set

[47] Sidney Fay, "New Light on the Origins of the World War, I., Berlin and Vienna, to July 29," *American Historical Review* XXV (July, 1920): 616–39; Sidney Fay, *The Origins of the World War* (New York: Macmillan, 1929), Vol. II, pp. 350–58; Harry E. Barnes, *The Genesis of the World War* (New York: Alfred Knopf, 1926), pp. 651–59; Adler, "The War-Guilt Question," pp. 14, 28.

forth explanations for the war which placed greater culpability on other nations—principally Russia and France. Along with Senator Owen, Congressman Fish was especially vocal among those legislators who felt that the accounts of World War I and the treaty itself should be revised to absolve Germany of the stigma of guilt assigned to her by the Allies.

After his return from inflation-ravaged Germany in 1923, Viereck intensified his efforts to bring before Congress and the American public his views on the causes for the war and the need to revise the peace treaties and alleviate Germany's suffering. He was not alone in this endeavor. The Steuben Society, through its journal, constantly harped on the theme of vindicating Germany of war guilt. Other more reputable liberal magazines like the *Nation* and *New Republic* likewise led a rising chorus of dissent over the Versailles Treaty and its treatment of Germany. A sizeable minority in Congress reflected similar sentiments, but the majority of congressmen, including the revisionists, favored an isolationist foreign policy that meant the United States would not likely prod the European Allies to revise the terms of peace.[48] Nor would Congress consider canceling Europe's war debts to the United States, thus making it even less feasible for the European Allies to forego the income derived from reparations. Yet Congress could help alleviate Germany's recovery on a bilateral basis, if the majority of the legislators could be converted to a sympathetic view of Germany and the need for America to be just and even generous with her.

In early 1924 Viereck became an active lobbyist, writing to several legislators who had shown an interest in better relations with Germany and sending them copies of his *American Monthly* for their edification. He also had the support of August Heckscher, a wealthy businessman sympathetic to Germany who offered to pay the bill if Viereck could get one of his journal articles by E. D. Morel into the hands of every member of Congress. Among the legislators themselves, he had established contacts with Senator Owen. In February, 1924, Viereck wrote an abstract of one of Owen's speeches on war guilt and published it in his

[48] Adler, *Isolationist Impulse*, pp. 164, 169–70.

journal. Owen in turn had the abstract printed in the *Congressional Record*, and two weeks later he had 10,000 copies printed for distribution.[49] Owen's argument rested heavily upon evidence in Czarist diplomatic documents which convinced him that Russia's "militarist clique" had started the war with the aid of France.

Possibly influenced in part by Viereck's lobbying, two other congressmen sponsored bills to aid Germany. Representative Emmanuel Celler of New York, for example, offered a resolution in February, 1924, requesting the appropriation of $25,000,000 for the relief of Germany's suffering poor. This measure found few supporters and was soon defeated. Shortly thereafter, another New York representative, Hamilton Fish, Jr., proposed a bill to appropriate $10,000,000 for the purchase of foodstuffs in the United States and their transportation and distribution to the starving women and children of Germany. Although approved in the House, it met defeat in the Senate (53–23) in June, 1924, despite support from Senators Owen, La Follette, and others.[50]

There were other indications that pro-Germanism was unpopular. Harold Knutson, a Minnesota congressman and sympathizer with Germany, claimed to have incurred "humiliation and suffering" as a result of taking a "stand for justice" toward Germany. Likewise, Senator Owen admitted to Viereck that he had been harassed for his views on Germany and, possibly as a consequence of his controversial position, he declined renomination in the campaign of 1924 after having served eighteen years in the Senate.[51] During the next three years he continued to contribute to the *American Monthly*, and he served as an assistant editor on the editions in 1927 dealing with a "war guilt forum"

[49] August Heckscher to G. S. Viereck, November 23, 1923; Robert Owen to G. S. Viereck, January 7, 1924, and March 15, 1924, Viereck MSS; Robert O. Owen, "Russian Militarist Clique Started the War with the Aid of Paris," *American Monthly*, February, 1924, pp. 361–69; *Congressional Record*, 68th Cong., 1st Sess., 1924, LXV, Pt. 3, pp. 3068–75.

[50] Emmanuel Celler to G. S. Viereck, February 11, 1924, and March 6, 1924, Viereck MSS; *American Monthly*, June, 1924, p. 123; *Congressional Record*, 68th Cong., 1st Sess., 1924, LXV, Pt. 5, pp. 4818, 4827, 4863; Pt. 11, pp. 10984, 10994.

[51] Harold Knutson to G. S. Viereck, May 5, 1924; Robert O. Owen to G. S. Viereck, February 1, 1924, and May 13, 1926, Viereck MSS. Also see *American Monthly*, November, 1926, pp. 262–64.

which summarized the arguments of a variety of revisionist sources.

In this forum Viereck praised, in particular, Congressman Charles Lindbergh's revisionist views on the war and his diatribes against the so-called "Money Trust" which allegedly played a dominant role in American involvement. This emphasis also continued after October, 1927, when David Maier became the chief editor and publisher of the journal. Included in the February, 1928 issue, for example, was a letter from Congressman Fish suggesting that the war guilt issue be placed on the agenda of the Institute of Politics to be held the following summer in Williamstown. Fish said he feared that if the question were raised in Congress it would become involved in other political issues, including the League of Nations. He made a valid point in asserting that it did not seem fair to the German people or to history to let the issue of guilt rest solely upon an admission extracted from the German delegates who signed the Treaty of Versailles.[52]

Beginning in 1927, Viereck also attempted to interview and obtain articles from William E. Borah, the isolationist chairman of the Senate Committee on Foreign Relations, with little initial success. However, in 1929 Borah consented to the *American Monthly*'s publication of an article on the evacuation of the Rhineland and another entitled "In the Shadow of the Mailed Fist," which discussed the indemnity problem as a bone of contention attributable to the "crime of Versailles." Other 1929 journal contributors included fellow isolationist Senators George W. Norris and Hiram W. Johnson.[53]

This is not to say that the concerns and motives of these isolationist senators were necessarily identical with Viereck's. Their isolationism seemed to issue from an abiding faith in American democracy and a fear that involvement with a "decadent" Europe would contaminate or otherwise compromise domestic peace and freedom. Viereck did not share their disdain for the

[52] Also see *American Monthly*, October, 1927, pp. 3–6; November, 1927, pp. 7–9, 19.
[53] William Borah to G. S. Viereck, October 22, 1927, Gertz MSS. Articles by Borah, Johnson, and Norris are found in *American Monthly*, February, March, May, and July, 1929.

culture of Europe or its monarchical tradition. Their main area of agreement seemed to be the assumption that British-based "International Finance" and America's own "munitions makers" were the chief culprits behind the war. Perhaps it was their negative tie—a mutual distrust of England's imperial ambitions—as well as the positive search for a judicious verdict on the war that formed the basis for this affiliation of disparate personalities.

Nor did Viereck share the pacifism that characterized some of the congressional isolationists. He did not believe all wars were immoral, and during the 1920's he had called for large naval expenditures. By 1930, however, he too was becoming aware of the danger of a new war in Europe and the consequent need to establish rules for universal disarmament. He believed that America could exert moral influence in this direction and help enforce such a drive by threatening to withhold loans and other monetary income on military budgets. This would be done without compromising America's political independence of Europe.[54]

Besides making use of dissident politicians, Viereck found it expedient to exploit the revisionism of two American professors and of several foreign publicists and writers. One of the professors was noted social historian Harry Elmer Barnes. Barnes came to Viereck's attention in 1924 when he published in *Current History Magazine* an assessment of the war which concluded that Germany was not responsible for starting it, and that blame should be assigned to Austria, Russia, France, Germany, and England in that order. The article was republished in the *American Monthly*. The next year Viereck publicized Barnes's new assessment that revised the order of guilt, placing both France and Russia in first place, followed by Austria, Germany, and England. Viereck also said he agreed with a speech by Sidney Fay attacking the "war guilt lie" but disputed his conclusion that a militarist spirit prevailed in Germany prior to the war. Fay became a friend of Viereck's in the 1930's and an apologist for him in the 1940's. Barnes meanwhile kept up his barrage against the "war guilt myths" with several articles on this subject in the *American*

[54] G. S. Viereck, "Europe Arms for the Next War," *Saturday Evening Post*, February 8, 1930, pp. 20–21.

Monthly during 1929.[55] It is safe to say that these iconoclastic and somewhat impassioned interpretations did not enhance Barnes's reputation among the majority of American historians.

Among the polemical works and supposed exposés by foreign observers and writers, Viereck drew on several British revisionists including Edmund D. Morel and C. Raymond Beazley, German propagandist Max von Montgelas, Italian Prime Minister Francesco Nitti, and the Bolshevik accounts implicating the Czarist war minister and foreign minister in the prewar plotting against Germany.[56] The point is that Viereck was willing to accept from and offer support to any individual who made Russia, France, or England relatively more culpable for the war or who presented evidence that tended to exonerate Germany. His use of such evidence could not be called objective or balanced, and he made no secret of his partiality for the German point of view. But by operating on the premise that the prevailing American views of the war were biased toward the British and French points of view, he could claim that only by appreciating the German side of the question could the impartial American come to a balanced perspective of the entire issue.

Early in 1929 Viereck noted that public opinion was changing on the war guilt question, but he claimed that Allied statesmen dared not at present permit a modification of Article 231 "because their whole financial structure depends upon its retention." He added that the United States should show the way by eliminating this clause in its own treaty with Germany. If the American public was changing its mind about the extent of Germany's guilt, Viereck himself was on the eve of a view reversal. In the fall of 1929, under circumstances described later, he became an enthusiastic friend of Colonel House. From House and his letters to President Wilson in World War I, Viereck received new insights into the causes of the war and the sincerity of Wilson's

[55] Note especially Harry E. Barnes, "A Rejoinder to M. Poincare," *American Monthly*, December, 1925, pp. 296–97, 314–19.

[56] For revisionist articles, see especially *American Monthly*, February, 1924, pp. 357, 361–69; May, 1924, pp. 78–89; April, 1925, pp. 112–17; September, 1925, pp. 240–49. On war guilt issue see the "War Guilt Forum" in *American Monthly*, January, 1927, to February, 1928; and October, 1929.

motives. By 1931 he confessed his belief that "all nations stumbled blindly into the abyss" and that no nation could be singled out as the guilty party. He even claimed now that he "never was" concerned with the question of war guilt—that is, with the rights and wrongs of the case—but that his rising to Germany's defense was "instinctive."[57] One might think that he had experienced a "conversion," but later events involving his support of Nazi Germany and his continued apologia for the ex-Kaiser indicate that much of the "Old Adam" remained.

In saying that he had not been concerned with war guilt, he seemed to mean that he had not considered it a moral issue in which metaphysical ideas of right and wrong were involved. In fact, referring to the matter in 1931, he denied that there was a right or wrong side and confessed his disbelief in moral law in nature or society.[58] This mood of resignation and moral confusion was aptly expressed in a poem written in 1930, entitled "After the Battle—1930":

> I struck for what I deemed the right.
> I saw the Truth. I was her knight.
> My foemen, too, were thus aflame,
> Blind chessmen in the obscure game
> Of some malign divinity.
> Now, with unfolding eyes, we see
> The paradox of every fight,
> That both are wrong and both are right,
> That friend is foe, and foe is friend,
> And nothing matters in the end.[59]

Viereck's mood after the war paralleled that of the majority of German-American editors who criticized Wilson, castigated the League of Nations, and supported Harding in 1920. But, whereas most of these periodicals reverted after 1920 to a concentration on domestic issues and to encouraging the revival of traditional cultural activities in local German-American societies,

[57] *American Monthly,* March, 1929, p. 3; Viereck, *My Flesh and Blood,* pp. 276, 307.
[58] Ibid., pp. 288, 307.
[59] Ibid., p. 306.

Viereck remained involved with "hyphen politics" and foreign affairs.

Most German-Americans apparently wished to return to normalcy—to forget about the troubles of Europe. Viereck could not forget so readily or easily. He was, to be sure, in a minority. He was not able to enlist any appreciable support for his strongly pro-German journal, nor was he able to arouse German-Americans to unify for the purpose of achieving stronger political representation and influence. In fact, his vocal and militant efforts to identify the German-American vote with Harding in 1920 and with La Follette in 1924 antagonized many German-American editors who wished to avoid the issue of "hyphenism" in politics and who did not accept Viereck's claim to speak for the bulk of Americans of German descent. Although he could not bring himself to admit it, except to complain about the indifference of the "silk stocking" or wealthy men to his cause, most German-Americans in the 1920's seemed not to share his feeling that German-Americans must agitate and lobby to promote ethnic causes.

Viereck could feel more successful in his promotion of revisionism; yet this movement was not specifically identified with German-Americanism. It won converts from a wide variety of ethnic groups. Moreover, it was closely linked with the popular isolationist mood of the American people. Both of these causes found support from Viereck and presumably his readers, as well as from the vocal and militant Steuben Society. Indeed, Selig Adler contends that the efforts of German-Americans had "far-reaching" effects upon the formation of the isolationist sentiment, exceeded only, it seems, by the influence of the Irish-Americans.[60] In this context Viereck's contribution should not be minimized—but again we must recognize that he was only one of a host of revisionists and isolationists, many of whom were more popular and reputable than he.

Less representative of German-American sentiment was Viereck's support of Debs and La Follette. His activity on their behalf stemmed largely from his sense of frustration with the politics of

[60] Adler, *Isolationist Impulse*, pp. 85, 88–89.

normalcy. His frustration and his narcissism were evident in his tendency to react to defeat with bad grace, to admit no wrong, and to impute bad motives or inferior sensibility to the opponent. His aesthetic orientation also came to the fore in the latter half of the decade, when he returned to literary pursuits and denied that his involvement in the war guilt question implied belief in any ultimate law of moral rights or wrongs. In brief, Viereck altered his rhetoric and his behavior in a variety of ways after April, 1917, to meet changing exigencies, but his characteristic values and beliefs remained unchanged. This consistency of attitude was also to be reflected in his strong advocacy of nationalist revival in Germany during the early 1920's.

In its treaty with Germany, the
United States did not demand any reparations of consequence
for itself. But it did expect full payment of debts contracted by
the Entente powers, and partly to meet these debts the Allied
nations in turn demanded that defeated Germany meet its indemnity charges promptly and completely. In this way the United
States indirectly laid a burden upon the infant and feeble Weimar
Republic that far outweighed the value of free food and other
necessities which Americans donated to destitute Germans in
1919. Indeed, it took time, at least two or three years, for general
American hostility toward Germany to subside. In the meantime,
seeking a return to normalcy, the American people turned their
attention away from European politics to focus on interests closer
to home. Understandably, in this climate Germany's need for
large American loans or credits went unmet. Some Americans did
buy German bonds prior to 1922, to an amount of several hundred million dollars, but rampant inflation in 1923 resulted in
their losing most of the investment.[1]

It was the eruption of financial chaos in Germany in 1923 that
brought the first noticeable wave of American sympathy for the
fledgling republic. When France anounced its plan to occupy the
Ruhr to force Germany to speed up its lagging reparations payments in late 1922, American Secretary of State Charles Evans
Hughes warned that such action would bring disaster rather than
a solution. After the French troops began to march, the President,
at the behest of the Senate, ordered the last contingent of Amer-

[1] Sidney Brooks, *America and Germany, 1918–1925* (New York:
Macmillan, 1925), pp. 55, 128, 140; Adler, *Isolationist Impulse*, p. 144.

ican occupation troops out of the Rhineland. The occupation spurred the German government to allow disintegration of the German mark and cost France more of her American friends. It is notable that virtually all the liberal American isolationists, including Robert La Follette and Oswald Garrison Villard, defended Germany's position.[2]

The crisis ended when Secretary of State Hughes initiated a proposal, later known as the Dawes Plan, which helped Germany rehabilitate her economy and resume a schedule of smaller but progressively increasing reparations payments. As the Ruhr episode receded into the past, American interest in European affairs likewise waned. But Germany's image continued to brighten as American tourists began visiting Germany in greater numbers than before the war; many of them came back to report that the German people were more cordial to them than were the French or English. American ambassador to Germany Alanson B. Houghton declared before he left his post in 1925 that German militarism was dead, that Germany was a bulwark against the expansion of Bolshevism, and that the Weimar government's only great ambition was to restore economic prosperity. A similar attitude was reflected in the American press as more and more editors demanded a revision or termination of the punitive features of the Versailles Treaty. The moderate policies and apparently peaceful intentions of German Foreign Minister Gustav Stresemann further enhanced American good will toward the German nation. American citizens also showed their new confidence in the burgeoning German economy by investing an unprecedented amount of over $2 billion in German public bonds and industrial securities in the latter half of the decade.[3]

As German prosperity increased, then, and it became possible to ignore such things as the Nazi movement and see the republican government functioning successfully, Americans in general took a new and more positive interest in the German nation. For Viereck, the process was just the opposite. In the late 1920's, his

[2] Adler, Isolationist Impulse, pp. 155–56.
[3] Charles H. Sherrill, "Our Friends, the Germans and Japanese," Review of Reviews LXXVI (December, 1927) : 635–37; Adler, Isolationist Impulse, pp. 163, 175–76.

concern about German affairs declined. It was during the early postwar years that he was most deeply and emotionally involved in efforts to secure official aid and assistance to the beleaguered German people. And while his efforts at that time were largely unsuccessful, he did prove, in retrospect, to be a prescient forecaster of German nationalist sentiment.

It should be stressed that even among Americans of German descent, few shared Viereck's militant concern about the fate of German nationalism. The Steuben Society came closest to his position, but this group was relatively small. In his promotion of German nationalism, therefore, Viereck mirrored not the majority of German-Americans, but only a small core of activists.

Along with his support of anti-Wilson politicians, revisionists, and isolationists at home, Viereck in the 1920's spoke out for the interests of German nationalism abroad. This first became evident in June, 1919, when he raged about the terms of the Versailles Treaty: "Henceforth the dream of every German will be consecrated to a greater Germany. French occupation of the Saar Valley will be a daily reminder of 'revanche.' We shall wake Barbarossa from his sleep. Every German in the world will become an irredentist."[4] Unfortunately, these words proved prophetic.

While helping Germany in a more positive way by organizing a relief drive which produced about $500,000 in clothing and food for destitute Germans, Viereck kept up a barrage of criticism toward those countries he felt were victimizing Germany. He was especially vociferous in his denunciations of France. He felt that Germany's western neighbor had been instrumental in imposing the huge reparations burden upon her and in compromising Germany's sovereignty in the Rhineland and the Saar. Especially distasteful to him was the 1921 French occupation of certain cities in the Ruhr to force reparations payments. On November 25, 1921, he set forth his response to Briand's suggestion that Americans of German descent act as intermediaries between Germany and France. Implying that he spoke for most German-Americans, Viereck said that this segment of the population would like to play such a role, but it could not do so in good faith because of

[4] *Viereck's*, June, 1919, p. 102.

such unredressed grievances as the French occupation, the veto of an *Anschluss* between Germany and Austria, the problem of Danzig and the Polish corridor, the excessive reparations, the Allied commissions that "violated" German sovereignty, and the annexation of Alsace-Lorraine without a plebiscite. He then appealed for a revision of the Versailles Treaty, "not merely as an advocate of abstract justice, but because the self-interest, no less than the honor, of the United States demands a strong and prosperous Central Europe, content with its fate and in peace with its neighbors." He hoped Briand would begin a reconciliation with Germany by withdrawing French troops, abolishing sanctions, and agreeing to a conference for the reconstruction of Europe with Germany at the council table; hopefully, all German-speaking people contiguous to Germany would be allowed to unite under one flag.[5]

It was this last request, the union of all Germans in central Europe under one flag, that was the most impractical and the most ominous of Viereck's proposals. In the same issue of his *American Monthly*, he published two maps—one showing the current boundaries of Germany, the other indicating the borders of a Germany established by self-determination. The latter map included within Germany such areas as Alsace-Lorraine, the Tyrol, Austria, Moravia, part of Poland, and most of the Baltic republics. The latter arrangement, Viereck implied, was Germany's "manifest destiny," not to be thwarted by France. Then he set forth a prophecy uncanny in its prescience: "Sooner or later Barbarossa will arise. He may come crowned as an Emperor, he may come as a Dictator risen out of the ranks, or he may be the Elected Representative of the People; but sooner or later he will heed the call of his race. All countries speaking the German language will be united under the German flag, just as all people who speak French are united under the tri-colored banner of France. . . ."[6]

This dream of German unity was, of course, an old one with Viereck, but the context in which he discussed it had changed somewhat. Back in 1919 he had seen it coming as a part of a true "internationalism," a system in which the major powers would be

[5] *American Monthly*, June, 1922, p. 114; December, 1921, p. 293.
[6] Ibid., p. 299.

equal, race rather than dynasty would be the "determinant of nationality," and boundaries would be determined by the wishes of the people. Now, since the Versailles Treaty had destroyed all hope for such a system, he had become a nationalist, arguing that the best course for either Germany or the United States was to pursue its own national interest without regard to the claims of international bodies. In 1921, he opposed the Washington disarmament conference for fear that it would leave the American navy weaker than Great Britain's and would involve the United States in international obligations.[7] At the same time, he aligned himself with and developed an elaborate apology for German nationalism.

Almost unconsciously and instinctively, it seemed, Viereck became a mirror of the nationalist movement in Germany—a force only faintly visible to Americans and, in the light of later events, greatly underrated and unappreciated. Most American editors, judging from reprints in the *American Monthly*, looked upon Viereck as a transplanted German of dubious loyalty, but hardly any recognized that in him they had an index or barometer of the feelings and attitudes of a large proportion of the German people. He could still claim—sincerely, it seems—that he was for "America First," that in case of conflict between his two loyalties his obligations to America would always be the strongest, but in many respects he did represent the mirror image of a German nationalist.

But if one is to regard Viereck as a transplanted German nationalist, one should do so with some qualifications. For one thing, he should not be classified with the radical right-wing and anti-Semitic extremists who were responsible for the assassinations of Mathias Erzberger, the chief signer of the peace treaty, and Walter Rathenau, Germany's Jewish minister of reconstruction. It should be noted that the *American Monthly* published articles by Rathenau, and Viereck himself rejected assassination as a legitimate political weapon. The Germans, he said, should settle their differences by due process of law and, most important, they should unite "on a common basis of patriotism." The most

[7] *Viereck's*, March, 1919, p. 4; *American Monthly*, December, 1921, p. 302.

that one might say is that Viereck, sympathizing with the goals of the extremists, was slow to condemn them, and when Rathenau was murdered, he did give credence to a right-wing rumor that the crime had been plotted or provoked by France.[8]

Likewise, one should note that his support of German nationalist aims did not necessarily set him in opposition to republican government. At its outset in early 1919 Viereck held out the hope that the Weimar constitution might be the "greatest experiment in human freedom since the Declaration of Independence." He added that America should extend a helping hand to the new republic to help it become the "cradle of liberty" in the Old World. "It is either that or—the Deluge," he concluded. "Deluge" seems to have been a reference to Bolshevism. However, a year later he advised his German-American readers that the German people knew what was best for themselves, and that German-Americans should cooperate with Germany in "rebuilding bridges of international amity" if she "turns east to Bolshevism," if she decided for a conservative government, or retained Ebert. "Few" Germans were in sympathy with the doctrines of Lenin and Trotsky, he noted; "some" were in sympathy with the "semi-socialistic, semi-clerical" bloc of the Weimar government, and "many" would like to see the rule restored "under which Germany reached the acme of her prosperity." "All" Germans were "thrilled by such names as Hindenberg." He also alleged that America had lured Germany to her destruction with the "political gold brick" of the Fourteen Points and thus the "moral duty" to reconstruct Central Europe devolved chiefly upon the American people.[9]

It is clear that Viereck felt committed to the task of helping reconstruct Germany and Austria—not necessarily on democratic lines, but in whatever manner would help them recover their former status and power. It is evident, too, that he was one of very few German-American editors that felt this kind of obligation. In May, 1922, he criticized the Ridder family—publishers of the *New York Staats-Zeitung*, perhaps the leading German-language

[8] *American Monthly*, October, 1921, p. 235; January, 1922, pp. 349–50; July, 1922, pp. 134–35.
[9] *Viereck's*, March, 1919, p. 5; April, 1920, p. 38.

publication in the country—and other German-language newspaper editors for their lukewarm attitude toward German interests and affairs. He also implied that most German-American
publications were ineffectual and dull because they avoided controversy and polemics.[10] Nevertheless, it is clear that his own
brand of extreme partisanship appealed to only a few German-
Americans. A key to his own psychological attitude toward controversy is provided by his eulogy of his father upon the latter's
death in mid-September, 1922. He described his father as a genial
type with an accommodating disposition that made him what
Americans call a "good loser." Then he added: "This last trait
seems at times to have been present in excess as the foundation of
a character too disposed to withdraw from controversy before it
reached the point of open rupture, too disposed to avoid even
those personal triumphs that entail the temporary discomfiture of
an opponent."[11]

His singular efforts did not go unnoticed in the German press.
According to a Berlin newspaper, in late 1921 there were only
three American journals notable for their unequivocating opposition to the Versailles Treaty and to the imputation of war guilt
to Germany: the *American Monthly*, Singer's *Neue Zeit* in Chicago, and Frederick Schrader's *Issues of Today* (the primary organ of the Steuben Society of America).[12]

Disturbed as he was by conditions in Germany, Viereck was
finally able to make his first postwar trip to Europe in September,
1922. Finding an employer in Bradford Merrill, editor of the
Hearst newspaper chain's Sunday supplement, "The March of
Events," he agreed to interview leading figures in Germany and
elsewhere; for each interview published he was to receive $500.
Of course, these same articles were also destined to be printed in
his own journal. Viereck took his wife and two sons with him,
remaining in Europe for seven months. It was his intention to give
his impressions "without bias." Unfortunately, his trip coincided
with a worsening of German-French relations, which reached
their depths in the French occupation of the Ruhr in early 1923.

[10] *American Monthly*, May, 1922, pp. 74–76.
[11] *American Monthly*, October, 1922, p. 232.
[12] Cited in *American Monthly*, January, 1922, p. 387.

Subsequent articles by the roving journalist bore titles like "A Trip through Topsy Turvy Land," "The Smileless Land between Rhine and Ruhr," and "French in Ruhr War on Children." In the course of this extensive reportorial tour, he interviewed the foreign ministers of several countries, the Socialist speaker of the Bundestag (Loebe), famed Marxist revisionist Eduard Bernstein, and Socialist editor Karl Stampfer; such nationalists as Karl Helfferich (leader of the German National Peoples party), Hitler (the "German Mussolini"), and Ludendorff; several major industrialists (Carl Siemens, Felix Deutsch, Krupp von Bohlen, and Fritz and August Thyssen); the executive officers of the "Deutsche" banks; authors Hauptmann, Sudermann, Fulda, and Shaw; Oswald Spengler; Steinach, Freud, Havelock Ellis, and Magnus Hirschfeld; British labor leaders Ramsay MacDonald and Philip Snowden; pacifist Edmund D. Morel; and various members of the former imperial house, including the exiled Kaiser and the Crown Prince. Most of these interviews were published in subsequent issues of Hearst's *New York American* as well as in other Hearst papers and in Viereck's *American Monthly*. Thus Viereck's sympathetic feelings toward Germany received wide exposure in the 1920's and presumably contributed to the American public's growing disillusionment over the war and its aftermath.

Predictably, Viereck's trip served to reinforce his animosity toward the French and the League of Nations and strengthened his sympathy for the nationalist point of view. Upon his return he called for the mobilization of world opinion against France. Especially galling to him was France's use of black African troops in the occupation; this reaction reflected his attitude of condescension toward the Negro, a common prejudice of white Americans at that time. He also arranged to have Karl Helfferich, a nationalist party leader and former vice-chancellor under the Empire, contribute articles periodically to the *American Monthly*. The experience likewise deepened his cynicism about the future of democracy in Europe and about the possibility of right instead of might governing relations between nations. He declared in October, 1923, that Mussolini's defiance of the League of Nations over the Corfu issue proved that "strength alone counts today," and that "only a Mussolini can save Germany from the pit!" Turning to the chaotic situation in Germany in mid-1923, Viereck counseled against any capitulation to France and proclaimed: "A government composed of Hindenburg, Ludendorff, Tirpitz, Helfferich, fortified by Escherich and Hitler, would inspire respect. It would breathe courage into German hearts and impress Poincare; weakness, surrender, compromise, inspire only contempt." In case of capitulation, he asserted that Germany's sons in other lands "must maintain the race spirit" and "support the national nucleus from which some day Germany's savior will rise."[13]

One important source of Viereck's uncertainty about democracy may be found in his amoral and aesthetic orientation toward life in general and politics in particular. This type of approach was exemplified in his first contact with a man destined to be one of democracy's fiercest foes—Adolf Hitler. Early in 1923 Viereck sought out this "upstart" in German politics for an interview. To Viereck, Hitler looked "more like a poet than a politician." Hitler told his interviewer how he planned to undercut the Marxists by restoring true "Aryan socialism" to Germany and how his scheme for a German state would allow no room for "the alien . . . no use for the wastrel, for the usurer or speculator, or anyone incapable of productive work." He declared, in particular, that the Jews would be disfranchised because they were a "disturbing influence" and an "alien people in our midst" and were guilty of making "a virtue of weakness." He even claimed that Marxism was a Jewish invention. To Viereck's rejoinder that Germany owed much to the Jews and that some of her most respected citizens were Jews, Hitler replied, "The fact that a man is decent is no reason why we should not eliminate him." At the end of Hitler's diatribe, Viereck observed, "For the moment there flashed, out of his eyes, something of the Blonde Beast of Nietzsche." Viereck decided that Hitler was a self-sacrificing "idealist, however mistaken," and concluded, "If he lives, Hitler for better or for worse, is sure to make history."[14]

It is interesting to note that in mid-1923, a short time before Hitler's ill-fated putsch, Viereck's article on Hitler was rejected

[13] *American Monthly*, May, 1923, p. 70; October, 1923, pp. 230–31.
[14] *American Monthly*, October, 1923, pp. 235–38.

by the mass-circulation magazines to which he had submitted it. According to Viereck, the editors of these publications thought the subject was of too little public interest. Consequently, he had to publish it in his own journal.[15]

There is no evidence to suggest that Viereck was particularly appalled or frightened by the irrational, egoistic, and even brutal implications of Hitler's message. The implicit dangers in Hitler's philosophy seemed to be lost on Viereck—the "poet of passion"—who unfortunately was dealing now not with poetry but with the life-and-death realities of politics. In early 1924, when Ludendorff was released from custody after being jailed for his role in the "Beer Hall Putsch," Viereck asserted that Hitler should have been freed, too, "unless patriotism is a crime in the German Republic." The fact that Hitler was a devoted nationalist appeared to be justification enough for his actions, in Viereck's view. Viereck then rationalized his position as follows: "Internationalism is a higher phase of human evolution. But its day has not yet come. Until it comes, the German, whether Catholic, Protestant, Jew, or social reformer must be a German first. We have no respect for a German who does not put Germany first, just as we have no respect for an American who does not put America first."[16] Despite the concluding note in his interview with Hitler, Viereck did not seem to appreciate the potential of Hitler's band of fanatical nationalists, and between 1924 and 1932 he paid little further attention to the future Fuehrer, briefly mentioning the Nazi leader on only three or four occasions in his journal.

For the most part, the *American Monthly* continued to reflect sympathy for the aims and policies of German nationalists. Thus in 1924 it gave currency to the myth of the *Dolchstoss*—"stab in the back." Viereck reprinted material from articles collected and published in Germany that allegedly documented the *Dolchstoss*.[17] This myth, attractive to conservative nationalists in particular, held that the German army had not actually been defeated in the war but that the nation had surrendered under the

[15] *New Yorker*, June 15, 1940, pp. 15–16.
[16] *American Monthly*, May, 1924, p. 72.
[17] *American Monthly*, August, 1924, pp. 171–76; September, 1924, p. 246.

The aesthete: Viereck around 1904, on the eve of a short-lived career as a highly respected neo-romantic poet. As a latent propagandist, he also would shortly style himself an "American barbarian" ready to interpret his German fatherland to his American adopted mate.

Probably taken in 1931 when Viereck was at the height of his success as a novelist, "interviewer deluxe," and literary psychoanalyst.

Viereck, at 65, Is a Poet of Passion Reborn

Propagandist Dreams
Of 3d Trip to Top

By HARRY GABBETT

You, too, are stung by the self-
*   same power,*
Your quick breath tells in its
*   shuddering fall:*
There is naught so strong as
*   love this hour—*
Call him god or beast, he is lord
*   of all!*

Thus, one-half a century ago, did a young and vibrant George Sylvester Viereck sing in his little-known "Love Triumphant," a poetic effort which he subsequently dismissed as "the cause of my failure in mathematics."

A gifted stripling at the time, this German-born poet of passion was destined to scale within the next few years literary heights from which few singers are permitted to gaze in their own lifetimes.

Reached Front Ranks

Within those next few years, George Sylvester Viereck's pen propelled him into the front ranks of American lyricists. Early 20th century critics hailed this young unquestioned master of two languages as another Shelley, another Heine, an inordinately winning wooer of the Muse elusive.

Nor could the most discerning of his champions foresee themselves before the very decade was done referring to him as "a venom-bloated toad of treason," an unreasonably wanton fellow who had plunged the very shaft of his ringing pen into his adopted country's vitals.

Almost to a man, and approximately in a trice, they forgot the lilting lines with which he had opened "The Love Seal" . . .

A silver sea beneath the stars—
*   We paid to love his mystic*
*   rites,*
And from thy lips I kissed the
*   scars*
Of fiercer joys and stranger
*   nights . . .*

By a howling majority was Viereck voted out of the nation's various literary societies, many of which he had helped to form. Of such a nature were his crimes—real or imagined in the chaotic mass psychoses of World War I—that they left no room for compromise. This "venom-bloated toad of treason" still strummed his lute, it was agreed, but the sounds he brought forth were the paeons of international discord. The poet of passion was spawning in his lyric incubator now the deadly, pro-German, germs of propagandistic hate.

Seeks Police Aid

George Sylvester Viereck, poet, became George Sylvester Viereck,

Times-Herald Staff Photo
GEORGE SYLVESTER VIERECK
At the 65th milestone in his first 2,000 years.

Flower" he had lamented so neatly . . .

Once thought I to kiss with
*   unperishing kisses*
Your lips that as mantles of
*   queens are red,*
Once thought I no love in the
*   world as this is,*
O beautiful love, O dream that
*   is dead!*

Within the next decade, however, George Sylvester Viereck's restless pen was at it again—writing him slowly at first, but ever faster, out of his incredible obscurity into a brand new sun. He was literarily reincarnated, so to speak, as George Sylvester Viereck, author.

His Trilogy Appears

From his seemingly inexhaustible spring there flowed his best-selling trilogy, "My First 2,000 Years," his deafeningly acclaimed "Glimpses of the Great," and his own account of his World War I activities, "Spreading Germs of Hate." In between was his poetic autobiography, "My Flesh and Blood," an impish experiment that was destined to play a part

In due course, too, he installed himself in a 10-room penthouse on forbiddingly fashionable Riverside drive, surrounded himself with b.s easily won luxuries, became only idly bemused at the ominous rumblings of World War II—rumblings which became for him the old siren call to calamity.

It Was Inevitable

His involvement was as inevitable as he now believes his extrication will be.

Almost involuntarily he marshaled and mushroomed his myriad of propaganda mills and arrayed them for another duel with destiny.

He was about to board a Hamburg-bound luxury liner when the FBI touched his well-clad shoulder for the first time in 1938. He came quietly, the man who touched his shoulder was able to report. There was no shouting, no tumult, no riotous uproarious scenes such as were within the next few years to accompany Viereck's most recent tumble down the rugged stairs he had only just reascended.

There followed, of course, his three trials here on federal

Ready to Unleash
New Flood of Words

charges that he failed to fully disclose his activities as a German agent.

From among Viereck's voluminous writings the prosecution plucked for their own purposes such 20-year-old prophecies as "If he (Adolf Hitler) lives, he will make history for better or worse."

Helping Hitler to fulfill the prophecy at the time were Viereck's own two sons, Peter, a Pulitzer Prize-winning poet in his own right, and George jr., both American Army corporals fighting in Africa. The latter was killed in action there, the announcement of his death almost coinciding with a District court jury's decision that the erstwhile poet of passion was guilty as charged.

By the suitcaseful this jury of his peers had listened impatiently to the government's recital of the wrongs it said Viereck had written in an effort to crystallize American sentiment in the Fatherland's behalf.

No Poetic Spice

Not a single surging line of the bleak defendant's "Monads" did they conjure up to spice the tedious testimony:

Sweet is the highroad when the
*   skylarks call,*
When we and love go rambling
*   through the land,*
But shall we still walk gaily
*   hand in hand*
At the road's turning and the
*   twilight's fall?*

In the spring of 1947 Viereck strode out of the federal penitentiary at Lewisburg, Pa., with the same jauntiness that attended his step into the District jail some five years before to begin the sentence imposed.

In New York last week his recollections of his prison service here, in Atlanta and in Lewisburg were fitful. He remembered, for instance, the written reply to his request for writing paper—in short, the little things well-calculated to sear the caged artistic soul.

More Sonnets Written

"It is not understood," the warden wrote to an undistinguishable number named Viereck, "why you persist in writing sonnets."

But write sonnets he 'did; as he whiled away his debt to society, on the meager supply of paper he was allowed to import and on toilet tissue when that supply gave out. He will publish them, he promises, when there can be found at long last a publisher who will not cringe at the name, George Sylvester Viereck.

His only note of pessimism in this regard is detectable in his admission that it's a long road back. He was 65 yesterday—or 50

By 1950 Viereck had behind him a prison experience as well as a broken home, personal tragedy, and the defeat of a nation he still felt impelled to defend. But his main concern at this point was the publication of his prison memoirs and the writing of an erotic novel.

In the late 1950's G. S. Viereck found reconciliation with his surviving son, expressed regret (to his son) over his "Nazi interlude," and continued intermittent efforts via his memoirs to vindicate himself and his career.

Rundschau Zweier Welten

Review of Two Worlds

Inhalt der Märznummer für 1912

Nachdruck nur bei Quellenangabe gestattet.

Owned by the VIERECK PUBLISHING COMPANY, and published monthly at $2.00 per year by the VIERECK PUBLISHING COMPANY, at 134 West 29th Street, New York. President, George Sylvester Viereck; Vice-President, Max R. Hein; Treasurer, Alfred Rau; Secretary, Ely Simpson; Assistant Treasurer and Assistant Secretary, Rudolph Bergman. Entered at the New York Post Office as Second Class Matter. Copyright, 1911, by the Viereck Publishing Company. German Representative, Louis Viereck, Friedenau-Berlin, Südwestkorso 8. Subscriptions may be sent to the office of the VIERECK PUBLISHING COMPANY, 134—140 West 29th Street, New York. Cable Address: Viereck New York.

Jahresabonnement · · **$2.00** **Einzelnummer** · · **20 Cts.**
(Yearly Subscription)   (Single Copy)

Jahresabonnement für Europa Mark 9.—

☞ Zur Beachtung! ☜

Wir machen diejenigen unserer werten Abonnenten, die ihre Nummern der RUNDSCHAU ZWEIER WELTEN nicht mehr so prompt erhalten, als es bis vor kurzem der Fall war, darauf aufmerksam, dass dieser Umstand der neuen Einrichtung des Postamts, Zeitschriften per „Schnellfracht" anstatt wie früher per Post zu versenden, zuzuschreiben ist. Wir hoffen, dass dies nur eine zeitweilige Verzögerung bedeutet und bitten unsere Leser um freundliche Nachsicht.   Die Redaktion.

One of the last issues of Viereck's German-language journal. It could not survive declining interest among its American readers in preserving the German language, nor did it apparently attract very many German subscribers.

Weather Forecast: GENERALLY FAIR.

The World To-Day—86 Pages

FIRST NEWS SECTION	16 Pages
SECOND NEWS SECTION	6 Pages
THIRD NEWS SECTION	6 Pages
WANT DIRECTORY	14 Pages
EDITORIAL SECTION	6 Pages
METROPOLITAN SECTION	6 Pages
COMIC SECTION	4 Pages
MAGAZINE SECTION	20 Pages
PICTORIAL WEEKLY SECTION	8 Pages
And SPECIAL "FUN" SECTION	

The World.

"Circulation Books Open to All."

NEW YORK, SUNDAY, AUGUST 15, 1915. 86 PAGES. PRICE FIVE CENTS.

HOW GERMANY HAS WORKED IN U. S. TO SHAPE OPINION, BLOCK THE ALLIES AND GET MUNITIONS FOR HERSELF, TOLD IN SECRET AGENTS' LETTERS.

LETTERS MR. VIERECK AND DR. ALBERT WROTE TO EACH OTHER.

VIERECK'S REQUEST for MONEY

OFFICE OF GEORGE SYLVESTER VIERECK
1123 BROADWAY, NEW YORK

June 29, 1915

Dear Dr. Albert:-

In thinking the matter over, I do not think that Mrs. R. would be the proper intermediary inasmuch as she does not attend to her financial affairs herself. If it must be a woman, Mrs. G., the mother of our friend Mrs. L., would be far better.

However, personally I see no reason why this payment could not be made every month through Mr. Meyer just like the other payments. If there is any objection to that, I would suggest that the payments be made to my personal friend and lawyer, Mr. Ely Simpson, whose standing as my legal adviser exempts him from any possibly inquiry.

As I have already received $250 this month I enclose a statement for $1500 for June. Will you please O. K. this and I shall then send my secretary for the cash. I am sending this letter by boy as for obvious reasons I do not wish it to go through the mails.

Sincerely yours,

G S Viereck

GEORGE SYLVESTER VIERECK

June 29, 1915

For June | $1750
of which I received | 250
Leaves a balance of | $ 1500

VIERECK'S STATEMENT for JUNE

New York, den 1. Juli 1915.

Lieber Herr Viereck:

Ihre Rechnung über die $ 1.500 – Zuschuss, die sich nach Abzug der bereits erhaltenen $ 250 – für Monat Juni 1915 ergeben, habe ich erhalten.

Ich hoffe, Ihnen im Laufe der nächsten Woche Zahlung leisten zu können. Inzwischen bitte ich um Vorschlag einer geeigneten Persönlichkeit, welche die finanziellen Verhältnisse Ihres Blattes gründlich prüfen könnte. Von dem Augenblick an, wo wir Ihnen einen regelmässigen Zuschuss gewähren, muss ich

1. eine neue Aufstellung der Verhältnisse Ihres Blattes haben,

2. eine Kontrolle wegen der finanziellen Verwaltung ausüben.

Ausserdem müssen wir uns über die von Ihnen zu verfolgende Politik verständigen, was bisher nicht erforderlich war. Sie haben vielleicht die Freundlichkeit, die Angelegenheit auf Grund dieses Briefes mit Herrn Fuehr zu besprechen.

Ihr ergebener

Herrn George Sylvester Viereck
1123 Broadway
New York City

Dr. ALBERT'S REPLY to VIERECK (Translation Below)

SHUCKS HIS CLOTHING ON TELEGRAPH POLE

But Discarded Raiment Falls in Bits on Women and Causes —Well, Consternation.

From a telegraph pole at Twenty-ninth Street and Madison Avenue a shoe dropped late last night on girls leaving the Madison Square Telephone Exchange. Near there also is the Martha Washington Hotel.

It was a man's shoe. And as the girl who got hit on the Panama by the first shoe screamed another shoe dropped. Then a man's collar and necktie and his straw hat—and his shirt and his collar button and—here the screams became deafening, because the man, with stolid consistency, kept dropping his clothing.

The telephone at the East Thirtieth Street Station began ringing riotously. Calls were being frantically registered from the Martha Washington, the telephone exchange and the Hotel Seville.

Lieut. Seiffert's operation of the flashlight signal system soon got Patrolman Grim at the bottom of the pole, atop of which Yackim Phillipo-

WIFE AND GIRL FIND HIM SLAIN IN HOME

John Hildenbrandt Blackjacked, Then Shot, in His Apartment

Dr. Albert Demands Control of the Fatherland's Policy

Translation of Dr. Albert's letter to Mr. Viereck.

New York, July 1, 1915.

Dear Mr. Viereck:

Your account regarding the $1,500—bonus, after deducting the $250 received—for the month of June, 1915, has been received.

I hope, in the course of the next week, to be able to make payment

Chancellor, Ambassador, Financial Agent and Bankers Chief Figures in Vast Scheme Revealed in Documents Obtained by The World—Fatherland Financed, Author Fox's Expenses Paid, Plans Laid to Buy Press Association and Otherwise Control News of the War.

COST PUT AT $2,000,000 A WEEK; BERNSTORFF DRAFT $1,100,000.

Big Arms Plant and Powder Works, Which Outwardly Dicker With Allies, Secretly Owned by Germany and Preparing to Deliver Munitions Sept. 1—Edison's Supply of Carbolic Acid Taken Over for Shipment—Plan to Buy Wright Plant Considered—Poisoned Gas Supply of Allies Crippled—Strikes in Munitions Plants Fomented.

Copyright, 1915, by The Press Publishing Co. (The New York World).

The World to-day begins the publication of a series of articles raising for the first time the curtain that has hitherto concealed the activities and purposes of the official German propaganda in the United States.

The facts set forth are based upon correspondence exchanged by representatives of the German Government, its agents, and sympathetic allies in this country, which has come into possession of The World.

This correspondence reveals unmistakably that the leading officials of the German Government have had a hand in the promotion of ventures directed not alone at its belligerent enemies with whom it is at war, but, in some instances, at the laws of the United States as well.

The most surprising fact in this connection is that no less a personage than Herr von Bethmann-Hollweg, Chancellor of the German Empire, has actually participated from Berlin in some of the secret undertakings of his Government in this country.

MEN HIGHER UP IN THE SCHEMES.

The facts set forth in the correspondence show that the chief actors selected to perform the duties assigned to them:—

Count Johann von Bernstorff, the German Ambassador at Washington;

Capt. Franz von Papen, the Military Attache of the Embassy;

Dr. Heinrich F. Albert, the chief financial agent of the German Government in this country;

Herr Hugo Schmidt, Western representative of the Deutsches Bank of Berlin;

Hugo Schweitzer, a German-American chemist;

S. Sulzberger, a banker in Frankfort, Germany;

Herr Waetzoldt, trade representative of the German Government in this country;

Agents of the German Bureau of Information (Secret Service), and various other agents who are not officially

Viereck's friend, Heinrich Albert, was caught off guard by a Secret Service agent who seized his briefcase. The result was a sensational exposé for the *World* in August, 1915, and a major setback for the pro-German propaganda effort in the United States.

American Monthly, January, 1920: Viereck was one of the first postwar "revisionists" dedicated to condemning American involvement in World War I, but his revisionism went to the extreme in vilifying America's former allies and in polishing the tarnished reputation of Germany's military leaders.

Hitler the German Explosive

By GEORGE SLYVESTER VIERECK

ADOLPH HITLER must be handled with care. He is a human explosive. The very mention of his name induces percussions. Some look to him as a German Mussolini, the savior of his country; others regard him as a violent agitator, thriving on religious prejudice and race contention.

Idolized by his followers, execrated by his foes, he is welcomed by Big Business as the only man in Germany who can take votes away from the Socialists. To some, however, the encouragement given to Hitler by conservative circles seems like an attempt to drive out Satan with Beelzebub.

Both friend and foe pay tribute to Hitler's power. He and those whom he marks as his own defy with impunity the Federal Court at Leipzig. They defy no less flagrantly the government at Munich. The Bavarian Government is inclined to look upon Hitler as a spoiled Baby that must needs be humored. In fact they are glad to have him. Hitler and his armed guard keep the Communist from painting the map of Bavaria red. Bavaria prefers Hitler to Eisner.

I met Hitler at the house of a former Admiral of the German Navy. Over the tea cups we discussed problems, temporal and eternal. Through the window we saw the celebrated Meadow of Theresa where Munich foregathers annually to celebrate the October Feast. The dying sun illuminated the gigantic statue of Bavaria gazing straight at us from the meadow.

Hitler is not a native of Bavaria. His cradle was rocked in German Moravia, a region which, though one hundred per cent German, was dished out by the four foolish men at Versailles to Czecho-Slovakia. Like every son of that soil, Hitler looks upon himself as a German.

We are afforded a glimpse of the Greater Germany to be of which every German dreams, from the fact that a former Austrian subject is the leader of the German Fascisti. Hitler's shock troops are Bavarians. But his influence extends far beyond Bavaria. Though not permitted to organize in Prussia and in several other states, he has followers everywhere.

There is no one in Germany who does not recognize the importance of his emblem, the "Hakenkreuz," the ancient swastika, sometimes standing by itself and sometimes superimposed on a cross or a shield, a mystic symbol of militant Germanism.

The pugnacity of the man appears from the very choice of the name by which he designates his Party. He calls himself a "National Socialist." However, his party program is the very antithesis of that commonly accredited to Socialism.

"Socialism," he said to me, "is the science dealing with the common weal. Communism is not Socialism. Marxism (the doctrine of Karl Marx, the father of orthodox Socialism) is not Socialism. The Marxians have stolen the term and confused its meaning. I shall take Socialism away from the Socialists."

His face was slightly flushed. The vein on his forehead rose. He talked excitedly.

Hitler's appearance contrasts strangely with the aggressiveness of his opinions. No milder-mannered reformer ever scuttled ship of state or cut political throat. Hitler looks more like a poet than like a politician. There is about him nothing of the "rough neck." He can sip tea or imbibe delicate cordials with any "high brow."

Nevertheless, he fascinates his audiences, drawing followers both from the intelligencia and from the peasants. He overcomes them with his eloquence. He storms their reserve with his passion.

Hitler refuses to be photographed. I do not know if his attitude is inspired by caution or by superstition. It may be part of his strategy to be known only to his friends, so that in the hour of crisis, he can appear here and there, and everywhere, without being recognized.

A self-made man who has thought much and read much, Hitler is not afraid to meet the challenge of debate. He holds his own in controversy with remarkable skill. Of his past little is known. He admits that art claimed him before he became a tribune of the people. His friends say that he was a portrait painter. His enemies insinuate that he practiced the art of painting only by white-washing walls. I do not know if he can wield a brush. There is no doubt that he can wield his tongue.

"Socialism," Hitler insists, "is an ancient Aryan, an

Is it true that he appears in public masked?   His striking facial trait is the luring eye.   Or is his mouth the thing?   Or that nose?
WHAT DOES HITLER LOOK LIKE?

According to Viereck, this article on Hitler—perhaps the first interview with the future Fuehrer by an American—was rejected by American editors because they believed their readers were not interested in the subject. So Viereck published it in his own journal—just a few weeks before the notorious "Beer Hall Putsch."

influence of supposedly disloyal politicians and liberals at home who had undermined the monarchy and weakened the patriotic spirit. Right-wing advocates of this view used it to make scapegoats of socialists, liberals, and Jews, and to weaken public confidence in the Weimar Republic.

Viereck simultaneously criticized the socialists in Germany for trying to suppress rising nationalism; Germany, he said, could be free only by being strong. In the same vein, he accused the Reichstag of selling the German people to foreign domination by approving the Dawes Plan, which scaled down reparations payments but empowered an international commission to supervise German finances, in particular the operations of the Reichsbank and the state-owned railroads. To the *American Monthly*, the terms of the plan meant the German republic had become "the satrapy of international capital whose agents are politicians from Paris, London, and Washington." Moreover, when Poland in 1925 began expelling residents who kept their German citizenship, Viereck retorted that the Poles were not fit to govern their "superiors" and that if Poland (a "robber state" erected by "Wilsonian ignorance") stood in the way of German reunification, it would have to be destroyed.[18]

Although considering both Wilhelm Marx (a Centrist) and Marshal von Hindenburg acceptable candidates, Viereck predictably extolled Hindenburg's victory in the 1925 German presidential election. He sent a letter of congratulations to Hindenburg on April 27, saying that his election proved that the German people "are again masters of their own household, refusing to be governed by foreign politicians or foreign financiers; Germany has found her soul and has recovered her self-respect."[19] Hindenburg's reply, sent on May 3, stated in part: "Your message pleased me all the more because it comes from a man who as a faithful citizen of his new country was one of the most courageous champions in the cause of preserving the intimate cultural association with the old Fatherland."[20]

[18] *American Monthly*, July, 1924, p. 151; September, 1924, pp. 181, 253; September, 1925, p. 190.

[19] *American Monthly*, May, 1925, p. 70; June, 1925, pp. 101–2.

[20] *American Monthly*, June, 1925, p. 102.

There was one notable exception to this spirit of harmony with the German nationalists. In November, 1925, Viereck approved the Locarno Pact as new recognition of Germany's importance to the West. Noting the strident opposition of German nationalists to the pact, he said, "The Nationalists have no right to regard every supporter of Locarno as a traitor." Displaying unusual objectivity, he explained that Germans must learn to "temper practical politics with common sense," and to "respect the opinions of their opponents." He added, "the fact a man disagrees with us does not make him necessarily a scoundrel or an ass." It seemed that Viereck finally was recognizing the dangers in a society where exchanges of personal insult and invective were becoming a substitute for rational and courteous debate. Yet, unable to surrender all his illusions, he claimed to see in the Locarno Pact the possibility that Germany might still exact concessions from its Western neighbors, including the return of Alsace-Lorraine.[21]

While approving the Locarno Pact, Viereck remained adamantly opposed to the League of Nations, even after Germany became a member in 1926. When questioned about this by Samuel Colcord, an eccentric promoter of schemes for world peace, Viereck replied that he still opposed American membership and disclaimed any intimation that he owed or acknowledged loyalty to Germany. He said that he and his associates may be "sentimentally and intellectually attached" to Germany, and that they may believe the interests of the United States "depend to a certain extent upon the well-being of Germany" and upon fulfillment of the Fourteen Points, "but our loyalty belongs solely and exclusively to the United States."[22] Viereck was unwilling to give up his premise that England and France, in particular, were more enemy than friend to the United States and that American interests could best be served by so-called "magnificent isolation."

Meanwhile, in the winter and spring of 1924–25 the Fatherland Corporation underwent another financial crisis. Viereck told his readers that income had declined appreciably from every source except subscriptions to the journal. He attributed the problem to a so-called "business depression" following the elec-

[21] *American Monthly*, November, 1925, pp. 261, 293, 294.
[22] *American Monthly*, October, 1926, p. 241.

tions of 1924, but it is more likely that certain enterprises, particularly his investment firm, had become the victim of Germany's monetary inflation and subsequent economic readjustments. He noted, too, the typical lack of advertising support, again faulting wealthy German-Americans for their aversion to unpopular causes. He appealed to his readers for aid; by October, 1925, their contributions reached the $5,000 goal.[23] This reaction indicates that a small but hard core of pro-German American citizens still looked to the *American Monthly* for leadership in "unraveling the conspiracies of secret diplomacy" and in overturning the Versailles Treaty—as Viereck explained its goals.

In its sustained attack on the Versailles Treaty, the *American Monthly* in 1926 and 1927 focused more closely upon two issues— the alleged "war-guilt lie" contained in the treaty, and the vindication of Germany's exiled Kaiser. At the same time, the journal devoted less attention to German domestic politics—a change in emphasis that may be attributed largely to the seeming economic recovery of Germany and the apparent normalization of relations with France following the Locarno Pact. The *American Monthly* also began to reflect more interest in literary events, and Viereck himself in 1925 resumed work on a novel. As his literary work became more pressing, Viereck appeared to become less intense in his political polemics. In mid-1927, after announcing that the magazine was now being distributed on newsstands, he claimed that the policy of the journal was to deal only with live issues which are "naturally extremely controversial," but that the staff was "eager to present all sides" of any issue it covered.[24] Subsequent numbers showed a more liberal policy, but the tone remained decidedly pro-German. Indeed, at that time Viereck was in process of releasing his reins on the publication. His other literary interests had become dominant. On October 8, 1927, he announced his resignation as editor of the *American Monthly* and as president of the Fatherland Corporation. He was succeeded in these positions by David Maier, who also was chairman of the political committee of the Steuben Society of America. In his

[23] *American Monthly*, July, 1925, p. 157; August, 1924, p. 168; October, 1925, p. 236.
[24] *American Monthly*, July, 1927, p. 17.

resignation announcement Viereck said, "If ever the bugle sounds again, if I am needed, I shall not be found wanting. I am not deserting the ship. I am merely stepping back into the ranks." He explained that he planned to devote himself to writing.[25] He contributed an occasional article thereafter to the journal until May, 1929, when his work as a contributing editor finally terminated.

From evidence adduced thus far, the *American Monthly*'s slogan could well have been "America First, Germany a Close Second." Previous chapters have, in various ways, revealed some of the precedent conditions and motives which help explain Viereck's close identification with German nationalism in the 1920's. There is one factor, in particular, that seemed to be an inseparable part and a causal force in all of his German affiliations. This force was the figure of Kaiser Wilhelm II, the last "father" of Imperial Germany, deposed by his "sons" in 1918 and esteemed as a martyr by many German nationalists and a very few unusual Americans (like Viereck) in the 1920's. Thus it is appropriate to investigate his unique relationship to the Kaiser in the 1920's and note how this affiliation affected his view of the political system and role of republican Germany.

Viereck's first meeting with Kaiser Wilhelm, then in exile in Doorn, Holland, took place in the fall of 1922 after an exchange of letters. Of course, the Kaiser was well aware of Viereck's reputation as an apologist for Imperial Germany and of his kinship to the Hohenzollern family.[26] Indeed, during Viereck's first trip to Europe in 1908 he had made arrangements to interview the Kaiser; but, as already noted, these plans were canceled by German officials in the aftermath of the international furor created by Wilhelm's interview with a *London Telegraph* correspondent on German-English relations. At that time Viereck accepted the view of some friends of the Kaiser that *Seine Majestät* was too shrewd not to have foreseen the repercussions of this interview, and that it actually was calculated to serve "some far-seeing

---

[25] *New York Times*, October, 1927, p. 19:4.

[26] Elmer Gertz, a friend of Viereck's from the late 1920's, reports that Viereck told him that the Kaiser occasionally greeted his American visitor as "cousin" in French (interview with Elmer Gertz, March 12, 1966).

plan."[27] Viereck's view of the Kaiser, in other words, was neither critical nor objective. Nevertheless, because of the special confidence placed in him by the ex-Kaiser, Viereck was able to shed new light on Wilhelm's personality and activities in the 1920's which helped dispel the opposite illusion built upon the wartime portrayal of Germany's leader as the "Beast of Berlin."

In anticipation of his first meeting with Wilhelm II, Viereck thought he might encounter an embittered and enfeebled man as had been rumored. Thus he claimed to be surprised in finding "a radiant figure, simple, dignified, intellectual, with the physical buoyancy of an athlete and the mental elasticity of the neophyte paying his pristine devotions at the austere shrine of science. . . ." He added that he had gone to Doorn not to interview the Kaiser, but only to be his guest. He had come to pay tribute to one of the "most remarkable men of our time if not of all time." He departed with a picture of his host which he would treasure for himself but which he would also share with the world, if Wilhelm would permit it, as a means of dispelling the "clouds of poison gas which still cling to his image and to his country." The Kaiser, in turn, revealed no trepidation about allowing his young admirer to publish his impressions of the visit to Doorn. Speaking for the Kaiser, his aide-de-camp Lieutenant Colonel Count D. Molthe informed Viereck:

> In view of your years-long manly struggle for truth and right, I feel no hesitation in authorizing you to publish the impressions you gathered at Doorn as the guest of His Majesty. I do this the more willingly because I know that the communications entrusted to you by his majesty will be made use of by yourself in a manner calculated to promote the true, just interests of Germany.[28]

Count Molthe added that this was the first time since his exile that Wilhelm had authorized a correspondent to publish an interview with him.

Trying to forestall criticism from those who would see him only as a "rubber stamp" for the Kaiser, Viereck asserted, "A

[27] Viereck, *Confessions of a Barbarian*, p. 38; Viereck, *My Flesh and Blood*, p. 275.

[28] *American Monthly*, January, 1923, p. 326; *New York American*, December 17, 1922, pp. ME-1, 2.

sympathetic interpretation of the Kaiser does not necessarily imply that I identify myself with all his opinions. . . ." He explained further, "no artist can work well unless he attunes his mind to the mind of his model." In spite of the Kaiser's confidence in him, Viereck proceded cautiously in reporting his first interview. On the Kaiser's opinions concerning German culpability for the war, he drew repeatedly from Wilhelm's published memoirs. Not surprisingly, he offered agreement with the Kaiser of the various arguments being promoted to vindicate Germany's role in the war, and the Kaiser's in particular. Viereck, for instance, helped perpetuate the Kaiser's contention that there were informal "gentlemen's agreements" as early as 1897 between the United States and England, and in some cases with France, to thwart the further spread of the German Empire. He also gave credence to the Kaiser's assumption that his position above the quarrels and divisions of politics helped account for Germany's remarkable progress toward power and prestige. At the same time, Viereck subscribed to the fiction that the Emperor "was far more hedged in with constitutional restrictions than the President of the United States."[29]

Rather than admit the role that personal kinship may have played in motivating his infatuation with the ex-Emperor, Viereck claimed to be animated by the belief that the German people could not be "cleared" without clearing the Emperor—and, vice versa, the Emperor could not be vindicated without vindicating his people. As a corollary, he asserted that one could not assail Wilhelm II without assailing his country. He added that this feeling was shared by Alfred Niemann, another friend and European spokesman for Wilhelm, and that the Emperor's recognition of this same "fact" moved him "to continue his campaign for the truth."[30] A sampling of the correspondence between Viereck and the Kaiser in the 1920's indicates that each of these kinsmen found the kind of ego support in each other which perhaps more than compensated for the defeats they both had suffered as a result of World War I events. A favorite theme of the Kaiser was

[29] *American Monthly*, January, 1923, pp. 328–36; *New York American*, December 24, 1922, pp. LII–1–2.
[30] *American Monthly*, December, 1924, p. 315.

that Germany's problems and defeats could be traced to a variety of conspiracies, fomented primarily by Great Britain and supported by the interests of "International Freemasonry" and "International Capital," which led to nefarious "gentlemen's agreements" (between England, the United States and others), to *Einkreisung* (encirclement of Germany), and finally to war.[31]

Viereck's implication that the Kaiser was a popular ruler and that his policies were supported by the vast majority of Germans seems to be correct. However, one need not conclude from this assumption that to disparage the Kaiser was to belittle Germany—especially in a period when Wilhelm was no longer in command. Indeed, because he had identified himself so closely with the Kaiser, Viereck could easily feel that an attack on the intelligence and intentions of the Kaiser was at least indirectly an assault upon his own affiliations and personal judgment. As for his consanguinity with the Emperor-in-exile, Viereck claimed in 1931 that he had "never presumed" upon his blood relationship and had never discussed the subject with him. At the same time, he admitted it amused him "to play with the idea when I delve into history."[32]

Although obviously a friend of many German monarchists and favorable to the restoration of the Hohenzollern dynasty, Viereck did not agitate openly for a monarchical overthrow of the republican form of government established by the Weimar constitution. He seemed to share the Kaiser's position, expressed in November, 1923, that only the plea of a united people could persuade him to accept the throne again. Noting the Kaiser's unwillingness to "resort to bayonets" or cause civil strife over the issue of his restoration, Viereck concluded, "He is a German, before he is a Monarch. He loves his country more than himself."[33] Indicating where his preferences lay, Viereck a year earlier had spoken out against the German government's suppression of some of its nationalist or right-wing opponents. He implied that there were dangers to the government in this kind of so-called "drastic pun-

[31] Letters on deposit at Harvard University Library. See especially Wilhelm II to G. S. Viereck, December 3, 1925, and March 30, 1927.

[32] Viereck, *My Flesh and Blood*, p. 275.

[33] *American Monthly*, December, 1923, p. 296; *New York American*, November 11, 1923.

ishment" for its enemies. He then revealed his own political (or apolitical) stance, as follows:

> We ourselves are citizens of a republic. Other things being equal, we prefer the republican form of government. But government terrorism is unpalatable at all times. . . . In the last analysis, the external form of government is of no importance. It is the spirit that counts. The Germans may prefer to be free under a Kaiser to being slaves under a President. Such a feeling will be reinforced, if the German Government leans more heavily upon the extreme left. . . .[34]

Viereck's association with the Kaiser grew into a warm and active friendship. By the end of 1923 Viereck noted that he had been a guest of Wilhelm on three occasions and was the only person authorized by him "to perpetuate in writing his impressions of Doorn." He also at that time presented a character sketch of the Empress Hermine and said he aimed to dispel false rumors about the alleged marital discord between Wilhelm and his wife.[35] As an official spokesman of the Kaiser, Viereck obtained notable success in exposing the Kaiser's views outside his own *American Monthly*. Among such examples, in late 1923 the *New York American* published an exclusive cablegram from Wilhelm to Viereck in reply to a note from the latter on rumors of the Kaiser's plan to return to the Fatherland.[36] And, more important, *Current History* magazine of the *New York Times* in October, 1924, published in full one of his interviews with the Kaiser. The ex-Emperor as usual defended his own motives and intentions and attempted to make the Allies most responsible for the conditions that led to the war.[37] On occasion it appears that Viereck performed a positive function in helping "set the record straight" regarding the Kaiser. For example, in May, 1925, Viereck published in his journal a letter to Wilhelm in which he asked the latter for a comment on newspaper reports that Hindenburg would accept the nomi-

[34] *American Monthly*, August, 1922, p. 165.
[35] *American Monthly*, January, 1924, pp. 335–40; December, 1923, p. 295.
[36] *New York American*, November 15, 1923, p. 1.
[37] *New York Times–Current History Magazine*, October 26, 1924, p. II–5:1.

nation for president only with the approval of the Kaiser and that he would help restore the Hohenzollerns. Wilhelm replied that he had no communication from Hindenburg on his candidacy and that he intended to continue his policy of noninterference in Germany's internal affairs.[38]

Beginning in 1922 Viereck made almost a yearly journey to Europe for the rest of the decade, visiting each time with the Kaiser. On his return in August, 1926, from an especially productive sojourn, he told the *New York Times* that he had been asked by Mussolini if he thought that Wilhelm II would ever return to the German throne. Viereck said he replied to *Il Duce* that "a man once schooled to rule could never be satisfied with a lesser part, and that the Emperor at Doorn was no different from Napoleon at St. Helena."[39]

In 1926 Viereck published his most extensive series of articles on the Kaiser in his *American Monthly* and in the *New York American*. One article covered the Emperor's views on the supposed "gentlemen's agreements" between his adversaries. Another dealt with his reactions to Wilson's Fourteen Points. Predictably, he pictured Germany as being grossly deceived by the promises contained in these points. He felt deceived in that he was told his departure from the throne would result in "peace with honor at home and abroad." The latter article was also published by the North American Newspaper Alliance.[40] In another study of the Kaiser, translated from a work by Professor Dietrich Schaefer, various pieces of evidence were drawn together to show that republics historically were no more peaceful than monarchies. In a subsequent article, Viereck published extracts from and comments on a letter received by Wilhelm from Colonel House in July, 1914, in which the latter said that President Wilson had responded with a "thrill of deep pleasure" over House's report on his meeting with the Kaiser. In reflecting on this response from Wilson, Wilhelm now felt exonerated of charges that he sought war. Instead, he accused England's Foreign Secretary Grey of "engineering" events with France and Russia in a way that made war

[38] *American Monthly*, May, 1925, pp. 69–70.
[39] *New York Times*, August 24, 1926, p. 9.
[40] *American Monthly*, February, 1926, pp. 365, 367–68.

against Germany virtually inevitable. The series concluded with an article in which Viereck helped the former Emperor defend the wisdom and intention of his alliances and other policies prior to the outbreak of World War I.[41]

The more appealing side of the ex-Emperor's personality was brought out in 1927 in an article by Viereck which was published in *Liberty* magazine. Viereck quoted the Emperor as saying that two things sustained him in exile—his "sense of duty" and his "sense of humor." The exiled monarch confessed to missing only "the opportunity to work on a larger scale for the redemption of my people and those of the world." Some of the material in this article was used later in a character sketch of Wilhelm which Viereck published in his book, *Glimpses of the Great*. At the exiled Emperor's request, the latter article concentrated upon his religious views. He was portrayed as a man of sensitive conscience who believed in man's moral freedom and accountability, and as a man who professed Christianity but was not interested in dogmas, "Calvinistic or otherwise." He was depicted as a man humbly accepting his new status as part of a divine plan or command. On the other hand, he could not accept Germany's defeat as the will of God. Rather, it was the result of the German people refusing in the end "to face all risks in preserving faith." This "faith" upon examination bore a closer resemblance to belief in the German spirit than it did to a Christian God.[42]

Viereck's visits with Wilhelm II at Doorn continued into the 1930's and came to an end on the eve of World War II. He also established, in 1922, a lasting friendship with Wilhelm's son, the former Crown Prince Wilhelm. At Viereck's instigation, the latter's memoirs were serialized in *Liberty* magazine in the spring of 1933. Although devoting most of his attention to the Hohenzollerns, Viereck likewise became a friend of other German and Austro-Hungarian royalty. Especially notable in the latter regard was his acquaintanceship with Crown Prince Rupprecht, pre-

[41] *American Monthly*, March, 1926, p. 15; April, 1926, p. 56; September, 1926, pp. 207–9. Also see *New York American*, October 5, 1925, p. LII–1?; December 6, 1925, p. LII–1; May 30, 1926, p. CE–3; June 18, 1926, p. LII–1?; August 8, 1926, p. CE–3.

[42] G. S. Viereck, "What Life Means to the Kaiser," *Liberty*, October 15, 1927, pp. 79–82.

tender to the Bavarian throne, and with Countess Elizabeth Salm of the Austro-Hungarian royal family. Viereck corresponded frequently with the latter two during the 1920's, and Crown Prince Rupprecht allowed Viereck to interview him in 1927, the first interview he had granted in many years. The prince received a hearing for his views in Viereck's book, *Glimpses of the Great*, published in 1930.[43]

It is evident that Viereck secured considerable publicity for the Kaiser and his opinions concerning his role and that of Germany in world affairs. The articles served a positive purpose in deflating various false rumors about the Kaiser's plans or activities, but their contribution to the historical record and to public enlightenment seems not to have been very constructive. They obviously perpetuated the prejudices of the Emperor and his distortions of history—such as his belief that "gentlemen's agreements"[44] existed between the United States, England, and France after 1897 to thwart Germany's proper imperial ambitions, and his statement that "Woodrow Wilson's ambition to be remembered by history as the greatest Englishman of his generation" contributed to America's involvement in the war.[45] Perhaps most Americans recognized the Kaiser's words for what they were—special pleading. Nevertheless, they probably made some contribution to the revisionist and debunking mood that emerged among biographers and other writers in the 1920's. One may assume that not many Americans took the Kaiser seriously; except for the Hearst newspapers, the American public media gave him relatively little attention, in spite of Viereck's yeoman efforts. Many years later he confessed disappointment in that "no important figures commented upon his articles although they were regularly read by over ten million people."[46] He was evidently

[43] G. S. Viereck, *Glimpses of the Great* (London: Duckworth, 1930), pp. 146–55; *American Monthly*, December, 1927, p. 11.

[44] *American Monthly*, January, 1923, pp. 332–33. One of the sources used by the Kaiser in support of the validity of this rumor of secret gentlemen's agreements was the book by Roland Usher (*Pan-Germanism*, pp. 139–40), which does not, however, offer any documented proof or even reasonably substantial evidence to support such an insinuation.

[45] *American Monthly*, February, 1926, p. 367.

[46] Synopsis, G. S. Viereck Autobiography, ca. 1960, p. 12, Gertz MSS.

citing the total readership of the Hearst network, but one can only speculate as to how many of these individuals actually read the material on the Kaiser. In view of the Hearst chain's opposition to American entry into World War I and its support of postwar isolationism, one may surmise that the Kaiser articles served the newspapers' editorial purposes.

In conclusion, it is worth emphasizing that Viereck's promotion of German nationalism in the 1920's reflected certain tendencies in his character which had become apparent before 1914 and which were reinforced by his experiences during and after the war. First, one should note the aesthetic bent of his personality, which included the tendency to personalize the abstract, to emphasize the role of personality and understress the importance of political principles that restrain and control the individual's will to power. As a prewar poet he had admitted that Nietzsche was one of the few German writers to have any influence upon him. Accordingly, he expressed an empathy for the dynamic personality, like that of Roosevelt or the Kaiser, and he attached little significance to differences in ideology. He likewise was inclined to endow nations with peculiar personalities of their own, but he did not go to the extent of some German nationalists who made a religion out of *Volkstum* (German folkdom), which presented the Germans as a race of gods upon earth. Nevertheless, Viereck did periodically indulge in the excesses of frustrated German nationalism. He shared at least implicitly in the German romantic tradition, going back to Herder, that viewed nations as organic growths peculiar and unique in themselves. Likewise implicit in his rhetoric was the Darwinist analogy which assumed that each nation occupied a different level on an evolutionary "fitness" scale. Probably because of his conditioning by American culture he did not consciously subscribe to these assumptions or beliefs, but at a subconscious level he seemed to accept them.

Associated with Viereck's aestheticism (mixed as it was with diluted Darwinism) was his tendency, noted earlier, to indulge in narcissistic or egocentric behavior. The praise that he received as a young poet had led him to think of himself as a genius. Operating from this premise, he showed no inclination to defer to the opinions of others. Thus, in supporting a cause, he tended to be dogmatic and unwilling to concede anything to the adversary. He was not entirely unbending in this regard, as one may conclude from his actions in conforming to wartime censorship controls. But he remained consistent in viewing himself as a superior person and Germany as a superior nation—even though both had experienced failure and persecution. Impressed—or perhaps fixated—by this self-image, he found it impossible to accept the reality of defeat for himself or the Fatherland. He could accept the idea that American power had stopped Germany from expanding her frontiers, but he allowed his wishes, his ingrained Germanophilism, to father the thought that the Fourteen Points offered peace without victory—in effect, a stalemate which would do Germany no more harm than her enemies. This *status quo ante* was the least he had hoped for; the ideal role he seemed to have envisioned for Germany was as dominant land power of Europe and guard over the continent's interests, just as the United States stood like a colossus over the other nations of the western hemisphere.

Certainly there are a number of other variables which would help account for Viereck's tendency to identify his own interests with the nationalist aspirations of Germany. The impact of his father's example and of Muensterberg, his associations with aristocratic Germans of the ruling class between 1914 and 1917, his support for a "peace without victory", and (not least of all) his first-hand encounter with a sullen, resentful Germany at its nadir in 1923—all these incidents and influences bear upon his oftimes irrational support of German nationalism. Furthermore, one of the most significant ingredients was his familial relationship to the former ruling family of Germany, which was supplemented by his fascination with the "great man" view of history. Even before the war he had come to an inflated view of the Kaiser's virtues, and he had speculated that there was something special about the blood or genes of traditional ruling dynasties.

Finally, Viereck's implicit hopes for a restoration of at least a limited monarchy under the Hohenzollerns did not, of course, bear fruit. On the other hand, his calls for the emergence of a strong national leadership did come to fruition—in a twisted form —in the triumph of Adolf Hitler and his National Socialists. As later events proved, Viereck was mistaken in his belief that the interests of the Hohenzollerns would be promoted by the resurgence of a fascist-style nationalist movement. The relationship of Viereck and Nazi Germany forms another chapter in his life, but before turning to that, it is important to note Viereck's other activities which illuminate his world view and the ideas of various prominent figures of the interwar period.

Apologizing for German na-
tionalism and promoting historical revisionism did not exhaust
Viereck's energies or concerns in the 1920's. His aesthetic, egoistic, and erotic interests could not be fulfilled by these activities
alone. Already by 1920 he had taken a special interest in the
nascent Freudian school of psychology, and he would soon become one of its popularizers. Feeling little inspiration to write
poetry, Viereck turned to fiction in the latter half of the decade;
in collaboration with another author he composed three novels
around the theme of eternal youth, blending eros, fantasy, and
history in a manner that attracted a fairly large number of readers. Concurrently, he developed into an interviewer deluxe; in
book and magazine he published accounts of meetings with many
of the great men of Europe and a few in America. Viereck enjoyed
basking in the aura of these luminaries of the age; especially
pleasing to him were his visits with Freud, Shaw, and Wilhelm
II. Near the end of the decade he made his way to the Kremlin and discovered that he was basically bourgeois. He likewise
rediscovered himself in a Freudian-flavored autobiography he was
inspired to write during his most productive literary period—1928
to 1932.

At the end of the decade Viereck felt sufficiently expansive
and liberated from the past to write about his experiences as a
propagandist in World War I. His attitudes had mellowed to the
point that he freely (if wryly) complimented his English adversaries when the occasion called for it. This episode brought him
into contact with the aging Colonel Edward M. House of war-

time fame, and from this encounter developed a close and productive relationship that became strained, however, toward the end. At the same time, Viereck sustained friendly communication with the exiled Wilhelm II, an experience that culminated with a unique biography of the ex-Kaiser which did not, however, please the latter. In these and other ways Viereck indulged his talents, his curiosity, and his desires for fame and perhaps for fortune, but in a larger sense he also held up a mirror to his times. His own agnosticism, eroticism, and subjectivism were in large measure duplicated—if not inspired—by the metaphysical and ethical confusions of the interwar period.

In the world west of Russia the 1920's was a decade of conservatism and reactionism in politics and economics, but it was a time of bold innovation and experimentation in culture. The war had something to do with the uprooting of traditional value systems and structures of authority, but movements in this direction had already gained considerable momentum by 1914. Already by 1900 sociologists had observed and rationalized the dislocating effects of rapid industrialization and urbanization and the breakdown of the Judeo-Christian value system. Sensitive observers noted evidence of growing anomie or a sense of purposelessness in the new industrial society. Europeans in turn reacted to the mechanization of life by becoming ready converts to the gospels of nationalistic myths such as Germanic *Volkstum* (folkdom), to the will to power, to various other forms of elitism, and to cults of the irrational and the intuitional.[1] One of the most significant new developments was Sigmund Freud's exploration of the unconscious functions of the mind and the role of sexual drives in determining human behavior.

The Freudian conception of man had made relatively few converts by 1914. But the way had been prepared by the dissolution of Victorianism in Europe and of Puritanism in America.

[1] See H. Stuart Hughes, *Consciousness and Society: The Reorientation of European Social Thought, 1890–1930* (New York: Random House, 1958), pp. 126–40, 148–51, 282–83; Fritz Stern, *The Politics of Cultural Despair: A Study in the Rise of the Germanic Ideology* (Garden City, N.Y.: Doubleday, 1965), pp. 212–18 and passim.

The war itself intensified feelings of disillusionment and skepticism toward the conventional standards and moral codes of western civilization. In the bold insights of Freudian analysis, many found an antidote to middle-class hypocrisy and a way of liberating themselves for the happy life promised since the Enlightment and not yet delivered. There was, in fact, a variety of motives for individuals rallying to the banner of Freud. With its emphasis on the primacy of individual feelings and personal gratification, Freudianism did not appeal necessarily to the social reformer, although it became a guide to many who were in revolt against society. Indeed, it was the individualist rebel and perhaps the hedonist who felt a special attraction to a philosophy that encouraged freer expression of instinctual desires. At least, that is what many thought it implied. And for those like Viereck who had already proclaimed the gospel of sexual liberty, Freudianism seemed to offer a form of reinforcement and scientific respectability for something they already believed. As Viereck was to write in 1931: "Wherever you touch life you touch the libido. . . . God, patriotism, and art may inspire the singer, but God and art and patriotism are merely sex in solution. . . ."[2]

Prior to 1918 Viereck displayed a favorable but only casual interest in the theories of Sigmund Freud. Nevertheless, his erotic poetry in the first decade of the century anticipated the sexual emphasis in Freudian psychology. It is not surprising, therefore, that as Freud's theories became better known in America Viereck became increasingly impressed with this system of thought that paid homage to the spirit of Eros. He found in this philosophy reinforcement for his romantic and vitalist tendencies; thus he was prepared to accept the Freudian premise that sexual energy—the libido—comprised the dominant and primary life force, and from it were derived the secondary forces that shaped and reflected human behavior. He also was impressed with the potentialities of the concept of "ambivalence" in elucidating apparent contradictions of feelings between individuals. As already noted, he used the latter principle in 1918–19 to explain his estrangement from Theodore Roosevelt. Meanwhile, in response to his

2 Viereck, *My Flesh and Blood*, p. 14.

growing admiration for Freud, immediately after the Armistice in 1918 Viereck dispatched to the founder of psychoanalysis some newspaper articles and clippings, and he offered to send him food. The latter offer was subsequently accepted.[3] From this beginning a friendly correspondence developed between the two which was not terminated until 1933. Moreover, in his first postwar journey to Europe in 1922–23 Viereck was able for the first time to visit the Columbus of the Unconscious. There were several more visits during the remainder of the decade.

The work that especially impressed Viereck and drew his attention to Freud was the latter's "Reflections on War and Death," written in 1915 and subsequently translated by A. A. Brill and Alfred Kuttner for distribution in America. Viereck published portions of it, with a commentary, in his journal in September, 1918. This article was undoubtedly enclosed in his initial letter to Freud in November. He said of the author, "Freud is the first great teacher who explains the many contradictory impulses in our natures; he shows us how to sublimate our unsocial impulses; he also indicates the limits beyond which suppression cannot go." He noted that in this essay Freud theorized that mankind was living morally and psychically beyond its means. Man had not progressed as far beyond his primitive forebears as he had been led to believe. At first glance, Viereck noted this theory seemed pessimistic, but on deeper reflection it struck him as the "most idealistic creed ever pronounced" because it proved "that we are all idealists striving to live up to some impossibly high standards." Alluding to Oscar Wilde, Viereck alleged that an ideal would no longer be such if it were attainable, but the fact that man had idealistic aims seemed to him one of the greatest compliments ever paid to the human race. The effect of Freud's exposition was to reinforce in Viereck the wishful thought that man was still god as well as animal. No animal could have set up the unattainable ideals which man had created; yet the beast in man made it impossible to realize his self-made ideal.[4] Viereck

[3] Ernest Jones, *Sigmund Freud: Life and Work* (London: Hogarth Press, 1957), Vol. III, p. 11.

[4] *Viereck's: American Monthly*, September, 1918, pp. 9–11.

appeared pleased that this explanation helped rationalize the contradictions of war; it also served him as a substitute for the Christian view that war manifested the innate or endemic sin in man and demonstrated his need for repentance before a transcendent God.

Viereck told his readers that he enjoyed the distinction of being the first journalist to be granted an interview with Freud "to interpret himself and his message." Freud obviously had come to respect the sympathy and judgment of Viereck on the subject of psychoanalysis. Their first meeting took place on August 1, 1923, in Vienna. Freud's American visitor was eager to spread the gospel. The interview was published in two parts in the *New York American* and other Hearst newspapers. Viereck described psychoanalysis as the science that leads man through the mazes of his own subconscious mind and as the "thread pointing the way out of the labyrinth where his repressed desires, like fabulous monsters, lie in ambush to pounce upon him in unguarded moments." He said that Freud denied free will, that psychoanalysis had as yet shed only a dim light on man's motives and instincts, and that Freud's outlook seemed sad rather than cheerful. He noted principles such as the embryo's recapitulation of evolution, the significant role of childhood experience in shaping the pattern of future behavior, the important role of infantile regression in criminal behavior, the ambivalence of the psyche, and the use of sublimation by civilization as a defensive mechanism. He reported that Freud emphasized the antisocial instincts of childhood and the importance of proper education to restrain what Viereck called "the beast, the criminal, and the savage in ourselves." He reported that there was meaning in slips of the tongue and in symbolic dreams. Psychoanalysis, he learned from Freud, teaches that drives which are genuinely antisocial must be sublimated, to protect oneself and society, but that many repressions are needless and cause unhappy complexes. Releasing these latter repressions by acknowledging the legitimacy of the repressed drive offers hope of making the person whole and happy and even charitable in his relations with others. Viereck concluded with Freud's assertion that the child is not the father of the man, but is the man himself, in that what happens to the child by the age of five determines the essence of the adult personality.[5]

Viereck sent his host a copy of his account of the interview, and Freud responded that it was correctly reported although somewhat accentuated to meet American tastes, and also perhaps too pessimistic.[6] Shortly after the interview Freud also acknowledged receipt of Viereck's book on Eugen Steinach, another controversial Viennese biological experimenter; he complimented him on the clarity, cleverness, and intelligent manner in which he had presented the subject.[7] In early 1925 Viereck wrote an article, published in an obscure journal, which suggested psychoanalytic principles that might apply to the Loeb-Leopold case. He reported Freud's view that man has a mania for authority and that if the authority of the priest is taken away, one must find a new authority in science (including presumably psychoanalysis). The scientific approach recognizes the need for some inhibitions, and it is psychoanalysis that can show how to achieve a proper balance between "release and repression." Viereck spoke of a king-slave complex, a kind of regressive trait in which the will to power coexists with the will to die or the desire to return to the equilibrium of the womb. Moreover, the object of this death or destructive impulse may be transferred from one's self to another individual. Thus sadism blends with masochism.[8] Again he received compliments from the founder of the psychoanalytic method, who viewed the article as correct on all essential points and said that the author was an "excellent interpreter of psychoanalysis." Freud added that the prevention of crime is basically an educational problem and not necessarily a psychoanalytic one (since the two are not strictly identical), but he stressed, with Viereck,

    [5] [G. S. Viereck], "Freud's First Interview on Psychoanalysis," *New York American*, August 19, 1923, p. ME–3; [G. S. Viereck], "How Freud Unveils the Subconscious Mind," *New York American*, August 26, 1923, p. LII–6.
    [6] S. Freud to G. S. Viereck, October 25, 1923. From excerpt in Charles Hamilton (bookseller), *Autographs*, New York City, List No. 3, n.d., Gertz MSS.
    [7] S. Freud to G. S. Viereck, August 12, 1923, Gertz MSS.
    [8] G. S. Viereck, "The Loeb-Leopold Case and Psycho-Analysis," *Haldemann-Julius Monthly*, February, 1925, pp. 151–59.

that education should be in the hands of those guided by the insights of psychoanalysis. Freud pessimistically allowed that even the psychoanalyst can be frustrated by youthful obstinacy.[9]

Another extensive interview with Freud was published in Viereck's *American Monthly* in October, 1927, and was repeated in his book, *Glimpses of the Great*, in 1930. At one point in his conversation with Freud, Viereck mused, "I wonder what my complexes are!" Freud replied:

> A serious analysis takes at least a year. It may even take two or three years. You are devoting many years of your life to lion-hunting. You have sought, year after year, the outstanding figures of your generation, invariably men older than yourself. There was Roosevelt, the Kaiser, Hindenburg, Briand, Foch, Joffre, George Brandes, Gerhardt Hauptmann, and George Bernard Shaw. . . .[10]

Viereck interjected that this was all part of his work. Freud continued: "But it is also your preference. The great man is a symbol. Your search is the search of your heart. You are seeking the great man to take the place of the father. It is part of your father complex."[11] Viereck said that at that time he vehemently denied Freud's statement, but after reflecting upon it he concluded there may be a truth unsuspected to himself in Freud's "casual suggestion." Viereck averred that he himself would be a difficult patient for a psychoanalyst because being "too well versed in psychoanalysis," he would constantly anticipate the intentions of the analyst. Freud responded that intelligence in the patient was no handicap, and could even facilitate the task.[12]

In spite of Freud's encouragement and his own commitment to Freudian psychology, Viereck did not submit himself to analytic treatment. He did harbor the ambition to be analyzed by Freud himself, but he could not find the time for the lengthy residence in Vienna that it would have required.[13] He undoubt-

---

[9] S. Freud to G. S. Viereck, published in *Haldemann-Julius Weekly*, April 4, 1925; G. S. Viereck Scrapbook, Vol. XXI.

[10] G. S. Viereck, "Surveying Life at Seventy," *American Monthly*, October, 1927, p. 10.

[11] Ibid.

[12] Ibid.

[13] Psychiatric Consultation Report on G. S. Viereck by Dr. Wendell Muncie, Johns Hopkins Hospital, December 27, 1940, p. 2, Viereck MSS.

edly had other, less conscious reasons for avoiding analysis. He said offhandedly to Freud that perhaps like Medusa he would "die from fright" if he saw his own image.[14] Actually, Viereck seemed remarkably free from inhibitory complexes, although one might charge him with varying degrees of narcissism, delusions of persecution (against Germany and German-Americans, as well as himself), and a fixation on the Fatherland. He noted in 1931 that he dreamed little, and he had attributed this phenomenon to mental censorship. He added, however, that Freud's first American pupil, Dr. A. A. Brill, suggested that this paucity of dreams might be attributable to his "comparative freedom from repressions."[15] Nevertheless, as a follower of psychoanalysis, Viereck accepted Freud's comment concerning the "father complex" and used it to explain a conflicting relationship with both parents. Also in the 1920's he projected many of his concerns and complexes onto the fictional Wandering Jew, but he worked out his primary catharsis in the preparation and 1931 publication of his unorthodox autobiography, *My Flesh and Blood: A Lyric Autobiography with Indiscreet Annotations.*

It is evident that Freud respected his American admirer primarily because of Viereck's sensitive understanding of psychoanalysis and his ability to communicate its principles to the public. But it is also relevant to point to their common sharing of Germanic culture as another cause for the rapport between them, although this same culture was carrying seeds of latent disaffection. In the 1927 interview Freud acknowledged his identification with and debt to German culture, but he also asserted that his attitude was undergoing a change as a result of rising anti-Semitism in Germany and Austria. In the context of this situation he disagreed emphatically with Viereck's comment that "to understand all, is to forgive all." He admonished Viereck that psychoanalysis teaches one not only what to endure or tolerate but also what to avoid or exterminate. "Tolerance of evil is by no means a corollary of knowledge," he concluded.[16]

One might question the meaning of "evil" in the context of

[14] *American Monthly*, October, 1927, p. 10.
[15] Viereck, *My Flesh and Blood*, p. 96.
[16] *American Monthly*, October, 1927, pp. 9–10.

Freudian psychology. In any event, Freud was not the kind of amoralist that Viereck presumed him to be. Especially noticeable in the latter respect was Viereck's inability to appreciate or understand Freud's reasons for wanting to avow himself a Jew instead of a German in response to the rising tides of anti-Semitism in his native land. To Viereck this reaction reflected "prejudice of race" and "personal rancor," but it also was "honest wrath" and evidence of a "complex" that made him "more endearingly human." In other words, Viereck was betraying an unseemly indifference to the reality or seriousness of evil. Ironically, this tendency seemed to be enhanced by his espousal of the principles of psychoanalysis.

In the mid-1930's the friendly relationship with Freud broke down over Viereck's affiliations with Nazism. Freud severed the bond in April, 1933, when he expressed deep regret that his American apostle had "debased" himself by taking sides with the Kaiser and his sympathetic opinions of the Nazi movement.[17]

Related to Viereck's fascination with psychoanalysis was his interest in the myth of eternal youth, a theme that had also appeared in his early poetry. Taking a practical approach, in the early 1920's he wrote a book about the work of Dr. Eugen Steinach, a Viennese physician who was experimenting with the use of hormones to arrest the aging process. In the last half of the decade, he exploited this topic most successfully in a series of three fairly popular novels about the legendary Wandering Jew. He wrote them in collaboration with Paul Eldridge, an American novelist of Jewish descent.

It is significant, in view of Viereck's later connections with Nazi Germany, that in his Wandering Jew trilogy he indicated a liking for Jews. Commenting on this in his poetic autobiography in 1931, he wrote:

> The quickness of the Jew, the restlessness of his mind, his immediate response to nervous and cerebral stimuli, under the veil of Oriental languors, excites me. It is this attraction that makes me the chronicler of Cartaphilus and Salome, the Wandering Jew and the Wandering Jewess.

[17] S. Freud to G. S. Viereck, July 20, 1928. Reprinted in Ernst Freud, ed., *Letters of Sigmund Freud* (New York: McGraw-Hill, 1964), p. 416.

However, Cartaphilus is not merely the Wandering Jew. He is Wandering Man, Faust-Don Juan. And Salome is not merely the Wandering Jewess, but the Eternal Woman, with a dash of Lilith and a dash of feminine Faust. I refuse to make the vulgar distinction of sex or race.[18]

Subsequent events cast doubt on the depth of Viereck's conviction concerning racial tolerance. Nevertheless, the friendships he had with Jews (such as Ludwig Fulda, Ludwig Lewisohn, and Paul Eldridge) and his sympathetic treatment of them in the Wandering Jew trilogy indicated clearly that he was not anti-Semitic. His psychological affinity for the Jews even drew Albert Einstein's attention. In a 1929 interview Einstein told Viereck that he had the "psychic adaptability of the Jew," and that there was something in his psychology "which makes it possible for me to talk to you without barrier."[19]

Another major facet of Viereck's personality, already alluded to, was his intense interest in the "dynamics" of great men. It was part of his apolitical or nonideological stance, of his supposition that the character of the ruler was of more significance than the system of government in which he operated. This kind of "personalism" may thus be seen as the obverse side of his aestheticism. It is thus appropriate for the next phase of this account to deal with his endeavors as a journalist and historian to fulfill his own undefined desire to interact personally with the great men and events of his own time.

It is perhaps already evident that one of Viereck's favorite sports in the 1920's was "big-name" hunting. In trips that he made almost every year after 1921 he added more trophies to his collection, many of them reaching public display through not only his own journal and the Hearst newspapers, but eventually in the Saturday Evening Post and Liberty magazine. Some remained unpublished—that is, until 1930, when thirty-two of his interviews were published in a book called Glimpses of the Great. Viereck styled himself the "interviewer deluxe." What impelled him to seek out and persuade these personages to bare their

[18] Viereck, My Flesh and Blood, p. 145.
[19] Ibid., p. 375.

thoughts to the world? One might agree with the suggestion that he was "searching for the father" as part of his alleged father complex, or one could more simply conclude that he was searching for fame. In his own view, like the Wandering Jew he was "compelled by an immense curiosity to seek out my most eminent contemporaries." "I am not satisfied," he continued, "until I have wrested their philosophy of life from their lips, until I have acquired something I need to complete my own universe."[20]

He denied that his motives or techniques were those of the ordinary journalist. He told Clemenceau, for instance, that he had no use for conventional journalism and that he considered himself a poet rather than a journalist.[21] In his introduction, he declared that he was motivated not only by a desire to complete his own world view but by a belief that each individual represented a special expression of a world spirit. He explained:

> By birth a Protestant, by temperament a pagan, by persuasion a pantheist, I look upon all life as an expression of the World Spirit of which we all, however feeble and remote, are a part. The sum of all intelligence is God. I see a God in the making. He is neither perfect nor omnipotent, but forever in process of evolution.
>
> To me the men to whom I have talked and whose thoughts I record are flashes of the great World Brain. Some are incandescent in their intensity; in others the divine flame burns more dimly. Their colours are more varied than the spectrum. I am the spectroscope that reveals the stuff of which they are made, or, translating color into sound, I am the trumpet through which they convey their message.[22]

This testament of faith, nebulous as it is, diverged somewhat from his earlier profession of materialism and "glandular determinism." Viereck's profession of belief in a World Brain should not be taken too seriously. In fact, it bore a close resemblance to the metaphysical creed expressed by an unlikely model—Henry Ford. Ford told his interviewer that he believed there was a "Master Mind" or a "Brain of the Earth" sending thought waves to

[20] G. S. Viereck, *Glimpses of the Great* (London: Duckworth, 1930), p. 9.
[21] Ibid., p. 54.
[22] Ibid., p. 10.

earthlings, and that it might even be part of a "Brain of the Universe." Yet, if Viereck was becoming attuned to pantheism, it probably drew more inspiration from the influence of stellar thinkers like Einstein and Shaw than from the car-maker of Detroit. Einstein admitted being fascinated by Spinoza's pantheism, and Shaw spoke of civilization's need for some kind of religion if mankind were to survive, but one could give this divinity any name he preferred, such as "Life Force, World Spirit, Elan Vital, or Creative Evolution."[23] Agnosticism mixed more ominously with militarism and supernationalism in such figures as Mussolini, Ludendorff, and former Crown Prince Wilhelm. Each individual had his own gods, reflecting a self-image and also mirroring the moral confusions of the age.

Indeed, in the early 1930's Viereck confided to his friend Elmer Gertz that he was not sure of his own philosophy. He speculated that it might be based on the idea of vibrating with a great aesthetic or racial creed, or with a great philosophy. More specifically, he proclaimed himself an "Einsteinian in morals," a believer in the relativity of all things, an admirer of any philosopher "who gives me the illusion of a thrill or a hope." He continued, "Nietzsche appeals to me; likewise in some moods Schopenhauer; in others Hegel; but none means as much to me as Freud. . . ."[24] In his application of relativity to morals, Viereck apparently did not take to heart Einstein's warning that the physical theory of relativity "merely denotes that certain physical and mechanical facts, which have been regarded as positive and permanent, are relative with regard to certain other facts in the sphere of physics and mechanics. It does not mean that everything in life is relative and that we have the right to turn the whole world mischievously topsy-turvy."[25] Yet, as noted earlier, Viereck did impress Einstein and others as a tolerant individual, open to and appreciative of the contributions made by individuals of many races and nations.

In these expressions of confusion about belief and faith, Viereck might be seen as a child of his time. He professed to see in

[23] Ibid., pp. 15, 347, 373.
[24] Gertz, "Stormy Petrel," Ch. 16, pp. 4–6.
[25] Viereck, *Glimpses of the Great*, p. 357.

the twentieth century the doom of old orthodoxies and funda-
mentalisms, the rejection of absolutes or final truths. The thirty-
two personalities interviewed for his book demonstrated the
"polyphony of human thought," the complex and conflicting
lines of belief which characterized the age. The varieties of
thoughts, emotions, and beliefs expounded by these witnesses
served to reinforce Viereck's own belief in the ambivalence of
truth and in the complex role of the unconscious. There was insight in Viereck's statement that the "self," as each one conceives
it, is only a part—a conscious factor—in a compound personality
which also responds to an unconscious element. "The unconscious," Viereck explained, "is a mansion harbouring myriads of
ancestors as well as innumerable complexes imposed upon us
from without." Every personality tends to be schizophrenic; the
glimmer of hope, for Viereck, was his belief that modern man
possessed a clearer perception than in previous centuries of the
limits of the human mind and the cosmos. It might be possible,
he implied, for man, equipped with his expanding knowledge of
the mind, to "recover human dignity from the wreck of ancient
faiths and taboos."[26]

In view of the prominence of his subjects and of the broad
spectrum of interests and areas they represented, Viereck's
Glimpses of the Great could well be considered his tour de force.
Besides his conversations with people already mentioned, he in-
terviewed such disparate personalities as Hindenburg and Henri
Barbusse, Briand and Joffre, Ramsay MacDonald and Marshal
Foch, Grand Duke Alexander of Russia and Henry Ford, Ein-
stein and Hjalmar Schacht, playwright Arthur Schnitzler and
Queen Elizabeth of the Belgians, sexologist Voronoff and nov-
elist-playwright Israel Zangwill, occultist Baron von Schrenk-
Notzing and German Chancellor Wilhelm Marx, and Frank
Harris and Gerhardt Hauptmann. From most of these individuals
he elicited opinions on philosophy, religion, or sex, as well as their
views on more practical affairs of state or techniques of their art.
There was a preponderance of German-born or German-related
figures, many of whom represented the spirit of Imperial Germany. Yet Emil Ludwig, for instance, was permitted to voice his

[26] Ibid., p. 11.

criticism of the Kaiser, and both he and Israel Zangwill took the opportunity to speak out against anti-Semitism and supernationalism. At the same time, Viereck offered a forum to the likes of General Ludendorff, who expressed his hatred of "supranationalist" forces—meaning Jews, Freemasons, and Catholics.[27] Viereck admitted that "this transposition of hatred [from the French and English] has wrought a transformation in the General which astonishes and, at times alarms, his friends."[28] Yet on political matters the tone of Viereck's questions revealed his underlying sympathy with German nationalism.

Among the "great men" Viereck included in his book, he no doubt felt closest in his affections to the former Kaiser; of course, he had already acknowledged his special debt to Sigmund Freud. Yet there was a third distinguished personage—George Bernard Shaw—who in some respects occupied the most endearing position in his pantheon of idols. Viereck had long been awed by Shaw's great talent, and he could hardly forget the playwright's sympathetic words during the crisis of World War I. He first met the great playwright in 1911, and on all of his subsequent trips to Europe he included Shaw in his itinerary.[29] Commenting upon his interview of Shaw in June, 1926, Viereck called him "the greatest dramatist, the keenest wit in Europe, and, now that Anatole France is dead, the last of the sages." Captivated by Shaw's wry Irish wit and his "Mephistophelean smile," Viereck decided the latter was only a "defensive mechanism to conceal from the casual observer the kindliness of his heart. Bernard Shaw for all his cynical attitudes is more saint than Mephisto."[30] Viereck's interview published in *Glimpses of the Great* placed emphasis on Shaw's ideas concerning creative evolution. Shaw had remarked in jest to his interviewer, "Don't say I authorize the publication of this interview. I don't. If you get me into hot water, I can always say: 'You know Viereck—he is a poet, endowed to a marvellous degree with the creative imagination.'" Shaw con-

[27] Implied ibid., p. 111, but explicit in G. S. Viereck, *As They Saw Us: Foch, Ludendorff and Other Leaders Write Our War History* (Garden City, N.Y.: Doubleday, Doran and Co., 1929), p. 51.
[28] Viereck, *Glimpses of the Great*, pp. 110–11.
[29] Ibid., p. 15.
[30] *American Monthly*, October, 1926, p. 247.

cluded, however, that the interview did reflect his philosophy of life.[31]

But the Irish sage was not always happy with the results of these interviews. A few years earlier Viereck had to recant a statement in a prior interview in which he had quoted Shaw to the effect that he was a foe of Bolshevism.[32] Then, in the early 1930's, Viereck quoted Shaw as saying that his interviewer was "80 percent clever and strong minded, and 20 percent an impenetrable blockhead. He generally brings the 20 percent to bear on me. . . ."[33] On a couple of other occasions he complained of subjectivity and inaccuracy in drafts of interviews submitted to him, but he remained tolerant of his American admirer. In 1935 one of Viereck's friends asked Shaw for his opinion of Viereck's place in literature, to which Shaw replied, "Ask me three hundred years hence." He added that Viereck was *echt Deutsch* (pure German), and he professed to like the German touch in him and considered him to be pleasant company.[34]

Viereck's file of great men did not include any builders of Communism. But his "immense curiosity" would not let him rest until he had gotten a closer look at this new phenomenon which was transforming Russian society and threatening the capitalist system around the world. Consequently, for the first and only time in his career, Viereck extended his journalistic tour into the Soviet Union in 1929. He also was able to sell the *Saturday Evening Post* on publishing his impressions, thus giving them wide dissemination among the American public. It is evident that if he had shown a strongly anti-Communist stance he would not have gained admittance to the Soviet Union.

[31] Viereck, *Glimpses of the Great*, p. 15.
[32] G. S. Viereck, "Bernard Shaw's Paean on Bolshevism," *New York American*, July 17, 1927, p. E–1. Also see G. S. Viereck, "Reason Alone Can Cure Ills of Social Organism: Shaw," *New York American*, June 13, 1926, pp. 1, 11; G. S. Viereck, "Bernard Shaw: Real Disarmament Is Impossible," *New York American*, July 10, 1927, p. E–1.
[33] G. S. Viereck, "Shaw as a Lover," *Contempo* (Chapel Hill, N.C.) I (October 15, 1931): 1.
[34] G. B. Shaw to G. S. Viereck, December 4, 1929, and April 10, 1937. Extracts in George van Nosdall's booksellers list 1,120, April, 1949, New York, pp. 2, 4; G. B. Shaw to Elmer Gertz, February 15, 1935, Gertz MSS.

We have already seen that he held a pragmatic attitude toward both the Bolshevik revolution and the socialism of Debs. He had no basic moral or ideological objection to either. He did believe that the idea of private property was firmly fixed in western civilization and would be most difficult to rout. Moreover, he himself held stock in various American corporations, and his scale of life approximated that of the upper bourgeoisie.

It has also been noted that Viereck cared little about structures or systems of government; he was concerned primarily with the personality of the leader. A dynamic leader invariably attracted him. Thus, when Lenin died in 1924, Viereck offered him an accolade. He wrote in his *American Monthly*, "For better or for worse, Nicolai Lenin, who more than any other 'big Bolshevik' incarnated Soviet Russia, proved himself the greatest figure in human annals since the first Napoleon." At the same time, he said that recognition of Lenin's greatness implied no approval of his economics.[35] In the next five years the *American Monthly* virtually ignored Soviet affairs. Meanwhile, Viereck had met and interviewed nationalist, socialist, and fascist leaders in Europe, as well as the pope, and others among Europe's dynamic elite; it seemed only a question of time before he would knock on the doors of the Kremlin.

To gain entry to the Kremlin was no easy matter—at least for those who had not shown themselves to be pro-Bolshevik or who did not have a technical skill to offer the state. Still, Viereck had not yet demonstrated any noticeable anti-Communist fervor, and of course there was the matter of his parents' onetime contribution to the Marxist cause in Germany. His first application for an entrance visa was submitted in early 1929. In April Senator William Borah wrote a letter of commendation for him in which he assured whomever it might concern that Viereck was a "brilliant writer" and sympathetic to the Russian people.[36] Borah, who was chairman of the Senate Foreign Relations Committee, had long favored American recognition of the Soviet government, and Americans traveling to Russia found that a good word from Borah

[35] *American Monthly*, March, 1924, p. 8.
[36] William Borah to G. S. Viereck, April 26, 1929. Extract in George van Nosdall's bookseller's list 1,119, p. 3.

opened doors for them.[37] Along with his request for entry into Russia, Viereck also asked permission to interview Lunacharsky, Madame Lenin, and Stalin, as well as other lesser figures. He subsequently received a visa for himself and his wife, but Soviet officials ruled out his request to interview the foregoing three prominent individuals.[38]

Viereck found conditions in Russia grim. He noticed groups of urchins chanting for bread and saw people on the streets without shoes. He complained of the high expenses he incurred in Moscow and alleged that official delegations were treated much more royally than individual tourists like himself. Nevertheless, in his talks with government officials he was treated with unquestioned courtesy, and he moved about unhampered by the police. At the Marx-Lenin museum he was shown letters his parents had written to Engels and Marx. He talked to acting Foreign Minister Krakhan; to Kahan, who was in charge of Anglo-American relations in the foreign office; to Volin, acting head of the press bureau and chief censor; and to Vorobkov, director of the state bank. He reportedly told one official, "I am intensely interested in your experiment, but I am glad it takes place in Russia and not in America." He cited for his readers the rationing of food, a housing shortage, low pay, and the favoring of the industrial worker at the expense of the peasant.[39] He saw Bolshevism turning toward the East and stated that "in his heart Lenin was an Asiatic despot. Stalin, though lacking the genius of Lenin, is made in a similar mold." He reported that the Soviet ideal left no room for individuality and that the leaders were fanatical and doctrinaire, "lacking the milk of human kindness and the saving grace of common sense." He added that the Soviet state illustrated the "horrors of any government dominated completely by the intelligentsia," and that it was difficult for anyone nurtured in the Anglo-Saxon tradition "to comprehend the supineness with

[37] "Travelers Say Borah Letters Pierce All Barriers in Russia," *Washington Star*, June 28, 1929, G. S. Viereck Scrapbook, Vol. XXIII.

[38] S. P. Trevas, Anglo-American Referent, U.S.S.R. Society for Cultural Relations with Foreign Countries, to G. S. Viereck, July 4, 1929, Viereck MSS.

[39] G. S. Viereck, "Russia Marks Time," *Saturday Evening Post*, November 30, 1929, pp. 14–15, 94; Viereck, *My Flesh and Blood*, p. 240.

which the Russian people endure the incubus of Bolshevism."
The iron-willed idealism of the leaders frightened him; he felt it
could only accentuate their destructive force. It was beyond the
Machiavellian, which he felt still possessed something understandably human. In Viereck's view:

> Even the good-natured scoundrel, even the arrant fool, is prefer-
> able to the intellectual zealot, more interested in his formula than
> in human life. You can reason with a scoundrel or you can bribe
> him; you can twist a fool around your finger, but doctrinaires,
> imbued with perverted logic, are impervious to human persuasion.
> Such is the government of Soviet Russia in the hands of highbrows
> bereft alike of humanity and humor.[40]

In his third and final article, he pointed to the uniqueness of
the Soviet experiment, based as it was on the philosophy of Marx.
Yet he doubted that Bolshevik ideology would succeed in erad-
icating the "old Adam," which he presumed was what made the
world as it is. He included in this traditional world "monogamy,
and the desire of a man to profit from his own labor and to store
up a competence for his wife and children." For a metaphorical
comparison, he said, "The human heart beats more passionately
for the Holy Grail than for the threshing machine." Even in the
Soviet policy of encouraging the various ethnic groups to retain
their cultural customs, he saw a technique of "divide and rule"
and a device to entice outsiders to join the fold. He noted that
economic districts disregarded racial-ethnic boundaries. Bolshevism, he decided, was a disease of autocracy, "the elephantiasis of
authority," in that "Stalin is not only the state, he is the church
and the people." In fascism, he said, he found "much that I admire . . . much that repels me," but he claimed that fascism was
at least efficient, whereas Bolshevism was not—at least it was not
feeding its people as well. He alleged, too, that fascism rallied all
citizens into its ranks, whereas the Communist party was exclusive, admitting only about one-half of 1 percent of the people
into membership. Without being specific, he also condemned
Bolshevism as a creed that could not survive unless it conquered

[40] G. S. Viereck, "Prisoners of Utopia," *Saturday Evening Post*, December 14, 1929, pp. 23, 175–77, 181.

the world; thus humanity would sometime be faced with the either/or of becoming all capitalist or all Marxist-socialist. Finally, writing on the eve of the stock market crash and a capitalist crisis in the western countries, he decided: "The more I see of Fascism and Bolshevism, the better I like Americanism. The more I observe economic and political conditions existing in Italy and in Russia, the more I realize that capitalism tempered by democracy offers the greatest advantage to the greatest possible numbers."[41]

Undoubtedly to the chagrin of Soviet officials, Viereck's journey to Moscow turned out to be a reversal of what they may have hoped would be a propaganda asset. His account buttressed the anti-Soviet feelings shared by many Americans, but at least he did not yet have the liquidation of kulaks and the forced labor camps to write about. At the same time, however, his disinterest in economics partially blinded him to the positive goals of the first five-year plan. He did not appreciate the fact that the consumer would have to sacrifice living standards at least temporarily while available resources were concentrated on the building-up of expensive basic industrial facilities. He realized that his type of aesthetic personality had no place in this highly regulated society, but he again failed to realize that what he called the abstract ideals of Soviet managers actually represented a strongly utilitarian ethic. Plainly, the ideas of class struggle, a one-class state, and state ownership of the means of production lacked the mythic, poetic values that he could find in fascist Italy, where Mussolini made pretensions of restoring the spirit and splendor of ancient Rome.[42] Viereck could understand the latter, for pagan Rome had already supplied him liberally with poetic ideas and values.

In the 1930's, particularly after 1933, Viereck became a gadfly to the Communist movement. Inspired by the domestic economic crisis and also by the German-Nazi antagonism toward Bolshevism, he began warring on the American Communist movement, mainly through the pages of *Liberty* magazine. He

---

[41] G. S. Viereck, "Pyatiletka," *Saturday Evening Post*, January 18, 1930, pp. 17, 83–85, 89.
[42] Viereck, *Glimpses of the Great*, p. 67.

portrayed Communism as an international conspiracy whose tactic was to bore from within capitalist institutions. He wrote of the "Web of the Red Spider" in 1933, emphasizing those instances in which Communist sympathizers had penetrated into government, unions, big-city schools, and other groups. At one point he wrote, "Without being enamored of Fascism, one may concede that it may be necessary as an antidote against Communism."[43] He found one ready source of support in Congressman Hamilton Fish, Jr., of New York. Fish wrote Viereck that he agreed with his analysis of the Bolshevik danger and with his conclusion that Germany was better off fascist than Communist.[44]

Five years later Viereck wrote another four-part article, "What the Dies Committee Overlooked," which brought up to date the earlier charges of Communist subversion in the United States and accused the Communist party of planning to call a general strike, seize factories, and sow terror and confusion among the populace in preparation for a take-over.[45] None of the articles were adequately documented; much of the evidence was hearsay; his conclusions exaggerated the extent and nature of the menace. Nevertheless, he was likely sincere. The problem was that his judgment had been warped by his receptivity to fascist, and particularly Nazi, arguments against Marxism. Displaying a certain skepticism about the durability of democracy, Viereck tended to accept the Nazi portrayal of Communism as essentially foreign and alien to the spirit of the German nation, as an enemy of western culture in general, and as resistable only by a fascist ideology— at least in Western Europe.

Along with his articles on Russia, the *Saturday Evening Post* in 1929 carried a five-part story on propaganda in World War I

---

[43] G. S. Viereck, "The Web of the Red Spider," *Liberty*, Pt. I, June 17, 1933, pp. 5–9; Pt. II, June 24, 1933, pp. 38–39; Pt. III, July 1, 1933, pp. 32–35; Pt. IV, July 8, 1933, pp. 42–45.

[44] Hamilton Fish, Jr., to G. S. Viereck, April 21, 1933, and June 17, 1933, Viereck MSS.

[45] Donald F. Wickets [G. S. Viereck], "What the Dies Committee Overlooked," *Liberty*, Pt. I, December 24, 1938, pp. 13–14; Pt. II, December 31, 1938, pp. 37–38; Pt. III, January 7, 1939, pp. 47–51; Pt. IV, January 14, 1939, pp. 45–47.

"by one of the war propagandists," a byline that pretended to conceal its author—G. S. Viereck. This series was published in 1930 as a book, *Spreading Germs of Hate*.[46] By the time this story was written, Viereck's views on the war had mellowed somewhat and his account possessed surprising objectivity. For example, at one point he admitted that friends of the Germans and the Irish castigated Allied propagandists as "hired tools of Lord Northcliffe but rarely questioned sources of their own financial support." "The hypocrisy of this attitude," he explained, "is not, as a rule, conscious. The propagandist has a schizophrenic mind, a split personality." Moreover, in his summary of the work, he offered suggestions on how to detect and resist propaganda. He said that one must learn to examine news critically and to analyze one's own reactions. "We can defeat propagandists by laughing out of court those who preach hate, the historians who falsify history, and the blatant politicians appealing to our most primitive instincts under the guise of idealism," he declared. No one can make himself entirely immune to the cunning and insidious nature of propaganda, but the best antidotes are "a rugged sense of Americanism," "horse sense," and a "sense of humor."[47]

Harold Lasswell—perhaps the world's leading student of propaganda—told Elmer Gertz that Viereck's book was "one of the truly basic contributions to the study of propaganda."[48] The book received considerable attention from reviewers; most praised it for its objective coverage of both sides, its first-hand dimension, its good humor and sprightly style.

One of those deeply impressed by Viereck's articles on propaganda was Colonel House. After reading them in the *Saturday Evening Post*, he inquired about the identity of their anonymous author and was pleased and surprised to learn that Viereck had written them. House wrote Viereck at once (August 18, 1929), thanking him for the pleasure this story had given him. He explained further, "I seldom read articles or books relating to the

[46] "War Propaganda," *Saturday Evening Post*, June 15, 1929, pp. 3–5, 141–42; June 22, 1929, pp. 12–13, 158, 161–66; June 29, 1929, 20–21; 169–74; July 27, 1929, pp. 26, 28, 134–38; August 17, 1929, pp. 41, 43–44, 114, 117. Published in book form by Horace Liveright.
[47] Viereck, *Spreading Germs of Hate*, pp. 13, 297.
[48] Gertz, "Stormy Petrel," Ch. 22, p. 9.

war, for I got a full measure of that greatest of human tragedies while it was in progress, but I am glad my attention was called to your brilliant, informing and valuable contribution to one of its most sinister features."[49] He commented, too, on the quality of fairness toward both sides, and expressed his hope that they would be published in book form. This letter marked the beginning of a fruitful friendship. However, House's immediate fondness for Viereck is somewhat surprising in view of the fact that three years earlier Viereck had portrayed him as a bungler and hypocrite for his role in World War I. This interpretation of House came out in Viereck's review of Charles Seymour's *Intimate Papers of Colonel House*; the review was published in the *American Monthly*.[50] It is possible that House was unaware of these remarks.

The two newfound friends first met on October 14, 1929, in New York. According to Viereck, Colonel House told him that he was the "last person in the world" whom he would have suspected of being the author of these articles. He was astonished that anyone so closely connected with the war could be so impartial. "He [Colonel House] said that I must be like him, able to detach myself from the passions of the moment," noted Viereck.[51] House repeated to Viereck his feeling that neither he nor Wilson disliked Germany, but that they did fear German militarism which, if triumphant, they felt would have compelled the United States to become an armed camp. He added that, unlike Theodore Roosevelt, they did not fear an invasion by Germany.[52] With House's encouragement, Viereck proceeded to draft into book form his series of articles, and Horace Liveright agreed to publish it. Colonel House contributed a preface to the book, in which he complimented the author for his calm and fair treat-

[49] Quoted ibid., Ch. 32, p. 4.
[50] "Colonel House, Bungler and Hypocrite," *American Monthly*, March, 1926, pp. 5–6; "Colonel House a British Spy?" *American Monthly*, April, 1926, pp. 37–38.
[51] Memo for Record, G. S. Viereck, concerning Col. House, n.d., House MSS.
[52] Notes by G. S. Viereck, "Scraps from Conversations with House," 1929, House MSS.

ment of the subject while at the same time refusing his concur-
rence in all of the author's opinions and conclusions.[53]

While the foregoing project was underway, Viereck began to
work with Colonel House on other plans. In January, 1930, he
obtained House's consent to take part in a dialogue on freedom of
the seas to be recorded by Fox-Hearst Movietone Corporation. In
his request to House, Viereck said that his gracious consent
"would be the final and indisputable proclamation that I have
at last achieved both fame and respectability. This is far more
important to me than any financial consideration." There was no
monetary compensation for the dialogue.[54] Later that month,
Viereck asked the Colonel for a letter of recommendation in
preparation for a possible speaking tour of the country as proposed by the manager of a New York lecture bureau. House
obliged with a statement that Viereck's "knowledge of public
men and events throughout the world will give what you say the
stamp of authority, and will enlighten our people." He pointed
further to Viereck's unique range of contacts with notable leaders
and with the events of World War I and its aftermath.[55] For
reasons unknown, Viereck's plan for a lecture tour was not carried out. In February he proposed to House, who was planning a
trip to Europe, that if he met Paderewski perhaps he would suggest to the Polish leader the possibility of Viereck collaborating
with him on an autobiography, as had been done with Empress
Hermine and as he proposed to do with House, "if you are
willing."[56]

Viereck's suggestion that he collaborate with House in writing
the latter's memoirs remained dormant for several months. Finally, in October, 1930, House proposed that Viereck write an
account of his association and friendship with Woodrow Wilson.
Viereck readily agreed and asked House for access to unpublished
information. He also told his subject that the project could oc-

[53] Viereck, *Spreading Germs of Hate*, pp. v–vi.

[54] G. S. Viereck to E. M. House, January 2, 1930; G. S. Viereck to
E. M. House, January 8, 1930, House MSS.

[55] G. S. Viereck to E. M. House, January 29, 1930; E. M. House to
G. S. Viereck, January 30, 1930, House MSS.

[56] G. S. Viereck to E. M. House, February 25, 1930, House MSS.

cupy only part of his time, since he had "to keep the wolf from the door, which in the present state of business and the stock market, is no easy task." Like many others, in 1930 Viereck had incurred a substantial loss on his stock in investments, and he was feeling the financial pressure.[57] It is evident that the royalties on his books were insufficient to maintain his accustomed standard of living. The *American Monthly* had ceased as a source of revenue since he had turned it over to new management, and it was withering anyway.

Actually, the period between the first symptoms of the crash in 1929 and the depths of the depression in 1933 marked Viereck's most productive literary period; in this five-year span he authored or coauthored eight books. Nevertheless, as a journalist he had few magazine articles to his credit in 1929 and 1930 except those published in the *Saturday Evening Post*. It must have occurred to him that his work on House's memoirs need not be a financial sacrifice, but might be a source of gain. More than that, as he confided to House in mid-October, 1930, "there is a certain poetic justice in this, that I, who had been one of the most bitter enemies of Woodrow Wilson, should be selected by you and by fate to tell the true story resting in the lines and between the lines of your correspondence."[58]

Viereck designed a thorough plan of research for the first authorized account of House's relationship with President Wilson. Most important, of course, was his ready access to House and his ideas and materials which he hoped would shed a new and clearer light upon a most crucial period in American history. In the course of his research on this project he also consulted with former Central Power ambassadors, Dumba and Bernstorff, various members of Wilson's cabinet, Wilson's secretary Joseph Tumulty, Sydney E. Mezes (chief of the Inquiry, the body established by the President to prepare data and advice for the peace conference), Justice Charles Evans Hughes, Washington correspondent Louis Seibold, Professor Charles Seymour, and Fran-

---

[57] G. S. Viereck to E. M. House, October 7, 1930, House MSS. Viereck's son Peter estimates his father lost up to $250,000 in the stock market crash (interview with Peter Viereck, August 15, 1967).

[58] G. S. Viereck to E. M. House, October 17, 1930, House MSS.

ces Denton, the Colonel's secretary. Shaemas O'Sheel served as a research assistant. It is notable that Viereck did not obtain impressions from British or French political and diplomatic personnel—indicating his pro-German orientation, presumably.

In spite of his known inclinations, Viereck's account was not as biased as one might have expected. The restraining hand of Colonel House undoubtedly helped moderate his predispositions, but Viereck himself appeared to have become broader and more rational in his outlook. Working diligently on the manuscript in 1931, Viereck finished it in 1932. In that year it was published by Horace Liveright, titled *The Strangest Friendship in History: Woodrow Wilson and Colonel House.*

Most significant was Viereck's new understanding of Woodrow Wilson. Already by the end of November, 1930, he confided in a letter to Count Bernstorff that his reading of Wilson's letters to House had "completely revolutionized" his attitude toward Wilson. He confessed to Bainbridge Colby in June, 1931, "I now realize his sincerity and his desire to keep the country out of war."[59] In the final text he proclaimed that instead of a "hypocrite" he saw Wilson as a "tragic and solitary figure, not unlike Abraham Lincoln's, with the tongue of a poet and the dreams of a savior." Wilson's failure could be attributed partly to his temperament, but in the main his task was "too gigantic."[60] Sizing up the personalities in his story, he explained, "There are neither heroes nor villains in our drama—only poor struggling mortals, each striving vainly to play his part without fumbling his lines." This statement was quite an admission, especially in that it presumably included the Kaiser as well as Colonel House. In spite of this apparent diffusion of blame, Viereck repeated the old canard of the German nationalists that the German army was not beaten, although it was losing, and that the Kaiser was ill advised and misinformed when he was persuaded to abdicate in order to preserve Germany from revolution and enable his country to reap an honorable peace based on the Fourteen Points.[61]

[59] G. S. Viereck to Johann Bernstorff, November 28, 1930; G. S. Viereck to Bainbridge Colby, June 22, 1931, House MSS.
[60] Viereck, *Strangest Friendship in History*, p. 7.
[61] Ibid., pp. 8, 225–26.

Viereck's work may have been more dramatic in style than other books on this subject, but it generally failed to offer any startling revelations or new interpretations. Surprisingly, in view of his orientation in other works, he employed Freudian principles sparingly, but his comments on Wilson's psychology set it off from other works bearing on the topic. Most notably, he alleged that in converting from pacifist to warrior Wilson could not forgive himself the surrender of his dearest convictions; unwilling to censure himself or his alter ego—House—he unconsciously transferred the fury of his resentment for himself to "the military masters of Germany," as he usually labeled the enemy. According to the author, this dilemma produced schizoid behavior after April 2, 1917. Viereck also explained Wilson's "inconsistencies of behavior and judgment" in terms of the interplay of four dominant personalities within himself, each vying for mastery of his mental processes. Viereck claimed that in most people one facet of the personality dominates all the others; in Wilson's case, however, he detected a complex conflict of his intellectual, emotional, practical, and moral selves which upset his psychic balance.[62]

One incident emphasized as a revelation was Wilson's plan to arrange for the immediate succession of Charles Evans Hughes as president if Wilson had lost the election of 1916. Another aspect which had not been stressed before was the important role of the President's wife during Wilson's convalescence from his stroke. Viereck described her role frankly, asserting that from September 26, 1919, to April 13, 1920, she not only in effect was "Acting President, but Secretary to the President, and Secretary of State." He also produced evidence which convinced him that the cause of the rupture of relations between Wilson and House—an issue of long controversy—was the insidious intervention of Wilson's wife.[63]

In 1931 Viereck found a journalistic market for his House-Wilson account. Editor (Charles) Fulton Oursler, his friend of several years, agreed to serialize this work in abbreviated form in *Liberty* magazine. Accordingly, it was published in ten install-

[62] See ibid., pp. 194–96, 280.
[63] Ibid., pp. 150–53, 262–77, 293.

ments from February through April, 1932. Up to that time Viereck had authored less than a dozen articles in this magazine, but within the next six years he contributed more than fifty articles for this journal, which had a total circulation of more than 2,000,000 copies each week. It became his chief source of income, netting him $8,000–10,000 per year.[64]

With Viereck's encouragement and assistance, Colonel House also composed several articles on contemporary issues that were published in the magazine between 1933 and 1935. *Liberty* paid Colonel House $500 for each article and in addition remunerated Viereck with about one-third of that amount.[65] In one of their joint efforts in 1935, they used the terms "haves" and "have nots" to distinguish nations with colonial empires from those without. Viereck claimed that they thereby gave currency to these now-familiar terms. It should be noted, however, that the chief "have nots," in their view, were Germany, Italy, and Japan—the fascist nations lusting for empire. Their thesis was that the latter countries should be appeased (economically especially) if war was to be averted.[66] Perhaps it was this motivation which caused Viereck to take great interest in a remark by Colonel House that an American—a Mr. Hammond—knew of oil deposits in Bavaria. Viereck passed this information on to Dr. Hjalmar Schacht, Germany's economics minister, who asked for more details. But Hammond would not comment upon this matter, and Viereck complained to House that this unwillingness to comment might cause "my friends in Europe [to pay] much less attention hereafter to any suggestions from me."[67]

Liberty magazine agreed, apparently in 1934, to a similar financial arrangement for the projected publication of House's memoirs. Viereck had persuaded House to begin the autobiog-

[64] Memo, G. S. Viereck to Fulton Oursler, April 7, 1939, Viereck MSS.

[65] G. S. Viereck to E. M. House, April 16, 1937, House MSS.

[66] E. M. House, "Wanted—A New Deal among Nations," *Liberty*, September 14, 1935, pp. 44–47; G. S. Viereck to E. M. House, March 2, 1935, House MSS; G. S. Viereck, *The Kaiser on Trial* (Richmond, Va.: Wm. Byrd Press, 1937), pp. xiii, 460.

[67] G. S. Viereck to E. M. House, May 15, 1935, and May 24, 1935, House MSS.

raphy, with his assistance. The first two installments of the draft were completed in 1934. It appears that in the first phases of the project Viereck suggested how the material should be arranged and then edited and revised the drafts prepared by House. Viereck's technique was demonstrated in his remarks to House on the latter's draft of the second installment: "There should be some striking characterizations, some memorable phrase, and preferably some anecdote or some incident that characterizes the man and the situation." Some of the subsequent installments, however, were prepared by Viereck and reviewed and, where necessary, reworked by Colonel House. For reasons not discernible in their correspondence, in 1935 House appeared to lose interest in the project. In July Viereck complained to him that he still had not seen his diary, and he regretted that House had elected not to amplify or revise the thirteenth installment which Viereck had based entirely upon Seymour's *Intimate Papers*. He still lacked information, too, on House's career since the war. Meanwhile, he confided to Frances Denton that Farrar and Rinehart were no longer interested in publishing the book; he attributed this in part to the Colonel's keeping himself too anonymous and being too reticent. Under Viereck's prodding, House cooperated in the preparation of the final installments, but the manuscript was not completed until early 1936.[68]

In the meantime, *Liberty* magazine postponed indefinitely its plans to publish the memoirs, although it had paid advances to both of them. Nevertheless, in mid-1935 Viereck complained of financial difficulties caused in part by *Liberty's* plan to pay him for no more than ten installments on the memoirs. He had counted on this income to pay moving expenses, to outfit his youngest son for college, and to meet expenses arising in Europe from his mother's death. In June, 1935, the Vierecks moved from their large home at 627 West 113th Street to an apartment at 103rd Street and Riverside Drive. They finally had to abandon the house to the mortgagee at a reported loss of $20,000.[69] In the

[68] G. S. Viereck to E. M. House, November 28, 1934, July 18, 1935, October 5, 1935, and April 15, 1936, House MSS.

[69] G. S. Viereck to E. M. House, June 10, 1935; June 18, 1935; July 18, 1935; August 7, 1935; House MSS.

midst of these upsetting experiences, Viereck told House that he had made up his mind to find a job "where I will not depend entirely upon my ability of selling articles." He added: "It might be an editorial job, it might be connected with publicity, it may be almost anything in which I can use my personality, my contacts, my knowledge, but where I must not resell myself every day. It must be something that can take a good deal of my time, but it must leave me some time for purely literary work. But I wonder if there is such a job anywhere?"[70]

A few weeks later he noted that *Liberty* had eight of his articles—not including those on the memoirs—which they had not yet been able to publish. He averred that one needed "sensational smashes" to break into print now. He speculated that the government might be able to use him on a mission to Europe, alleging that "in Central-Europe I have contacts superior to those of anyone else in the United States."[71]

Viereck contemplated other possibilities, too, including publicity work for radio, the movies, and big business, as well as for the government. Following through on one of his ideas, he persuaded NBC in the fall of 1936 to try him as a speaker and producer of a radio program on science. This job required him to prepare a survey on scientific progress each week and to supervise its programming on the radio. The first broadcast was made in February, 1936. He resigned within a few weeks, ostensibly because of the "scant compensation" and the diminishing prospect that this project would lead, as promised, "to other and more important developments."[72] It is not clear whether Viereck attempted to establish relations with other mass-media organizations; if so, his efforts were unsuccessful. He may have felt inhibited by the adverse publicity he had begun receiving in 1934 because of his 1933–34 publicity work for German agencies in the United States. Thus he continued his dependence upon *Liberty* magazine.

Finally, in early 1937 Colonel House decided to repurchase

[70] G. S. Viereck to E. M. House, July 23, 1935, House MSS.
[71] G. S. Viereck to E. M. House, September 7, 1935, House MSS.
[72] Ibid.; G. S. Viereck to E. M. House, October 11, 1935; January 29, 1936; February 10, 1936; March 20, 1936; May 22, 1936; House MSS.

publication rights from *Liberty* for his memoirs, for which he paid the journal $10,000—presumably the amount that had originally been paid him. Viereck, in turn, decided to reimburse the magazine for the "larger part" of what it had paid him on the projected series. At the same time he told House that he was under the impression that the North American Newspaper Alliance would be permitted to publish them, but nothing came of it. Viereck expressed his disappointment, but he said he would rather forfeit his monetary interest in the memoirs than lose "one particle" of House's friendship.[73] The memoirs remained unpublished and were subsequently donated to Yale University. Charles Seymour later reviewed them and stated that they were based almost exclusively on *The Intimate Papers of Colonel House*, which he had prepared in the 1920's. He concluded that they did not add objective evidence, but reflected Colonel House's feelings after his memory had been refreshed, and that they also showed Viereck's influence as the ghost-writer.[74]

The lack of publishers' interest in the memoirs and House's decision to repurchase his literary rights chilled their friendship, but in July, 1937, House responded willingly to Viereck's initiative in renewing their old amity. Viereck told House that he still looked upon him as "more or less a Father Confessor." At the former's request, House reviewed and praised the final manuscript of Viereck's book, *The Kaiser on Trial*. On October 5, the two met for the first time in a long while; it also turned out to be their last meeting. The next day Viereck wrote Colonel House that he was "deeply touched" by the latter's tribute to his book.[75] Soon thereafter House's health began deteriorating; after a final attack of pleurisy he passed away in March, 1938.

Thus the eight-year friendship ended on the upbeat. It had been an unlikely alliance, considering the obvious differences in their backgrounds and personalities. Yet it is apparent that what they had in common exerted more force than what separated

[73] G. S. Viereck to E. M. House, April 14, 1937, and April 16, 1937, House MSS.

[74] Note by Charles Seymour, November 12, 1954, attached to MS of memoirs of E. M. House, House MSS.

[75] G. S. Viereck to E. M. House, July 7, 1937; July 12, 1937; September 15, 1937; October 6, 1937; House MSS.

them. One strand in this mutual attraction was the prominent though different role that each had played in World War I. There was common nostalgia and concern over the cataclysmic events and consequences of that world conflict. By 1929 each had revised to some extent his estimate of who or what had caused the war and where the guilt lay. Both tended to agree that the European nations had stumbled into the fray. Thus their views came to converge on some points (such as the relative innocence of the Kaiser) but remained divergent on other issues (such as the existence and effect of so-called "gentlemen's agreements" on crucial diplomatic matters). Both agreed that "have-not" nations—Germany, Italy, and Japan—envied the "haves," and that to avoid war some arrangements would have to be made to placate the have-nots. Their willingness to satisfy the land hunger and the imperial designs of these fascist "have-not" nations (presumably at the expense of more "backward" nations) as a means of preventing war attested to both their "realism" (acquiescence to power) and naïveté in international affairs. Neither seemed to realize, for instance, that the fundamental tenets of Nazism posed an implicit threat not only to non-Aryans but to democracy, freedom, and human dignity everywhere. Part of their blindness on the latter point seemed to stem from their belief that the impotency of idealism as a basis for conducting international relations had been amply demonstrated by the shambles made of Wilson's Fourteen Points and the League of Nations.

While working on the memoirs of Colonel House, Viereck was also involved in retracing the career of another famous—or notorious—figure of the Great War, the exiled German Emperor. As a trusted friend of Wilhelm II, Viereck was in a good position to study his thinking. Likewise, because of his fluency in German and his amicable relations with many German officials, especially in the foreign ministry, in the 1920's and early 1930's he had an unusual freedom of access to records and opinions dealing with the German Empire and the Kaiser's role in it. As for motivation, Viereck had a reputation to uphold as the Kaiser's chief American spokesman.

It remained for Viereck to present a full account of the Kaiser's position, of the circumstances and the rationale explaining his course of conduct up to the fateful day of abdication in November, 1918. The idea for such an account germinated during the 1920's, but he did not begin work on a manuscript until about the time the Weimar Republic came to a disastrous end. Presumably, the long delay between conception and execution derived in part from the extensive research the subject required and Viereck's preoccupation with several other projects in the 1920's, most notably his monthly journal. In addition, it might be partly attributable to the Kaiser's expressed reluctance to stir up civil strife in republican Germany by appearing to wish a "comeback," and to the fact that many of the figures in such a biography, including those playing the villain's role, would still have been living.

In fact, the Kaiser was still not officially exonerated of the Allies' charge that he was guilty of a "supreme offense against international morality and the sanctity of treaties." This accusation was contained in the Versailles Treaty (Part VII, Article 227), and the victors had intended to try him on this charge. Thus, when Viereck broached his project to Fulton Oursler (his "brilliant friend," as he called him), Oursler suggested casting the story in the form of a trial.[76] The appropriateness of the idea must have been readily apparent to the Kaiser's American apologist: here was the vehicle by which he could bring his case to the "High Court of History" and obtain a final acquittal on the charge in the treaty.

Although Viereck told Oswald Garrison Villard in 1937 that *The Kaiser on Trial*, then being published, had taken more than twenty years of collecting material and more than five years of actual preparation, he did not complete the draft of his first chapter until the spring of 1935. At that time he confided in Colonel House that the rest of the book would be "less rhetorical and less impassioned and more in the nature of gathering and presenting the evidence." A little more than a year later he told House that he had introduced him as one of the witnesses and that he defended him and Wilson, "while at the same time pointing out the inevitability of a misunderstanding between Germany and

[76] Viereck, *Kaiser on Trial*, p. xvi.

the United States." As the manuscript neared completion in mid-1937, Viereck asked House for a statement that might persuade David Lloyd George to write a preface for the work. At the same time, he noted that his elder son Peter, a Phi Beta Kappa student at Harvard, was revising the style, correcting historical errors, and making the text more concise.[77]

The completed work was published in an American edition in 1937 and by an English publisher in 1938. Failing to obtain the services of Lloyd George, Viereck succeeded in persuading James W. Gerard, American ambassador to Germany at the outset of World War I, to provide prefatory remarks. Gerard said he did not agree with all matters set forth as facts by the author, but he recommended the reading of this book because he believed the Kaiser had been unjustly maligned by modern historians. In his introductory chapter, Viereck asserted that irrespective of his relationship with the Kaiser, the "present venture is neither authorized nor inspired by William II." He added that frequently his conclusions were at variance with those of the Emperor and his circle. He claimed to offer little-known information on the Kaiser in many instances and to present psychological insights and interpretations probably not even known to the Kaiser himself. His list of sources was impressive. Among the latter was his correspondence with Dr. Gottlieb von Jagow, German foreign minister in 1914, and conversations with Friedrich Rosen, onetime foreign minister of Germany, whom he said enlightened him on matters "hardly touched upon in their reminiscences."[78]

Viereck admitted that his book was not history in the conventional sense. His method was to permit both sides to be heard by staging dialogue between a prosecutor and an attorney for the defense and their respective witnesses. As might be expected, the longest monologues are given by witnesses for the defense. For the prosecutor's arguments Viereck drew, sometimes literally, from state documents and the writings of "hostile historians." There are five judges, representing the principal belligerents, and

[77] G. S. Viereck to Oswald G. Villard, October 15, 1937, Villard MSS; G. S. Viereck to E. M. House, April 25, 1935; June 19, 1936; July 20, 1937; House MSS.
[78] Viereck, *Kaiser on Trial*, pp. xi–xii, xix.

twelve jurors, one of whom is masked. It is only in the last paragraph of the book that the reader discovers he is the masked juror and that the secrets of the jury and its decision are known only to him. The jury has ruled on three counts: on the Kaiser's competence, on his sincerity, and on whether he deliberately planned and provoked the World War. The verdict is presumably "innocent" on each count. Yet, as Viereck discloses in his introduction, the book "reveals how William II was drawn into the war as was Woodrow Wilson, by masters of intrigue at home and abroad, by accidents, blunders and misunderstandings, by madmen parading as statesmen, by lying friends and hypocritical foes."

More specifically, Viereck's portrayal presents the Kaiser mainly as a victim of devious, self-serving or short-sighted advisors —the most notable villains being his boyhood tutor Hinzpeter, Bismarck, foreign minister Holstein, Prince Eulenberg, and Chancellor Buelow. The effect on the reader, therefore, is perhaps not at all what Viereck aimed for—that is, the "masked juror" could well be expected to indict the Kaiser, at least for incompetence in his choice of and control over his subordinates. Viereck feebly tried to allay this kind of conclusion by perpetuating his own myth that the German Emperor was more restricted by constitutional and other legal restraints than were the British king or the American president.[79]

Viereck assured the reader that he had striven for utmost objectivity. One cannot say that he met this goal, but the fact that the portrayal did often castigate German foreign policy and indirectly show the Kaiser as neither forceful nor all-wise in certain crucial situations indicates that the author had reached a new level of maturity. It might be considered a sign of maturity, too, that while his work reflected Freudian and Adlerian premises, he did not employ such concepts in excess. On the other hand, he remained bound to his customary overemphasis on the role of personalities—as contrasted to policies and objective conditions— in determining historical events. The book cannot be considered a success as a reliable or complete historical guide, but as a work of literature it is praiseworthy for its novelty of organization and presentation, its lively and personalized style, and its vivid imag-

[79] Ibid., pp. xvi–xvii, 447.

ery. Viereck often employed his talent for metaphor to good advantage—as in these comments on Bismarck: "As Narcissus admired his image in the pool, so Bismarck gazed spellbound at his handiwork—the German Empire. It was a mirror reflecting his personality. He was annoyed when the mirror gave back the image of the youthful Kaiser, when the lustre of the crown was more dazzling than the laurel of the Empire-Maker."[80]

Viereck showed page proofs to a number of friendly critics and to one or two neutral reviewers of note. Among his revisionist-historian friends, Harry Elmer Barnes labeled the book an "extremely clever and dependable effort to make the lessons of 1914 available for the benefit of those who face the world crisis in 1937." Charles Beard complimented the author for his inclusion of unpublished materials but disapproved the courtroom approach because he felt it inappropriate to apply the terms "guilty" or "not guilty" to such historical matters. Sidney Fay considered the book audacious, interesting, and readable, but he felt that Viereck was too harsh on some of the Kaiser's advisors. Walter Millis agreed to a not-guilty verdict, commenting favorably on the book's original scheme of presentation. William L. Langer, an eminent scholar on foreign relations and less revisionist in his views than the foregoing three, disagreed with Viereck's treatment of Bismarck's dismissal and felt that Holstein's influence had been overestimated, but he was pleased that the book was being published and hoped that it would help correct popular misapprehensions concerning the Kaiser. Probably most pleasing to Viereck was the accolade of George Bernard Shaw, who considered the book to be a most effective way of writing history; this work, in Shaw's view, represented a splendid and unusual combination of the informative, the dramatic, and the judicious.[81]

The Kaiser was not pleased, but it is not known if or how he conveyed this feeling to his faithful American friend. Viereck had not intended to disparage the Kaiser, and the belittlement was

[80] Ibid., p. 66.

[81] Quoted in G. S. Viereck to O. G. Villard, December 21, 1939, Villard MSS; Sidney B. Fay to G. S. Viereck, September 12, 1937; Walter Millis to G. S. Viereck, September 21, 1937; G. S. Viereck to William L. Langer, September 21, 1937; Viereck MSS; G. B. Shaw to G. S. Viereck, January 27, 1938, Gertz MSS.

slight. But even a slight pinprick was enough to irritate the Kaiser, who by 1937 had truly become a man without a country and a relic of history—all of which seemed to exacerbate his aggrieved vanity. Talking to a friend before he died in 1941, Wilhelm asserted that what had been published about him thus far had been mostly of inferior quality and that his biography was yet to be written. He called Viereck's effort "amusing" and took exception to the author's method of putting him on the dock and resorting to "reconstructions and hypotheses." He labeled the final product "fiction." He was still awaiting a "fair" biography in which objectivity and justice would prevail, showing that "not everything he did was wrong"—an overreaction that might indicate the depth of his feelings of inadequacy and guilt. It is of interest, too, that according to a postwar biographical study, in order to receive their annual stipend from confiscated lands in Prussia, the Hohenzollerns agreed in 1934 to make no public comments forthwith about the Nazi regime.[82] This "blackmail censorship" made the Kaiser even more a prisoner of his past and poor copy for the publicist.

Viereck continued to visit the aging ex-monarch, at least through 1938, but these visits went virtually unnoticed by the American press after it became clear in the mid-1930's that there was no chance of a restoration of the German monarchy. Viereck's book met the same kind of public apathy. In December, 1939, the author was able to blame the war for killing whatever remained of public interest in the book.[83]

Viereck's personality and his impact on literature were held up to a mirror in 1935 by his friend Elmer Gertz, who undertook in that year to write a biography of Viereck. By vocation, Gertz was a Chicago attorney; by avocation, a writer. His first published work was a biographical study of Frank Harris, a controversial British-American biographer and editor, that appeared in 1931— the year Harris died.[84] In the research for this book Gertz con-

[82] Joachim von Kürenberg, The Kaiser: A Life of William II, Last Emperor of Germany, trans. H. T. Russell and Herta Hagen (New York: Simon and Schuster, 1955), pp. 419–21.

[83] G. S. Viereck to O. G. Villard, December 21, 1939.

[84] Elmer Gertz and A. I. Tobin, Frank Harris: A Study in Black and White (Madeline Mendelson, 1931).

tacted Viereck, who had written a memoir of Harris; from this correspondence a personal friendship developed.[85] Gertz viewed Viereck as a complicated and intriguing character, and both seemed to share a sympathy for the Freudian outlook and a neo-romanticism in regard to aesthetic taste. Gertz soon envisaged his literary friend as a fit subject for a biography, and while many Jewish friends were turning against Viereck, Gertz remained loyal to his decision to write an account of the latter's literary career, giving lesser emphasis to his role as a propagandist for Germany. Gertz saw Viereck as a man reflective of the age, a man of "contradiction, of dubious action and thought, of good conduct and bad motives, of high purposes and low attainment, of revolt and reaction, of understanding and obtuseness . . . of ill-motivated flitting from thing to thing, like a typical child of his day."[86] But the times were not propitious for the publication of a work sympathetic to an apologist for Nazism, and the document remained in limbo.

In the course of his research on this project, Gertz compiled a questionnaire and sent it to those acquainted with Viereck and his work, asking them for their opinions and reactions to him. The responses, most of them received in the spring of 1935, offer a commentary upon Viereck and his strained relations with many former friends. Sigmund Freud declined to answer the inquiry, replying to the effect that he had "broken off diplomatic relations" with Viereck. Thomas Mann felt he was not acquainted well enough with Viereck or his work to offer a public opinion; besides that, he commented that Viereck's position "toward the actual present problems promises me very little," referring evidently to Viereck's publicity work for Nazi Germany. Among other epithets, E. Haldemann-Julius labeled Viereck a "clever, second-rate Oscar Wilde," and "Hitler's prostitute." Upton Sinclair told Gertz that he was no longer a friend of Viereck. William C. Lengel, an editor for *Liberty* and an acquaintance of Viereck's since 1910, said that adjectives such as "impatient, impetuous, diffident, arrogant, superior, contentious, and disdainful" applied to him. Lengel, like others, pointed to the subject's extreme ego-

[85] Elmer Gertz to Niel M. Johnson, March 3, 1967.
[86] Gertz, "Stormy Petrel," p. 12.

tism, but also noted that he was "stuffed with words and ideas." Lengel observed, too, that Viereck had a limp handshake. Shaemas O'Sheel and Alexander Harvey looked on Viereck as a perpetual "sprite" and as a man of genius. O'Sheel and Colonel House were especially impressed with his "charm and graciousness." Fulton Oursler, on the other hand, said Viereck often lacked tact. Alfred Adler, the famed neo-Freudian psychoanalyst, had visited Viereck once in the latter's home and once in his own home. He observed that the subject, as an only son, was "a good species of a pampered child," on whom were burdened "great expectations." Finally, H. L. Mencken, who had not met Viereck personally, considered him an excellent journalist but said he was "not sure about him" as a poet.[87]

The tone and contents of the foregoing responses indicate how little agreement there was on either Viereck's personality and character or his place in American and world literature. There were few, in fact, who were willing to venture an estimate on his literary status. Many of the replies were also colored by Viereck's recent affiliations with Nazi propaganda agencies in the United States. However, most respondents would probably have agreed with the following summation, written by Shaemas O'Sheel in 1930:

> . . . a younger generation has grown up which is unaware of its debt to George Sylvester Viereck. It is true that American poetry, as to form and technique, has developed along quite other lines than those proposed, but it is also true that for its liberation from ethical preoccupations, its enfranchisement in aesthetic freedom, American poetry has George Sylvester Viereck to thank more than anyone else, with the possible exception of Ezra Pound.[88]

This juxtaposition of Viereck and Pound was apt from another standpoint. Both were soon to become notorious as apologists and even propagandists for fascism, and both were to suffer the penalties attached thereto.

[87] Elmer Gertz to Niel M. Johnson, December 30, 1966. Letters to Elmer Gertz from the cited individuals were written in 1935 and may be found in the Gertz MSS.

[88] Shaemas O'Sheel, "The Return of George S. Viereck," *The World*, April 13, 1930, G. S. Viereck Scrapbook, Vol. XXIII. Also quoted in Viereck, *My Flesh and Blood*, pp. 3–4.

If he lives, Hitler, for better or
for worse, is sure to make history."[1] With these words, Viereck
concluded his 1923 interview with the obscure leader of a radical
German nationalist political sect. Then, after mentioning Hitler
favorably on two or three other occasions in 1923 and 1924, Viereck lost interest in this German upstart. In fact, as already noted,
his interest in German politics waned rapidly in the latter part of
the decade as he became preoccupied with his role as novelist,
free-lance journalist, and confidant and biographer of Colonel
House. It seemed that he had become resigned to the fait ac-
compli of the Weimar Republic; in fact, in 1930 he said that
German-Americans were reconciled to the German republic.[2]

Nevertheless, from what has been noted of his own associations with the Kaiser and German monarchical traditions, his
echoing of German nationalist sentiment in the 1920's, and his
"personalist" politics (cult of the individual and indifference to
political structure), one might surmise that his acceptance of the
Weimar Republic was only tentative. Indeed, it has been in-
timated that he favored a restoration of the Hohenzollerns, although he followed the Kaiser's lead in not openly espousing it.
There was also a pragmatic disregard for political or moral absolutes in his thinking. In sum, Viereck's attitude seemed to be that
if democracy worked in Germany it should be retained; but if it
failed to unite and uplift the people, then another political system—probably a limited monarchy like that of the Second Empire—should be reinstituted. At the same time, he adhered to the

[1] See page 117.
[2] Viereck, *Spreading Germs of Hate*, p. 269.

principle that the German people themselves should be the arbiters of their own fate and that outsiders, including Americans, should not interfere in their political decisions.

Perhaps one could deduce from these behavior patterns and political beliefs that he would make a likely candidate for a radical, antiliberal movement of the type led by Hitler. But one should also consider the contrary signs. For instance, he espoused certain freedoms, especially of speech and press, which did not appear to fit in with the oppressive and militant philosophy of the National Socialist movement in Germany. He also did not share the anti-Semitic principles of this movement. Moreover, he professed to be repelled by physical violence. In his autobiography in 1931 he said, "To me nothing is more distasteful than to inflict or to suffer physical pain," and elsewhere he added, "In my catechism there is no sin save unkindness."[3] Admittedly, the latter statement was more or less an afterthought that followed a confession of confusion over the meaning or existence of good and evil in any metaphysical sense. If he shared some of the vices of the old German ruling class, one could also expect him to reflect in part its virtues, including a degree of the honor, integrity, and honesty usually ascribed in some measure to the aristocratic class of Imperial Germany despite its affiliation with *Realpolitik*. Furthermore, from his choice of American friends and associates one would hardly surmise that he preferred authoritarian or totalitarian types of personalities.

In short, on the eve of Hitler's rise to power in 1932, one could not say with certainty what kind of position Viereck would adopt in respect to a Nazi-ruled Germany. One could say that he would probably become involved in political or cultural relations between the land of his birth and the land of his adoption, since he still considered himself a foremost "interpreter" of Germany to the United States. It remains to be seen how he would appraise and carry out this function in a most crucial decade.

As the decade of the 1930's opened, it was unfortunately not republicanism, or even monarchism, but rather the *Fuehrer-Prinzip"* of the Nazi dogma that was gaining headway in Germany. The perception of this fact came slowly to Viereck, whose

[3] Viereck, *My Flesh and Blood*, pp. 131, 220.

attention was finally drawn again to the Nazi leader in 1932.[4]
Borrowing from his earlier interview with Hitler and from contemporary observations, especially by leading Nazi theoretician
Gottfried Feder, in July, 1932, Viereck published in *Liberty* magazine an article on Hitler in which he implied that the Nazi leader
was destined to become a dominant force in Germany. Viereck
explained the twenty-five points of the Nazi party's program and
made generally favorable comments upon them. Nevertheless,
he noted that the German public's reception of Hitler was mixed
with hope and distrust. He observed: "Hitler is welcomed by Big
Business as the only man in Germany who can combat Bolshevism. To some, however, the encouragement given to Hitler by
conservative circles seems like an attempt to drive out the devil
with Beelzebub."[5] Depending in part on Feder's evaluation, Viereck surmised that there was a left-wing of the NSDAP (National
Socialist German Worker's Party) that leaned toward republicanism (probably meaning socialism), while the right wing
favored monarchy. Hitler, he felt, was still undecided about which
of these two alternatives to implement, although he might learn
from Mussolini's example that "political dictatorship and monarchy are not irreconcilable." Viereck speculated that if Hitler decided for monarchy, the ruler would be elected by the people, but
"no one can tell if that monarch will be Adolf I or William II."

This "mask for monarchy," called national socialism, succeeded in exploiting the forces of conservatism and reactionism
in Germany in January, 1933, when it was able to capture the

[4] Interview with Elmer Gertz, March 12, 1966. In this interview, Mr.
Gertz stated that during a conversation he had with Viereck, presumably
in early 1932, he suggested that the latter write an article on Hitler for
Liberty; Viereck responded that he had not considered it but that it struck
him as a good idea.

[5] G. S. Viereck, "When I Take Charge: Hitler Shows His Hand,"
Liberty, July 9, 1932, pp. 4–7. This article contained little of Hitler's earlier
anti-Semitic diatribe (from 1923). Viereck claimed later that the editor
of *Liberty*, "unwilling to arouse racial rancor in the United States, ex-
punged my remarks on Hitler's proposed anti-Semitic measures. . ." (G. S.
Viereck, "What Will Hitler Do Next?" *Liberty*, May 14, 1938, p. 4).
However, he also claimed in an unpublished manuscript ("Is Germany an
Aggressor Nation?", Viereck MSS) that the anti-Semitic material on Hitler was omitted because the editor considered the prophesy "improbable."

chancellorship for Adolf Hitler by constitutional means. That this was an international tragedy in the making was not clear to many American observers, including George S. Viereck. Indeed, for him as well as for other German sympathizers, the turn of events offered new hope for a German "reawakening"—a shibboleth first used by Hitler on February 1 and then enshrined in a "Day of National Awakening" on March 21 when Hitler, President Hindenburg, and other members of the government assembled in Potsdam at the tomb of Frederick the Great to celebrate a revived German spirit. Especially important for Viereck was the attitude of his "alter-ego," the former German Emperor, who told his American friend and relative in the late summer of 1933 that he approved of "what Chancellor Hitler is doing." The ex-Kaiser added, according to Viereck, that Hitler had taken the "yellow streak out of the German flag." Asked about the possible restoration of the monarchy, Wilhelm II conceded that this action would not take place "unless Hitler so wills it; he is supreme."[6] Similarly, in early 1935 Viereck reported that the former Emperor sympathized with the "national re-awakening without sacrificing his convictions" and that the Empress Hermine "makes no secret of her admiration for Hitler." At the same time, he said that he believed the time was not far distant when Germany would use members of former reigning houses in its diplomatic forces. He had also gained the impression that Germany did not want war. Of course, subsequent events were to prove him wrong on both counts.[7]

The other important influence upon Viereck was his old friend Franz von Papen, vice-chancellor under Hitler. In the late summer of 1933 Papen told his American visitor that the German government was democratic to the extent that it was supported by an overwhelming majority of the people. Germany, he explained, was a democracy, "but democracy acting through the instrumentality of a leader." Viereck concurred, noting that Hitler "has not employed violent means to upset the state. . . . Aside from some Jew-baiting by hoodlums and the maltreatment of Communists by overenthusiastic young men, force played no part in

6 *New York Times*, October 1, 1933, II, p. 3.
7 *New York Times*, February 23, 1935, p. 14.

the revolution." Moreover, Viereck had become convinced that Germany's only choice was either Hitler or chaos. These judgments reveal a superficial understanding of the actual trend of events, but there is no evidence to suggest that either of these protagonists was purposefully deceiving the other. Indeed, Viereck's favorable view of the new regime was considerably bolstered at that time by conversations and interviews with several other top officials of the Nazi party, including Dr. Goebbels and the Fuehrer himself.[8] This interview with Hitler was the last formal conversation he was destined to have with the Fuehrer, although he subsequently met Hitler in casual encounters at the Kaiserhof Hotel—across from the Reichs-Chancellory—during his subsequent trips to Germany. Viereck made it a practice to lodge at the Kaiserhof while in Berlin.

The only policy Viereck could find objection to in the new regime was its anti-Semitism. Yet, even on this issue, his criticism was muted by his apparent assumption—at least until the infamous "Crystal Night" (*Kristallnacht*) in November, 1938— that this policy was only temporary, that it was not a central tenet of Nazi ideology, and that it was attributable in large part to what he viewed as a justified reaction against those Jews affiliated with Bolshevist, "Internationalist," or Zionist movements. His unwillingness to condemn unequivocally this particular pillar of Nazi ideology was destined to cost him the good will of many of his American friends, including most of his Jewish friends and acquaintances. Of course, it also casts further doubt upon his critical acumen and moral sensitivity.

More important to Viereck than the issue of anti-Semitism was the Nazi party's promise to revive German honor and unity. He seemed most impressed by what he considered Hitler's central goal—to end Germany's humiliation under the Versailles Treaty and to make her once again a powerful and prosperous nation respected by the other great nations of the world. But this view of the new German spirit was shared by only a minority in America. Generally speaking, the Nazi regime from its inception received adverse editorial comment in the United States.[9] Thus

[8] G. S. Viereck, "Hitler or Chaos," undated MS, Viereck MSS.

[9] For a sampling of adverse editorial comments on the Nazi program

the stage was set for Viereck to make his services available in improving relations between Germany and the United States—the two nations that claimed his paramount love and loyalty.

Reflecting his experience as a propagandist, Viereck tended to view foreign relations mainly in terms of influencing public opinion by projecting the kind of public image which is most likely to gain friends or at least minimize hostility between nations. Such an approach, he seemed to think, could offset the antagonisms generated by basic, objective disagreements in political philosophy and practices. This thesis was verified by his actions in 1933. Yet only three years earlier his *Spreading Germs of Hate* had given the general impression that he was writing an epilogue, not a prologue, to a career as a propagandist. In this book he showed propaganda as a kind of disease spread by agents of deceit and distortion; as a practitioner of the art, he offered his readers advice on how to detect and resist the infection. He did, on the other hand, imply that a cure for either one might be highly improbable, for he declared propaganda to be "omnipresent" and noted, "The Dr. Jekyll in the soul of the propagandist ignores the derelictions of Mr. Hyde." Thus within three years the "Mr. Hyde" in Viereck appeared to ignore the "Dr. Jekyll" that had written the book. It is appropriate at this point also to note Viereck's definition of propaganda as given in 1930: "Propaganda is a campaign camouflaging its origin, its motive, or both, conducted for the purpose of obtaining a specific objective by manipulating public opinion."[10]

In view of his pro-German background, his conviction that propagandists have split personalities, and his favorable reaction to the Nazi revolution, it is perhaps not surprising that he began early to establish personal contacts with the new regime. In March, 1933, he became involved with the German consul in New York, Dr. Otto Kiep, who, according to Viereck, sought out his advice on German-American relations. For this service, Kiep

---

at its outset, see "What Hitler's Rule Means to the World," *Literary Digest,* April 8, 1933, pp. 1–2; and "American Outcry at German Jew-Baiting," *Literary Digest,* April 1, 1933, pp. 3–4, 28–29.

[10] Viereck, *Spreading Germs of Hate,* pp. 7, 9, 11, 294–98.

offered his American advisor a monthly retainer of $500, an arrangement that lasted about four months. Viereck testified in 1934 that Kiep told him this money was secured from "friends in Germany," but he suspected that it came from Kiep's "own pocket," since he was a wealthy man.[11] Actually, as an examination of records after World War II was to show, the consulate-general in New York was designated by Goebbels, the German propaganda minister, as the headquarters for German propaganda in the United States.[12]

In the meantime, through long-time friend Carl C. Dickey, Viereck in 1932 became involved with the recently established public relations firm of Carl Byoir and Associates. Viereck agreed to search out the possibilities of getting "some German commercial business" for this firm, for which he would receive a commission of 15 percent on any contract thus obtained. In the summer of 1933 he decided to visit Europe and Nazi Germany to procure material for some projected articles and books and to consult with German authorities on the possibilities of a public relations contract with the Byoir firm. In addition to securing the interviews previously mentioned, Viereck successfully made arrangements that resulted in the German Railroads Information Bureau (a tourist information organization) entering into an eighteen-month, $108,000 contract with the Byoir firm which netted Viereck a monthly payment of $1,750—$1,000 as salary and the remainder for expenses. In addition, he was paid the rent of an office room and the salary of one stenographer.[13]

After his return from Europe, Viereck became involved in still another project for the German consul-general in New York.

---

[11] Transcript (copy) of *Examination by Congressman Samuel Dickstein of George S. Viereck*, June 9, 1934, Viereck MSS; U.S., Congress, House, Special Committee on Un-American Activities, *Hearings, Investigation of Nazi Propaganda Activities and Investigation of Certain Other Propaganda Activities*, New York, July 9–12, 1934, 73d Cong., 2d Sess., 1934, p. 94.

[12] Alton Frye, *Nazi Germany and the American Hemisphere, 1933–1941* (New Haven: Yale University Press, 1967), p. 34; G. S. Viereck, "My Intermezzo with Hitler," chapter in autobiography, ca. 1960, p. 20, Peter Viereck personal files.

[13] *Hearings, Investigation of Nazi Propaganda*, June 5–7, 1934, pp. 37–38, 57; July 9–12, 1934, pp. 98, 105.

Earlier in the year Herbert S. Houston, an American of pro-Nazi sympathies, had succeeded in arousing the interest of Macmillan in publishing a volume to be entitled "Germany Speaks." The book was to have an introduction by Hitler and chapters by other leaders in the Nazi government. It was expected that the book would define the views of the German government on the Jewish question and interpret Germany's program "to the world in general and America in particular." Houston received the approval and support of Consul Kiep and the German propaganda ministry for this plan. Probably at Kiep's urging, Viereck offered to edit the articles that were submitted. Houston and Viereck planned to have a book of about thirty-four "rightly edited" essays, and they hoped to have it ready by January, 1934, to help offset the effects of an anticipated congressional inquiry into Nazi propaganda. They were unable to meet this date, however, and the manuscript was not ready until the spring of 1934.[14]

Although the records do not clarify the point, it seems likely that Viereck himself prepared the foreword that was signed by Adolf Hitler on February 26, 1934—or perhaps Hitler prepared the original version and it was translated by Viereck. At any rate, it bore the earmark of Viereck's style. The foreword said, in part, that the book would bear witness to the "strivings and accomplishments of the New Germany," that it would "transmit to the World the knowledge that we desire nothing else except to build up a strong and free Germany on terms of equality with other nations." It concluded, "This Germany will be a better guarantor of peace than a Reich and a people suffering political and economic hardships and being ever a new source of unrest."[15]

Viereck presented the manuscript to German Ambassador Hans Luther for his approval, but Luther considered it unacceptable, mainly because the essays contained "too many superficial attacks on critics hostile to us." Luther forwarded the draft to Germany for reworking, but further work on the project was post-

[14] Frye, Nazi Germany, pp. 36, 49.
[15] Copied in George Van Nosdall's bookseller's list 1,118, Pt. I, April, 1949, Gertz MSS. Outline of book and statement of purpose also reproduced in Film 11273, frames K269171, K269273–77, U.S. National Archives, Foreign Affairs Branch.

poned. In the meantime, Macmillan likewise demanded drastic
revisions before accepting it.[16] Macmillan subsequently dropped
the idea of publishing it, but in 1938 the German government
managed to induce a smaller British publisher to print it.[17] The
whole project can be considered a fiasco insofar as it was intended
to exert an appreciable effect on American public opinion in the
crucial first two years of the Nazi regime. Although the project
had helped keep Viereck busy for several months, he managed to
avoid any public acknowledgment of his role.

While Viereck was becoming a well-paid publicist for the German tourist interests, other German sympathizers and pro-fascists
were becoming active in setting up Nazi-style organizations in
the United States. Various congressmen became increasingly
concerned about the growth of Nazi influence in America, and
in January, 1934, a resolution presented by Congressman Samuel Dickstein of New York to investigate Nazi and other alien
propaganda in the United States was approved by the House
of Representatives. A special committee on un-American activities was subsequently created to carry out this resolution. Chosen
to head the committee was John McCormack of Massachusetts,
and Dickstein was appointed vice-chairman. Although the committee's investigations were mainly concerned with the leaders
and officials of neo-Nazi organizations in the United States,
especially the Friends of New Germany (later renamed the
German-American Bund) and the Silver Shirts, they also included interrogation of publicity-firm personnel such as Byoir,
Dickey, and Viereck, who were doing work for German agencies.[18]

Both Dickey and Viereck were called upon in June and July,
1934, to testify before this committee on the terms and aims of
the contract between Byoir and the German Railroads Information Bureau. Dickstein, acting for the committee, first interro-

[16] Frye, *Nazi Germany*, p. 49.
[17] [German Foreign Office,] *Germany Speaks* (London: Butterworth,
1938).
[18] On the founding and functioning of this committee, see August R.
Ogden, *The Dies Committee* (Washington: Catholic University of America Press, 1942), pp. 32–35; and Robert K. Carr, *The House Committee
on Un-American Activities* (Ithaca, N.Y.: Cornell University Press, 1952),
pp. 12–13.

gated Viereck in secret session on June 9, 1934; a public hearing involving the same witness was also held a month later. Dickey explained to McCormack's committee in June that Viereck's main role was "to participate in any conferences that we might have had on this problem which was created here by anti-Semitism, in reducing German trade and travel."[19] Viereck asserted to the same committee, "I gave them advice. I made suggestions. I interpreted events and personalities for them. I gave them a number of articles which I had prepared myself, including an interview with Dr. Schmidt, the Minister of Economics, and another interview with Dr. Schacht, the president of the Reichsbank." Viereck also helped edit the *Economic Bulletin* which Byoir published under its contract, but he claimed that this project did not require him to publish propaganda or to engage in anti-Jewish activity.[20]

Despite the emphasis by these two witnesses on their intention to stimulate more tourist business with Germany, the testimony, especially Viereck's, would indicate that the German government's main objective with this contract was to counteract anti-Nazi publicity in the United States. This judgment is also supported by the fact that the first issue of the *Economic Bulletin* was entitled "Speaking of Hitler" and consisted mainly of press comments favorable to or praising Hitler. It was evident that these bulletins were intended to foster a better image of the "New Germany," and in particular to counteract the adverse publicity given by much of the American press to Nazi anti-Semitic policies. Between 3,000 and 5,000 of these bulletins were issued semi-monthly until the contract was terminated at the end of 1934, most of them distributed free to American newspapers and to various local chambers of commerce.

The interrogation of Viereck and Dickey bore prompt results of which the committee was undoubtedly not aware. On August 4, in a secret dispatch to German Foreign Ministry headquarters in Berlin, Richard Sallet, attaché and representative of the Ministry of Propaganda at the German embassy in Washington, in-

[19] *Hearings, Investigation of Nazi Propaganda*, June 5–7, 1934, p. 2.
[20] *Examination by Congressman Samuel Dickstein*, pp. 14–28; *Hearings, Investigation of Nazi Propaganda*, July 9–12, 1934, p. 97.

formed his superiors that since the "Dickstein investigation has resulted in exposing the links between German agencies and the two publicity firms, Byoir-Dickey-Viereck and Ivy Lee, their usefulness to us is almost entirely at an end." He therefore recommended that their services be terminated. On October 1, the German Ministry of Propaganda informed the Foreign Ministry that three months' notice of contract termination had been given that day, thus concluding the contract three months short of its scheduled eighteen-month duration.[21] Viereck's total remuneration on this project amounted to approximately $28,000.[22]

Meanwhile, at the hearing in July McCormack asked Viereck if he did not think it improper for an official of the German government (Consul Kiep) to pay for advice on the internal affairs of the U.S. government. Viereck replied that he did not think it improper and then claimed that Russia and France employed American public relations counsel for similar reasons. Under further questioning he admitted knowledge of such transactions only through hearsay and newspaper reports. After the hearing he added his objections to being labeled a "paid German propagandist," stating that the use of publicity in this country by the German government was "a proper defensive measure against a flood of billingsgate."[23]

Convinced as he was that Germany had a legitimate right to press its point of view in the United States, Viereck refused to break off relations with the land of his fathers, even though he was not employed by German agencies again until 1939. Although 1935 was a quiet year on the German propaganda front in the United States, in January of that year he traveled to Berlin and conferred with Ernst Hanfstaengl, foreign press chief of the Nazi party, on the problem of improving Germany's image in America. Viereck was especially concerned over the antics of Kurt Ludecke, a disaffected German propagandist who had said some damaging

[21] U.S., Department of State, *Documents on German Foreign Policy, 1918–1945,* Series C, III (Washington: Government Printing Office, 1959), pp. 1112–13.

[22] O. John Rogge, *The Official German Report* (New York: Thomas Yoseloff, 1961), p. 55.

[23] *New York Times,* July 11, 1934, p. 11; *Hearings, Investigation of Nazi Propaganda,* July 9–12, 1934, pp. 99–101.

things about the Nazi program in testifying before the Dickstein committee. Viereck convinced Hanfstaengl that he must try to dissuade Ludecke from carrying out his threat to divulge all he knew about Nazi propaganda plans in foreign countries. Ludecke had implied that he might not scandalize the German foreign office if the price was right. In mid-January Viereck and Hanfstaengl took their problem to Hans Dieckhoff, an expert on American affairs in the German Foreign Office and later ambassador to the United States. The idea of bribing Ludecke was broached, but Dieckhoff decided that he should be ignored; if he did speak out, the Foreign Office would show that he had tried blackmail. The strategy was successful; Ludecke remained silent.[24]

In the meantime, the Dickstein investigation had helped muzzle a few German-paid propagandists in the United States, and its disclosures finally prompted passage of the Foreign Agents Registration Act in 1938. But the number of neo-Nazi groups continued to increase after the committee's disclosures, and there was no letup in Germany's efforts to export propaganda into this country. In light of these trends, Congress again in 1938 decided to set up a special committee to investigate Nazi, Bolshevik, and Fascist propaganda and other activities in the United States. This body, patterned after McCormack's committee and called the Special House Un-American Activities Committee, functioned under the chairmanship of Representative Martin Dies.[25]

Having heard that Viereck was planning to meet privately with Hitler at his Berchtesgaden retreat, Chairman Dies moved quickly. On August 3, 1938, the day that Viereck was planning to leave for Europe, Dies's committee served a subpoena enjoining him to testify. Viereck in turn publicly denied Dies's allegation that he planned to visit Hitler. Dies had labeled his subpoenaed witness a "publicist and admitted propagandist for Nazi interests" and criticized him for allegedly seeking special introductions to American diplomatic representatives abroad through Senator Robert Wagner of New York. Viereck retorted that his work as a journalist required him to travel to Europe, and that "both Mr.

[24] Frye, *Nazi Germany*, pp. 59, 62.
[25] Carr, *House Committee on Un-American Activities*, p. 14.

[Hamilton] Fish and Senator Wagner, whom I also know, were good enough to ask the Secretary of State to give me introductions to all our diplomats and consular representatives abroad. . . ." As the time for departure neared, Viereck decided to abide by the subpoena and offered to testify as requested on August 18. He professed "highest respect" for the committee and its purposes.[26]

Nevertheless, he was able to avoid testifying after Congressman Fish interceded on his behalf, persuading Chairman Dies that his appearance would be unnecessary.[27] Viereck therefore left for Europe on August 12, parting with the statement that he might be walking into a world war. He added, "Judging by diverse symptoms, Europe is suffering from a high fever—nature's own process of healing. If Europe should resort to the old-fashioned process of bloodletting, I trust we shall keep hands off."[28] As a regular contributor to *Liberty* magazine, one of Viereck's objectives on this journey was to make arrangements for an interview with Hitler by Fulton Oursler, editor of *Liberty*. Viereck did not publicize this intention. According to a private memorandum he wrote to Oursler in early 1939, Hitler was amenable to the request until an article appeared in *Liberty* purporting to shed light upon his private life. The Fuehrer thereupon canceled plans for the interview.[29]

Viereck's narrow escape from the clutches of the Dies committee was attributable not only to the intercession of an influential friend; it also reflected his prudence in avoiding membership or active participation in organizations (such as the German-American Bund) obviously neo-Nazi in aim and method. There was one exception. He did lend his prestige and oratorical powers to a movement directed against the Jewish boycott of German-made goods proclaimed in 1933. The boycott was intended as a protest against Hitler's mistreatment of the Jewish minority in Germany. Viereck did not appreciate the psychological depth of

[26] "Dies Opens War on Propagandists," *New York Times*, August 4, 1938, pp. 1, 18.
[27] Rogge, *Official German Report*, p. 269.
[28] *New York Times*, August 13, 1938, p. 1.
[29] Memo, G. S. Viereck to Fulton Oursler, April 7, 1939, p. 2, Viereck MSS.

the Nazis' antipathy toward the Jews, inasmuch as he continued to overemphasize the importance of political and economic motives for Nazi anti-Semitism. At Madison Square Garden, on May 17, 1934, he joined with seven other speakers in denouncing "the unconstitutional Jewish boycott." The rally, attended by 20,000, was sponsored by the Friends of the New Germany (forerunner of the German-American Bund), and Nazi symbols and trappings were in bold display.[30]

At the outset of his address Viereck claimed to be speaking "in a sense" for 35,000,000 German-Americans who he said could be—as he was—friendly to Nazi Germany without being anti-Semitic. He admitted that he was not a member of the DAWA (the German-American Protective Alliance, established as a countermove to the Jewish boycott) but that he was "completely in sympathy with its defensive measures against the reign of terror foisted upon the United States and especially the city of New York by certain professional Jews and their Bolshevist confederates." He added, "The German boycott lasted one day. The Jewish boycott has lasted nearly a year and a half."[31] Actually, Jewish merchants were still being intimidated frequently by German Nazis—a fact that Viereck tended to ignore, possibly because such acts did not represent an officially sanctioned boycott by the Nazi government.[32] It should have been clear to him, nevertheless, that intimidation was an endemic Nazi tactic or style. The crux of his argument lay near the end of his speech when he said: "We Americans of German descent are Americans before we are German sympathizers. We resent the boycott not merely because it harms Germany. We resent it primarily because it interferes with the revival of American prosperity and lays the basis for racial strife in the United States."[33] Again, it is clear that Viereck failed to appreciate or understand the feeling of moral indignation or even outrage which motivated the boycott by the Jews. He also seems to have displayed poor judgment in overestimating

[30] "20,000 Nazi Friends at a Rally Here Denounce Boycott," *New York Times*, May 18, 1934, p. 1.

[31] Ibid., p. 3.

[32] See "American Outcry at German Jew-Baiting," *Literary Digest*, April 1, 1933, pp. 3-4.

[33] *New York Times*, May 18, 1934, p. 1.

the effects a repudiation of the boycott by its sponsors would have had on German policy toward the Jews. His third mistake was to exaggerate the boycott's potential for arousing racial discord in the United States.

Regarding the Nazi revolution in Germany, Viereck asserted, "Whatever our attitude toward Hitler may be, there is no doubt that there was no alternative for Germany except Hitler—or chaos." He also credited Hitler with saving Europe "from being inundated by the red sea of bolshevism," and added that Hitler had emancipated Germany from the bondage of Versailles and unified her people for the first time in her long history. Moreover, on the Jewish question it was his "hope and trust that when complete stability is established, the German people will differentiate Jews who are international plotters and Jews who are Germans before they are Jews." Finally, he expressed his hope that eventually a concordat similar to that established with the Catholic church would be arranged with the Jews in Germany, granting them "the largest measure of justice possible in this imperfect world."[34]

Viereck had first broached the idea of a concordat with the Jews in a letter to Colonel House on November 22, 1933, shortly after his interview with Hitler. He also suggested to House that President Roosevelt might "set the machinery moving by a confidential and personal letter to Chancellor Hitler." As a preliminary step, though, he recommended a canvass of this "extremely delicate" situation.[35] It is not clear if he expected House to initiate such a move, and nothing appears to have resulted from this suggested plan. Viereck himself had experienced little success in gaining the confidence of President Roosevelt. After his conversations with German leaders in 1933 he wrote the President about these contacts, noting that "Colonel House thinks that possibly some of the facts I learned may be of interest to you. If so, I shall be very glad to present these to you."[36] The President, however, declined to invite him to the White House. Roosevelt's secretary

[34] Ibid. The complete text of the speech was carried in two weekly issues of the *New York Deutsche Zeitung* in the latter half of May, 1934.

[35] G. S. Viereck to E. M. House, November 22, 1933, Viereck MSS.

[36] Quoted in Charles Tansill, *Back Door to War: The Roosevelt Foreign Policy, 1933–1941* (Chicago: Henry Regnery Co., 1952), p. 270.

invited him to contact Secretary of State Cordell Hull, who in turn referred the matter to Undersecretary of State William Phillips. Phillips subsequently arranged a conference with Viereck;[37] there is no record that anti-Semitism was discussed. Viereck did remember telling his hosts that *Anschluss* (merging of Germany and Austria) would be inevitable.[38] After this conference, he wrote a letter to "my old friend Dieckhoff" in Germany,[39] presumably to tell him of the mood of the State Department in regard to Germany. Dieckhoff was then chief of the Anglo-American Division of the German Foreign Office; four years later he was named German ambassador to the United States.

Viereck apparently had as little influence on Hitler as he had on President Roosevelt. He claimed, under questioning by Dickstein, that he had told the Fuehrer it would be much easier for any friend of Germany "to say a good word for Germany if the Germans would make a distinction between the good Jews—what the Germans call the good Jews—and the Internationalists who are opposed to any country." Hitler's response, he said, was that "he had not declared war on the Jews, but that the Jews had declared war on him; that he had done the Jews no harm; that he had merely curtailed some of their special privileges and prerogatives" (meaning apparently that he had removed Jews from positions of influence in various professions and industries). Hitler also referred him to the interview in 1923, when he had made some very bellicose and ominous statements on this subject.[40]

[37] Ibid., p. 271; G. S. Viereck to Cordell Hull, November 10, 1933, House MSS; Rogge, *Official German Report*, p. 149. See also Memo, G. S. Viereck to Fulton Oursler, April 7, 1939, p. 9, in which Viereck says he was invited by the "White House" to talk to the Secretary of State; but when he finally found time to go to Washington, Secretary Hull was in South America and so he consented to talk to Undersecretary Phillips.

[38] Memo, G. S. Viereck to Fulton Oursler, April 7, 1939, p. 9, Viereck MSS. Tansill, *Back Door to War*, p. 271, adds that Viereck told Phillips that Hitler was "the over compensation of Germany's inferiority complex"; Viereck also told Tansill that Secretary Hull had given him "a special letter which recommended me to all diplomatic representatives of the United States in Europe." Tansill's information is based on an interview with Viereck in August, 1948. No record was kept of the Viereck-Phillips meeting, and the whereabouts of the "special letter" is not known.

[39] Noted in G. S. Viereck to E. M. House, November 21, 1933, House MSS.

[40] *Examination by Congressman Samuel Dickstein*, June 9, 1934, pp.

It is not clear from such evidence what grounds Viereck had for believing that the Nazi government would either adopt or enforce a concordat with the Jews. It is interesting to note that he did not raise the concordat proposal with Hitler in his interview.

After the idea of a concordat was first made public in late 1933, Victor M. Bienstock, news editor of the *Jewish Daily Bulletin,* confronted Viereck with a list of charges made against him by Hellmut von Gerlach, a pacifist and writer on German affairs. One charge was that Viereck's proposal of a concordat was misleading in that "you knew quite well that Hitler is persecuting the Jews not on account of their religion but rather because of their race." Viereck replied that the idea was submitted in good faith, and that it could accommodate the racial as well as the religious aspect.[41] In the meantime, one may note that Viereck was assisting the Byoir publicity firm in trying to offset American public antagonism toward Germany's anti-Jewish policies.

It hardly needs emphasizing that Viereck could not bring himself to condemn unequivocally the immoral philosophy of the Nazi government regarding the Jews—a result largely of his inability to appreciate it as an ethical issue. Elmer Gertz, who remained a tolerant if somewhat exasperated friend of Viereck through the 1930's (a rare instance of Viereck retaining a Jewish friend), notes that on several occasions, beginning in the spring of 1933, he asked Viereck to raise his voice against the tyrannical regime in Germany. In his first reply in June, 1933, Viereck said he opposed anti-Semitism and racial discrimination but that he welcomed Hitler's unprecedented success in unifying the German people. Moreover, he claimed that much of what one heard about Germany was undoubtedly "propaganda pro and con"; then he added, "and the truth—what is the truth?"[42] In response to subsequent queries in the same vein, Viereck's replies consistently deplored "excesses" on both sides. He made excuses; he asked for

---

5–6; *Hearings, Investigation of Nazi Propaganda,* July 9–12, 1934, pp. 90–91; G. S. Viereck, "Hitler the German Explosive," *American Monthly,* October, 1923, pp. 237–38.

[41] Victor Bienstock to G. S. Viereck, November 29, 1933, and statement by G. S. Viereck attached thereto, November 29, 1933, Viereck MSS.

[42] Gertz, "Odyssey of a Barbarian," Ch. 38, p. 2.

calmness, but he could not judge the issue on its ethical or moral grounds.[43] Viereck could not even raise his voice in condemnation when the Nazi government included one of his books, *My First Two Thousand Years*, in its infamous book-burning campaign in 1933. The book was later banned in Germany.

Viereck's public reaction to the Nazis' banning of his book revealed a curious willingness to compromise literary freedom in the interest of political policy. In a statement issued for him by the Macaulay publishing firm on March 30, 1934, he declared that the rationalist philosophy espoused by the hero of the book (Cartaphilus) "clashed with the conception upon which National Socialism is building the New Germany out of the wreck of the old. . . ." This new conception was a "conscious protest against the overemphasis of the purely intellectual point of view, as against the instincts and feelings which may be more infallible than reason." Viereck concluded:

> For that reason, it would seem to me to be entirely logical if she could not harbor, for the time being, as disturbing a guest as my Wandering Jew. What is the fate of a book compared to the fate of a nation? Although I have warmly defended National Socialist Germany, I do not accept its anti-Semitic doctrine. Why should National Socialist Germany accept my Wandering Jew?[44]

With this final statement, Viereck appeared to be divorcing himself from a part of his own past—the part that was not welcome in the New Germany—although he entertained the hope that this situation would again be only temporary. It might be added that Viereck exaggerated the rationalism of his book's hero, who was primarily a romantic sensualist and only secondarily an intellectual skeptic. It is evident that this description fit Viereck himself. It is worth noting, too, that Eldridge had already repudiated his friendship with Viereck because of the latter's apologetic view of Nazism. Eldridge, who once had idolized Viereck, now saw him as a hypocrite whose "soul is dead if he is a Nazi propagandist for spiritual reasons."[45]

[43] Ibid.

[44] Viereck Kisses the Rod," *Nation*, April 25, 1934, p. 460; "Bans Books on Jews," *New York Times*, March 30, 1934, p. 14.

[45] Paul Eldridge, "Of Nazi-ism in the United States," *Panorama*, February, 1934, pp. 6–7, Gertz MSS.

Perhaps as early as 1934 Viereck had plans for further involvement in disseminating pro-German publicity in the United States
and did not wish to spoil future opportunities by protesting the
banning of his book. Other motives might also be adduced, including the possibility that he felt flattered to be important
enough to anathematize. More generally, this reaction might logically be attributed to his lack of consistent moral principles,
coupled with the pro-German psychological conditioning that has
already been noted in explaining his earlier affiliations with German nationalists and monarchists. In any event, when the book-
banning episode occurred, Viereck still had no inkling that within
three months a congressional investigating committee would help
bring an early termination of the Byoir contract and compromise
his value as a publicity agent for the New Germany. After the
Byoir job ended, Viereck became much more financially depen-
dent upon his free-lance writing for mass-circulation magazines.
Most of his writing was done for *Liberty* magazine, which had
begun publishing his articles in the mid-1920's.[46] It was not until
late 1939 that he was destined to become involved again in paid
publicity work for German-sponsored agencies (the *Muenchner
Neueste Nachrichten* and the German Library of Information).

Along with his partisan journalism for *Liberty*, in 1938 Viereck
contributed two articles to Father Coughlin's journal, *Social
Justice*, which portrayed fascism as a necessary antidote to communism in Europe.[47] Another article of note was published in *Nation's Business* in April, 1938, in which he pointed to the success
of totalitarian regimes in combining culture and sports with their
labor programs, and recommended that American business interests take the lead in copying some aspects of these programs.[48]
Less than a year later he contributed an article to the *Freude und*

[46] Memo, G. S. Viereck to Fulton Oursler, April 7, 1939, p. 1, Viereck
MSS. Viereck mentions in this memo that in the 1930's he had received
$8,000–10,000 per annum for his articles and editorial work for *Liberty*.
[47] G. S. Viereck, "Mussolini Knew . . . Twelve Years Ago," *Social
Justice*, May 9, 1938, p. 7; G. S. Viereck, "The 'Messiah' in the Sealed
Car," *Social Justice*, Pt. I, May 30, 1938, pp. 15–16; Pt. II, June 6, 1938,
pp. 3–4.
[48] G. S. Viereck, "We Can Beat Dictators at Their Own Game,"
Nation's Business XXVI (April, 1938): 16–21, 66–68.

Arbeit, the official organ of the German Labor Front, again extolling the *Kraft durch Freude* (Strength through Joy) approach toward enlisting workers in service to the state. He added that this new conception of labor promulgated by Dr. Robert Ley (founder of the Labor Front) was a "gospel of universal validity." It seemed to Viereck that the Nazis had established an exemplary program for eliminating the traditional conflict between labor and management. Elsewhere in this article, however, he qualified the universal acceptability of Nazi policy by asserting, "I admire many aspects of National Socialism without desiring to reproduce them in the United States."[49]

In his writing for *Liberty,* Viereck gained some prominence as a pundit on German affairs. In a May, 1938, article he prophesied what Hitler would do next, pointing out that the direction of Nazi policy held no surprises for one who had talked to Hitler and read his *Mein Kampf.* He predicted that Hitler's next series of moves would be "to make Germany impregnable on the Danube." In the Danubian basin Czechoslovakia, which had an alliance with Soviet Russia, was the only country unfriendly to Germany. It was, Viereck noted, "a pistol pointed at Germany's breast. Unless that pistol is muzzled, Czechoslovakia's hour of destiny will strike." He explained that if Czechoslovakia did not provide complete equality for her German citizens, Hitler would "march again at the psychological moment," although he doubted that Hitler was interested in adding non-Germans to the Reich by annexing purely Czech districts. Viereck did not moralize about these probable moves. On the other hand, he professed that Hitler had one "blind spot" in an "otherwise brilliant mind"—that is, his "anti-Jewish complex." He noted that the Nuremberg laws "surpassed the worst fears of Germany's well wishers."[50] These laws as first promulgated in 1935 denied the Jews full citizenship in the Reich and barred them from certain professions and all official organizations; much harsher laws followed in November, 1938.

[49] G. S. Viereck, "Germany Revisited," *Freude und Arbeit,* February, 1939, pp. 97–99, Viereck MSS.
[50] G. S. Viereck, "What Will Hitler Do Next," *Liberty,* May 14, 1938, p. 4.

With respect to German-American affairs, Viereck asserted that Hitler wanted friendly relations with the United States and could not understand the persistent antagonism of the American government and a large part of its press to a powerful Germany. He said Hitler noted that this feeling existed long before the advent of National Socialism. Hitler could understand American disagreement with his political philosophy, "but he cannot understand why the democracies do not appreciate his fight against Communism. He finds Japan more sympathetic in this respect." Viereck declared further that the Fuehrer was fully aware of the strength of the United States and "the inviolability of the Monroe Doctrine," and thus would offer no threat to American security. Hitler demanded only space in which to breathe, but expansion for this purpose would be neither to the west nor to the south, but rather to the east. Yet, with the recent retaking of Austria, the Reich's ancient eastern outpost, "his territorial ambitions may be satiated until Russia begins to crumble."[51] Viereck still felt he had a role to play as a mediator, as a kind of link between the foreign offices of both Germany and the United States. In October, 1937, he confided to Colonel House that he wished to establish a personal contact with Cordell Hull, possibly through House, and thus impress the Secretary of State with his desire to aid him as well as the German ambassador in finding means of "minimizing friction" between the two countries.[52] The contact was never made, and Viereck's proposal again reveals his lack of insight into the fact that less-than-cordial feelings between the two countries were due not so much to mutual misunderstanding but rather to well-understood differences in political philosophy involving the relationship of the citizen to the state and relations between states.

Developments thus far have tended to confirm the amoral and perhaps totalitarian quality of Viereck's political and social beliefs. But again, as one might expect of a poet, there was another side to his personality which continued to place high value on freedom and individualism. The question is rather obvious: How could he reconcile the latter values with his apparent sympathy

[51] Ibid., p. 5.
[52] G. S. Viereck to E. M. House, October 6, 1937, House MSS.

for fascist regimes which offered economic security at the price of extreme regimentation? Viereck attempted to give an answer in 1938 in a hardbound tract entitled *The Temptation of Jonathan*, which was also published as an article in *Nation's Business*. For one of the few times in his career, he appealed to moralistic judgments in support of his position. Jonathan, an unemployed American youth, is severely tempted by "Toto," the apostle of totalitarianism, but he is able to resist Toto's blandishments first by alluding to Christ's victory over similar temptation. Yet, since he is not a Christian, Jonathan must turn to another god; thus he elects to follow the "goddess of Liberty." The goddess tells him that he can earn the good things of life without selling out his soul, if he will cooperate with others, be patient, and exercise self-discipline—"discipline maintained, not for hate of your fellow men, of a race, or a creed or a class, but by love of me and love of your country." One may discern traces of the "old Viereck" in the goddess, however, when she tells Jonathan he should not be a missionary in her behalf. Responding to his dislike of dictatorship, she serenely advises him, "Leave other people to solve their own problems; grant them the freedom to order their house in their own fashion."[53]

There were intimations of "a new Viereck," too, in an article published in February, 1939. Under the pen name Donald F. Wickets he posed the question: "Will the Catholic Church be Hitler's Waterloo?" Referring to the papal encyclical *Mit Brennender Sorge* (With Burning Sorrow) issued by the pope in March, 1937, Viereck noted that although the pope had always striven for peace with Germany, the encyclical accused the Nazis of violating the "natural law," the law "written by the hand of the Creator on the tablet of the heart." Viereck concluded, "It is difficult, in view of recent events in Germany, to deny this." The recent event Viereck had most in mind was the infamous *Kristallnacht* on November 10, 1938, when the Nazis carried out widespread destruction of Jewish stores and synagogues in retaliation

[53] G. S. Viereck, *The Temptation of Jonathan* (Boston: Christopher Publishing House, 1938), pp. 25, 27, 31. Also published in *Nation's Business* XXV (December, 1937): 21–23, 108–10.

for the assassination of a German foreign-service official in Paris. He described this action as "inhuman vengeance wrought upon Germany's helpless and hapless Jews for the deed of one senseless boy." He feared that if Germany did not have the courage to repair these wrongs, she would find herself morally isolated. Yet there was a ray of hope in that "Hitler is a shrewd psychologist, with his ear to the ground." He may yet listen to the advice of Germany's friends; or he may, like Napoleon, refuse to heed his loyal advisors. He concluded, "Every Napoleon meets his Waterloo. The church may be Hitler's!"[54]

Liberty editor Fulton Oursler had authorized Viereck to use a *nom de plume* because of the latter's growing notoriety among Jewish and other anti-German readers and advertisers.[55] But one may question its use with the foregoing article, since for once Viereck had appeared morally indignant about Hitler's policies. It seems probable that Viereck used the pseudonym primarily as a shield against criticism from pro-German elements. Indeed, he had written an earlier article stemming directly from the *Kristallnacht* episode which he declined to publish, showing it only to close friends. In this article he conceded that a "radical neo-pagan ring" had gained at least temporary ascendancy over the Nazi party. He referred also to a conversation he had with Dr. Goebbels (presumably from an interview in the summer of 1933) in which he allegedly chided the Minister of Propaganda and Public Enlightenment for labeling anyone a Jew who had at least one Jewish grandparent. Nazi policy, he supposedly told Goebbels, implied that "one Jew is stronger biologically than seven Germans," and that 600,000 Jews were capable of having led 60,000,-000 Germans "by the nose politically." He said that Goebbels only smiled in reply, but that he later narrowed the government's definition of a Jew; Viereck implied that his interview might have had something to do with this change. Despite these reactions, he could not bring himself to condemn Germany in public. After all, America was his "chosen mate," but Germany was his "mother."

[54] Donald Furthman Wickets [G. S. Viereck], "Will the Catholic Church Be Hitler's Waterloo?" *Liberty*, February 4, 1939, pp. 6–7.
[55] Memo, G. S. Viereck to Fulton Oursler, April 7, 1939, p. 1.

He concluded, "If my mother did a thing I considered wrong, I might upbraid her in private, but I would not denounce her in public."[56]

It could be that the two articles just mentioned served as a catharsis for Viereck whereby he was able to rid himself of a bothersome psychic complex by bringing it to consciousness. At least, they seemed to mark the culmination of his moral indignation over the indiscretions of his ancestral motherland. The article on the Catholic church was one of the last written for *Liberty*. The break with this periodical and its editor came in April, 1939, when Viereck wrote a twelve-page memorandum to Oursler outlining his views on a spectrum of subjects and accusing Oursler of putting undue pressure upon him to conform to various standards or criteria of Americanism. He noted that the estrangement had been mounting for a year, during which Oursler rejected or canceled at least two series of articles Viereck had prepared or planned, with a resultant loss of expected income. Among these articles he claimed that Oursler rejected a series entitled "Red Termites at the Gate of Heaven" because Viereck would not agree "to assail Father Coughlin for bringing Nazism into the Catholic Church." Oursler had also apparently shown his displeasure over Viereck's failure to condemn Hitler's march into Czechoslovakia, a move that Viereck said "rectified some of the injustices of Versailles." Viereck defended his Americanism as a blending of love of liberty with neutralism, and he denied any sympathy with the Bunds, which he considered a "nuisance rather than a menace." He wanted "neither Silver Shirts nor Ku Kluxes, neither Communists nor Fascists under the Stars and Stripes. A plague on all their blouses." Oursler's reply was terse; he denied the motives attributed to him by Viereck and offered the opinion that the memorandum was a "self-serving declaration."[57]

There seems to be no evidence that Viereck attempted to establish connections with other mass-circulation magazines. His

[56] G. S. Viereck, "The German-Jewish War," unpublished MS, December, 1939, Viereck MSS.

[57] Memo, G. S. Viereck to Fulton Oursler, April 7, 1939, pp. 3–6; Fulton Oursler to G. S. Viereck, April 18, 1939, Viereck MSS.

memo to Oursler indicated that he felt *Liberty* was his only hope among periodicals that could afford to pay the fees to which he was accustomed. His European trip in 1938, unlike previous ones, had not been monetarily productive—in fact, it had set him back financially. On that journey he noted that material he had planned to obtain was "rendered unavailable by the swift march of events," and he complained that it was becoming extremely difficult for a writer to receive fair treatment or get a hearing if he did not join in with the "general hysteria" (in apparent reference to American public reaction against Germany's treatment of the Jews and of Czechoslovakia).[58] Viereck did not reveal his reasons for traveling again to Germany in June, 1939, but it is probable that he was motivated at least in part by the possibilities of securing a new source of revenue since he could no longer depend on the American journalistic market.

Whether or not Viereck was seeking a German source of income, he returned from Germany in early September, 1939, with a contract to serve as the American representative and correspondent of the *Muenchner Neueste Nachrichten,* a Munich newspaper. Hans Dieckhoff, German ambassador to the United States from 1937 to November, 1938, when he was recalled but not replaced, told an American judicial investigator after the war that he met Viereck in the summer of 1939 in Germany and that they discussed the "bad situation of our information" concerning the United States. Dieckhoff then proposed that Viereck accept a position as representative of a German newspaper and "inform us on what was really going on."[59] Viereck consequently entered into a contract, on July 20, with Giselher Wirsing, editor-in-chief of the aforementioned Munich paper. The contract obliged Viereck "to furnish reports [weekly] on the general situation, digests of the press, etc. as well as material for publication at regular intervals." He also agreed to "write at least once a month, one article of a political or economic nature" for publication in the newspaper. His immediate compensation was set at $2,000

[58] Memo, G. S. Viereck to Fulton Oursler, April 7, 1939, p. 2.
[59] Rogge, *Official German Report,* p. 133.

for travel expenses and salary for August and September, with a monthly salary of $500 to begin in October, 1939.[60]

Soon after his return to the United States, Viereck entered into a second contract, this one with the German Library of Information which had been set up in May, 1936, by the German consulate-general in New York. Under this contract, signed on September 27, 1939, Viereck agreed to edit and write articles for the library's weekly publication, *Facts in Review*. His remuneration for this job was $500 per month. He averred that he would be glad to set forth the German point of view, but he also demanded that the contract carry the following qualification:

> that I shall not be asked to prepare or edit any matter derogatory to the United States, or to undertake any editorial assignment which could possibly conflict with American laws and my duties as an American citizen. I welcome cooperation with you, because I can think of no more important task from the point of view of fair play and the maintenance of peace between your country and mine than to present to the great American public a picture unblurred by anti-German propaganda of the great conflict now unhappily waging in Europe.[61]

Facts in Review was a publication designed "to get over the boycott wall of the American press." In November, 1939, Hans Thomsen, German chargé d'affairs in the United States, reported to his superiors that the periodical was proving a success "and is quoted and occasionally attacked by the American press." By that time, too, its distribution had been increased to about 20,000 copies.[62] One of Viereck's first tasks in this position was to publicize Germany's excuses and rationalizations for launching war against Poland. Material for this latter purpose was drawn from *German White Book No. 3*.[63]

In the meantime, complying with a June, 1938, law which required "agents of foreign principals" to register with the State

[60] Ibid.; Michael Sayers and Albert Kahn, *Sabotage! The Secret War against America* (New York: Harper and Bros., 1942), p. 170.

[61] *Hearings, Investigation of Nazi Propaganda*, Appendix, Pt. 2, 76th Cong., 3d Sess., pp. 1046, 1050–51, 1289.

[62] U.S., Department of State, *Documents on German Foreign Policy*, 1918–1945, Series D, VII, pp. 432–33.

[63] Sayers and Kahn, *Sabotage!*, p. 171.

Department, Viereck filed a report denoting himself as American representative of the *Muenchner Neueste Nachrichten.* Shortly afterward he followed up with a similar report covering his association with the German Library of Information. In response to a question demanding a "comprehensive statement" of the nature of the registrant's business, he identified himself in both instances as an "author and journalist."[64] Investigation in 1941 and 1945 by Justice Department agents indicated that the weekly reports required from Viereck by the Munich newspaper were also being sent to Ambassador Dieckhoff, who, since his recall in late 1938, was in charge of the American committee in the Foreign Office in Berlin. According to a report by an Attorney General's assistant, O. John Rogge, who interviewed Dieckhoff after the war, these reports contained a "general summary and analysis of the American press, comments on American public opinion, a resume of propaganda activities in which he [Viereck] was engaged, and concrete suggestions as to the conduct of German propaganda activities and foreign relations."[65]

In a third important activity, Viereck in late 1939 intensified his efforts to influence federal legislation. It has been noted that Viereck's contacts with isolationist legislators dated back to the early 1920's. In 1930 he began to establish especially close rapport with Congressman Hamilton Fish, Jr., who was chairman of a special committee investigating Bolshevik propaganda in the United States. Another, and perhaps closer, friendship was struck up by Viereck in the spring of 1937 when he offered some of his books to Senator Ernest Lundeen of Minnesota, who was compiling a personal library on World War I. It was not a new ac-

[64] *Viereck* v. *U.S.,* U.S. Court of Appeals, D.C., *Federal Reporter,* no. 130, 2d Series, pp. 947–48; *Appellants Brief in U.S. Court of Appeals for the District of Columbia,* no. 8204, G. S. *Viereck* v. *U.S.,* p. 3, Viereck MSS. The statute defined an "agent of a foreign principal" as "any person who acts or engages or agrees to act as a public relations counsel, publicity agent, or as agent, servant, representative, or attorney for a foreign principal or for any domestic organization subsidized directly or indirectly in whole or in part by a foreign principal." Excluded of course were duly accredited official representatives of foreign governments (U.S. *Statutes at Large,* 75th Cong., 3d Sess., 1938, LII, p. 632).
[65] Rogge, *Official German Report,* pp. 131–34.

quaintance; Lundeen had come to Viereck's attention in World
War I when the former had been one of fifty-seven members of
Congress who voted against the declaration of war in April,
1917.[66] In the 1930's Viereck remained impressed with the Senator's firm opposition to any revision in America's neutralist and
noninterventionist foreign policy. Both men found much in common, and Viereck on occasion after 1937 assisted Lundeen in
preparing and editing speeches and articles.[67] In June, 1938,
Lundeen began a Senate campaign to exert pressure on the European nations who still owed war debts to the United States, and
during the October, 1939, debates on the U.S. arms embargo he
proposed that the United States threaten to seize the island possessions of England and France in the western hemisphere unless
they agreed to pay their debts by a certain date. Also in 1939 he
had proposed without success that the Constitution be amended
to require a public referendum on any resolution to declare war,
thus forcing Congress to share war-making power with the electorate.[68] Viereck's role in these latter moves is not entirely clear,
but he undoubtedly encouraged Lundeen in these actions, if he
did not actually instigate them himself. The next step by Lundeen, this time definitely with Viereck's encouragement, was to
create a Make Europe Pay War Debts committee; the formation
of this committee, with Lundeen as national chairman, was
announced on December 3. Prescott Dennett, an anti-interventionist public relations agent from Washington, D.C., was
named secretary and publicist for this embryonic group. The
other founders were Major General Smedley Butler and Lynn
Gale. Viereck had no official position, but he served as a key advisor and consultant.[69] By March 4, 1940, Dennett had persuaded

[66] Ernest Lundeen to G. S. Viereck, April 22, 1937, Viereck MSS;
Rogge, *Official German Report*, p. 266; WRD-WMAL, NBC News,
News Release, Washington, D.C., May 18, 1941, Viereck MSS.

[67] Ernest Lundeen to G. S. Viereck, January 4, 1938; March 21, 1938;
April 8, 1938; August 23, 1940, Viereck MSS; Rogge, *Official German
Report*, p. 267.

[68] *Congressional Record*, 75th Cong., 3d Sess., 1938, Appendix, p.
2999; *Congressional Record*, 76th Cong., 2d Sess., 1939, p. 411; *Congressional Record*, 76th Cong., 1st Sess., 1939, p. 1976.

[69] *Congressional Record*, 76th Cong., 3d Sess., 1940, p. 2286; *Viereck
v. U.S.*, p. 955.

several legislators to serve as vice-chairmen, including Senators Robert Reynolds of North Carolina and Smith Brookhart of Iowa, and Congressmen Martin Sweeney of Ohio and Jennings Randolph of West Virginia.[70]

The major purpose of the committee was to campaign for the fulfillment of war debts by compelling European debtor nations to cede their island possessions in the western hemisphere to the United States or to pay their balances in cash, possibly by surrendering their bank deposits in this country. A total bill of $14 billion was cited. The press release also claimed that a public opinion poll showed 66 percent of the American people favored Lundeen's earlier proposal that the West Indies be seized and applied as payment on the balance of war debts owed by Britain and France. Among other objectives, Lundeen asserted that the cession of the islands would create closer bonds of friendship between the American continents by eliminating foreign control in the hemisphere and would help insulate the Americas against involvement in Europe's recurring wars. The major task taken on by the committee in 1940 was to publicize the views of isolationist congressmen.[71] This activity indicates that the committee's principal motive was to forestall American intervention in the European war; the collection of the debt appears to have been a subordinate aim.

A fourth project undertaken by Viereck in early 1940 was to obtain control of an obscure publishing house—Flanders Hall—for the purpose of reinforcing those movements aimed at keeping America out of the European conflict. Viereck claimed, too, that as an experienced publicist he had had a long-time ambition to own a publishing firm and that he planned this enterprise as a successor to his position with the German Library of Information, which he assumed would only be temporary. Flanders Hall had been established in September, 1939, by the three sons of Sigfrid Hauck in Bound Brook, New Jersey. Viereck's attention was

[70] *Chicago Tribune*, December 3, 1939, p. 7; Rogge, *Official German Report*, p. 153.

[71] *Chicago Tribune*, December 3, 1939, p. 7; *New York Times*, December 3, 1939, p. 40; *Congressional Record*, 76th Cong., 3d Sess., 1940, p. 2286; *Viereck* v. *U.S.*, p. 955.

drawn to this firm in November or December when he received a complimentary copy of its *Scarlet Fingers*, a small book of anti-British polemic. He wrote the Haucks a letter of encouragement, and they in turn asked him for advice on book promotion. Later in 1940 Viereck obtained control of the firm with an investment of $10,000.[72]

Finally, it should be noted that through the Make Europe Pay War Debts committee (later changed to Islands for War Debts committee) Viereck was destined to become heavily involved in a 1940 campaign to have isolationist speeches in Congress reprinted from the *Congressional Record* in large quantities and then mailed out postage-free on the franking privilege of the congressmen involved.[73] The details of this activity, of Viereck's work for the two German agencies, and of his use of Flanders Hall as a sounding board for anti-British and neutralist propaganda are treated in the next chapter as part of the immediate background for his indictment and trial on charges of concealing activities encompassed under the Foreign Agents Registration Act of 1938.

It is appropriate, in conclusion, to evaluate Viereck's impact upon public opinion in the 1930's and to identify the forces that moved him to serve the interests of Nazi Germany. Clearly, he was not very successful in improving Germany's image in American eyes, nor was he able even to obtain much support from German-Americans. This fact is evident from a poll in May, 1938, which showed that less than 5 percent of the American people felt friendlier toward Germany than toward England and France, while another one-third claimed to have no preference.[74] Also, according to Wittke, a few German-language papers showed early

[72] G. S. Viereck, "The Story of Flanders Hall: Its Genesis and Liquidation," unpublished MS, January 29, 1942, pp. 1–2, Viereck MSS (document prepared by Viereck in his own defense prior to his trial in February, 1942); Rogge, *Official German Report*, pp. 135–36, 166–67; Copy of statement made by Sigfrid Hauck to F.B.I., January 14, 1941, Viereck MSS.

[73] See Rogge, *Official German Report*, pp. 154–72.

[74] Hadley Cantril, *Public Opinion, 1935–1946* (Princeton: Princeton University Press, 1941), p. 1061.

sympathy for the Nazi movement, and a few others took decidedly anti-Nazi positions; but most of them, including the largest circulators, seemed embarrassed about Nazism and avoided editorializing on it. Probably the most notorious pro-Nazi organ was the German-American Bund's journal, but it, like Byoir's and Viereck's *Economic Bulletin,* never had a circulation of more than 5,000 copies, most of which were distributed free.[75]

In the opinion of Selig Adler, the Nazi appeal in the United States was limited to "recent American immigrants and to a clump of American pseudo-fascists."[76] Most notably and fortunately, the movement was a fragmented one. One should not discount the show of early enthusiasm of the Friends of the New Germany in New York, but pro-Nazi or pseudo-fascist societies— numerous as they were—enlisted the loyalty of only a tiny fraction of the American people. True to past form, Viereck did not seek to identify with or work through these organizations after 1934, devoting himself mainly to writing for mass-circulation magazines.

For a time, Viereck had a tremendous forum for his views in the *Liberty* magazine, which apparently was popular in small-town, isolationist America. Yet there was a point at which isolationism parted company with pro-Germanism. This point was illustrated in Viereck's dispute with Oursler. In it we can see why it was so difficult for most American isolationists to feel sympathy with the German cause, and why Oursler rather than Viereck exemplified the climate of isolationist opinion. Conducting brutal and cynical pogroms against the Jews and annexing Czech territory were hardly calculated to appeal to Americans who, even though they might harbor racial prejudices, also had some sense of fair play. Furthermore, unlike other isolationists, Viereck in the 1920's had prophesied and even promoted the revival of a "greater Germany," and history was bearing him out. He had no clear idea of the limits to which German expansion should go; most isolationists did.

Still, there were a number of isolationists in Congress who

[75] Wittke, *German-Language Press in America,* p. 283.
[76] Adler, *Isolationist Impulse,* p. 293–94.

would, even after September, 1939, agree to further indirect appeasement of the German government. Keeping America out of the war transcended every other principle. Viereck found it possible to insinuate himself into this group, not because it espoused German victory but because it did not believe the political fate of the United States to be tied up with that of France or England, nor did it apparently believe that trade with the Allies was essential to American economic survival. In spite of their pro-American motives, this group, which might be called the "fanatical isolationists," would become unwitting tools for the promotion of pro-German propaganda. Viereck for a time would enjoy success in this endeavor, but his fate was not entirely in his own hands. It was, instead, mainly in the hands of the fascist powers—and they were yet to show any real inclination to alter their behavior to appease American public opinion.

Seemingly oblivious to such obstacles, Viereck refused to be discouraged. Clearly, he was strongly motivated. One such moving force was his persistent sense of mission. As he had declared in 1934, "The son of a German father and an American mother, I always regarded it almost a consecration to interpret the land of my fathers to the land of my children."[77] He was undoubtedly inspired by the example of his father, also a publicist concentrating on German affairs. Probably even more important was the younger Viereck's close, personal relationship to the former Kaiser. Moreover, if the Kaiser served Viereck as a father figure, Germany served as a mother image. For, as Viereck confessed in 1939, he could not turn his back on Germany because she was a mother to him, and while he might upbraid her in private, he would not denounce her in public. In the same metaphorical and romantic vein, he said that America was his "chosen mate"—his wife—to whom he owed his highest fidelity, even if she should go to war with mother Germany. But he would exert his utmost influence to prevent such a conflict.[78]

[77] "Statement by Viereck," (letter to editor), *New York Times*, June 7, 1934, p. 12.
[78] See G. S. Viereck, "The German-Jewish War," unpublished MS, 1939, Viereck MSS, and Memo, G. S. Viereck to Fulton Oursler, April 7, 1939, p. 7.

Related to this first explanation is a second insight he offered into his conduct. In early 1939 he told a friend that he advocated friendship with Germany and nonintervention in European affairs because of "certain integrities" or "complexes of my own which I cannot deny, without denying my very being." He conceded that his attitude undoubtedly was influenced by "instincts of race and memories of childhood. . . ."[79] He seemed resigned to, if not pleased by, this type of psychological determinism. Moreover, he did not seem to feel that his malady was serious enough to warrant catharsis by psychoanalysis, or that it would even be vulnerable to such means. He probably felt that individuals—especially creative personalities—must have their complexes in order to function, and that one complex did not differ morally from any other complex. In his aesthetic frame of reference the type of complex to avoid was that which inhibited one's enjoyment of sex and other pleasurable appetites and drives.

Among the more easily discernible motives, Viereck felt justified by the fact that his position on World War I—that it was a mistake for America to have intervened and that reasons for becoming involved had been more economic than idealistic—had gained currency in the interwar period. He believed that his anti-interventionism in the 1930's would likewise be vindicated by history.

As a fourth factor, he apparently had convinced himself that it was the German people—their ideals and ideas—to whom his friendship was committed, and not necessarily their government. Furthermore, he reasoned, if it was not a crime to be pro-French or pro-British, it should not be a crime to be pro-German.

A fifth motive has also been implied—that of economics. Viereck lost the major share of his income when he severed relations with *Liberty*, and his need for a new financial source was probably instrumental in his agreement to work for German "foreign principals." It should be emphasized, however, that Viereck could have remained with this magazine or undoubtedly could have been employed by others if he had been willing to condemn German foreign policy. Instead, he asserted he would not sacri-

[79] G. S. Viereck to Elmer Gertz, March 29, 1939, Gertz MSS.

fice his "integrity" as the price for remaining with *Liberty*. Actually, it was his lack of objectivity and critical judgment in the face of growing German belligerence that undoubtedly aroused Oursler's ire.

The foregoing reasons which Viereck employed to justify his position do not of course tell the whole story. One must also recognize the major contradictions and logical shortcomings in Viereck's position. For example, there was a one-sidedness in his role as "interpreter" of Germany to America in that he too often simply mirrored Nazi propaganda directed at Britain and France as well as at many other nonfascist countries. Slogans and shibboleths, such as "British imperial encirclement" of Germany, became substitutes for analysis and interpretation. Similarly, he employed the "conspiracy theory" in evaluating the policies of anti-Nazi nations, but he ignored this theory when examining German policy. In President Roosevelt he saw a "messianic complex" that blinded him to the true interests of the United States; in Hitler he saw a "genius" who should command admiration in spite of his ideology (which Viereck said he did not accept). In connection with the latter statement, he explained that it was Hitler's dynamic personality that deeply impressed him, and though he thought him to be a genius he would fight Hitler if he threatened to invade the United States.[80] As a "poet of passion," Viereck extolled the rights of the individual to experience earthly pleasures; yet he subdued any passionate repugnance he may have felt for the mistreatment of non-Aryans and dissenters by the Nazis. Most notably, he preached that America had no right to impose her will or system of government on other nations, especially Germany; nevertheless, he approved Germany's violation of this principle with respect to Czechoslovakia and Poland.

It is notable that Viereck seemed singularly successful in repressing conscious acknowledgement of these logical inconsistencies and moral ambiguities. But perhaps his ethical relativity was not so illogical—he professed that his creed was "pantheistic agnosticism", and he repudiated the claims of Chris-

[80] See Memo, G. S. Viereck to Fulton Oursler, April 7, 1939, pp. 7–8, 12.

tianity or any other absolutist basis for ethical conduct. Besides that, he had concluded early in his career, from reading Freud and his interpreters, that ambivalence (the simultaneous feelings of love-hate, joy-grief, etc.) was a natural property of the psyche, and thus was a psychoanalytic rather than a moral or logical issue. These influences, plus his aesthetic orientation, help account for the apparent inadequacies and naïveté in his political commitments. In summary, Viereck's special psychological conditioning was powerful and pervasive enough to cause him to suppress or distort logic and evidence, to accept the loss of some of his closest friends, and to cast his lot with the fate of a government devoted to the subversion or destruction of principles that he claimed to hold as his own.

*h*itler's invasion of Poland on
September 1, 1939, did not in itself reverse the noninterventionist
policies enacted by Congress in the previous four years. About
four days after the event the United States government issued the
routine proclamation of neutrality. Officially, America was neutral. Actually, as the director of the political department in the
German Foreign Office admitted, in September, 1939, "animosity
against Germany [is] already prevalent in broad sectors of the
population." As revealed in public opinion polls and editorial
surveys, the overwhelming majority of Americans clearly wanted
the Allied countries to defeat the Axis dictatorships, but they
still wished to avoid any direct involvement in the European or
Asian conflicts. And there was a vociferous minority that feared
any relaxation of strict military and political isolationism.[1]

As a consequence, there was a burst of agitated lobbying
against the Administration's plan—brought before Congress on
September 23—to repeal the 1937 arms embargo law and replace
it with a cash-and-carry provision that would especially benefit the
Allies, who still had control of the Atlantic sea routes. Yet a poll
in October showed that about 58 percent of the American people
favored such a revision, while 34 percent definitely opposed it.
Similarly, in Congress a two-thirds majority (mostly Democrats)

[1] U.S. Department of State, *Documents on German Foreign Policy*,
1918–1945, Series D, Vol. VIII, p. 127; Cantril, *Public Opinion*, pp. 967,
1061; Selig Adler, *The Uncertain Giant, 1921–1941: American Foreign
Policy between the Wars* (New York: Macmillan, Collier Books, 1969),
p. 219.

was persuaded of the bill's virtues, and in early November it became a law of the land.[2] Although a portent for the future, this act still preserved isolationism by requiring the use of foreign ships to carry war goods and by obligating the President to designate danger zones in the Atlantic that American ships must avoid.

By the end of 1939, pro-German propagandists obviously could not obtain a reimposition of the arms embargo, but they could hope to encourage a continuance of the isolationist policies that remained. German embassy officials in Washington did not need Viereck to convince them at the outset that German propaganda in the United States should avoid, first, any threat of the use of sabotage against this country, and second, any impression that American isolationists had the support of the German government. German charge d'affairs Hans Thomsen recognized that the isolationists' stance was not based on a rejection of German war-guilt; it stemmed mainly from their belief that America had no vital interests in Europe that needed protection, and that America was militarily secure because of her isolated geographical position. Therefore, pro-German propagandists had to be very careful in their use of these isolationists. It was clear also to Thomsen that the American people as a whole were a good deal more united in their hostility toward Germany at the end of 1939 than they had been in 1917.[3]

Seemingly German authorities could count on several hundred organizations in the United States by 1939 that were profascist or pro-Nazi. But these, the German foreign service officials felt, were of little—perhaps even negative—value because they lacked unity and capable leadership and also because they attracted an embarrassing amount of congressional investigation and threats of legal prosecution. Viereck, as noted previously, had avoided membership in such groups—partly, it seems, because their style was too crude; partly because their aim of regimenting America round an antidemocratic and anti-intellectual creed made him uncomfortable.[4]

[2] Adler, *Uncertain Giant*, pp. 222–24; Cantril, *Public Opinion*, p. 967.
[3] *Documents on German Foreign Policy*, 1918–1945, Series D, Vol. VIII, p. 127.
[4] Ibid., pp. 90–91; Gerson, *Hyphenate*, p. 116; Rogge, *Official German*

In their efforts to keep America neutral, then, the pro-German propagandists, including Viereck, largely ignored such groups as the Bund and the Silver Shirts and concentrated instead on news and information agencies. They worked, for example, through Manfred Zapp's Transocean News Service, with its wire services for American newspapers; the German Library of Information, which by late 1940 had thirty-seven employees; and the American Fellowship Forum, publisher of the journal *Today's Challenge*. Such organizations as the Railroads Information Office and the Flanders Hall publishing firm were also parts of the apparatus, and so were such journals as *Scribner's Commentator*, Lawrence Dennis's *Weekly Foreign Letter*, and Father Coughlin's *Social Justice*, all of which Viereck frequently quoted in his weekly reports to Germany. In addition, the German embassy and consulates distributed large quantities of literature to the American public. Shortwave broadcasts were beamed from Germany to North and South America, and a good deal of material was mailed to the United States by such German-based organizations as the German Information Office, the Fichte Bund, the League for Germandom Abroad, the Amerika Institut, and the German Labor Front.[5]

Some idea of how these propaganda efforts were faring in 1940 can be gleaned from the reports of the German chargé d'affaires in Washington. In September, for example, Thomsen was deeply concerned about the House Un-American Activities Committee, which, in his opinion, was trying to strengthen the widespread impression that German diplomatic and consular personnel were conducting subversive activity and espionage. He alleged that the committee was giving the 140 registered British agents an "entirely free hand," but was closely scrutinizing the agents of German principals; it seemed likely that Viereck, whom he referred to as "our well-known German-American writer and

---

Report, pp. 21, 117; Psychiatric Consultation Report on G. S. Viereck by Dr. Wendell Muncie, December 27, 1940, p. 2, Viereck MSS.

[5] Rogge, *Official German Report*, pp. 54–66, 117, 170, 428; "The War of Nerves; U.S. Front," *Fortune* XII (October, 1940): 143; Harold Lavine and James Wechsler, *War Propaganda and the United States* (New Haven: Yale University Press, 1940), p. 249.

our informant in many matters," would come under its scrutiny. In the same report, he also discussed plans to circulate the speeches and articles of Senator Rush Holt, advised against closing down such American agencies in Germany as the American Express Company, and claimed that the Make Europe Pay War Debts committee had declared itself "ready" to discredit the "Nazi-baiting," "socialist" organ *P.M.* It was perhaps no coincidence that the committee subsequently sponsored the reprinting and distribution under congressional frank of an editorial from the *Steuben News* entitled "P.M.'s Plot to Crucify Colonel Lindberg."

In another report in October, the charge d'affaires commented on the financing of the propaganda program. *Facts in Review*, he said, was now consuming $15,000 per month, and he had on hand a lump sum of $50,000 with which to subsidize newspaper publicity and pay informants. Shortly thereafter, he also emphasized that experience had shown that propaganda originating in Germany, to be effective in the United States, had to be revised and edited by American agencies and editors.[6]

In spite of Viereck's recognized talents as editor and writer, neither his work nor that of other anti-British or pro-German publicists had much chance of ultimate success in keeping America out of the European conflict. Words could not cancel out deeds. Hitler's *Blitzkrieg* was turned toward the west in early 1940 with frightening results. By the fall of 1940 the first peacetime conscription act was in force in the United States. Although there were many isolationists or non-interventionists (including Viereck) opposing it, the Administration had the support of the majority of congressmen for its policy of aiding Britain to a point "short of war." At the end of 1940 the President pointed to the possibility of an Axis victory and explained in a radio speech the threat to American security and democracy that would result from Nazi control of the Atlantic and its shipping lanes into American ports. The result, in March, 1941, was a lend-lease bill to aid those governments whose defense was considered vital to

---

[6] *Documents on German Foreign Policy*, Series D, Vol. XI, pp. 2–3, 243–44; Rogge, *Official German Report*, p. 162.

American security. In the meantime, a public opinion poll showed that at least 54 percent of the American people were willing to have the United States send Britain all the material aid she needed even if it had to be an outright gift. In May, 1941, an American freighter on its way to Capetown was sunk by a German submarine. In mid-June the President ordered the freezing of all Axis funds in the United States; two days later he demanded that all German consulates be closed and their staffs withdrawn by July 10. By late 1941 polls indicated that two-thirds of the American people felt that peace should not be purchased at the expense of a Nazi victory.[7]

Throughout this interim, from the invasion of Poland to the attack on Pearl Harbor twenty-seven months later, anti-British as well as pro-German propagandists played a part in reinforcing a hard core of isolationist doctrinaires that delayed but did not prevent the offering of various forms of material aid to the Allies. Although American public opinion drifted away from them, the majority of noninterventionist congressmen remained loyal to their cause until the bombing of Pearl Harbor.[8] Viereck's involvement in this cause was for a time financially remunerative, but it was destined eventually to cost him his freedom. A few die-hard isolationist congressmen likewise were to find their political careers damaged or cut short as a result of their persistent promotion of anti-British (and by implication—pro-German) propaganda.

At the end of 1939 Viereck had again become embroiled in the business of supporting and defending the policies and principles of a Germany at war with its neighbors. According to *Facts in Review*, which Viereck helped edit, the Poles had committed a host of atrocities against their German minority, and Germany was compelled "to take drastic countermeasures."[9] Viereck himself, in a letter to Elmer Gertz, reasserted the same myth. He said

---

[7] Elmo Roper, *You and Your Leaders: Their Actions and Your Reactions, 1936–1956* (New York: William Morrow, 1957), p. 49; Cantril, *Public Opinion*, p. 974.

[8] Adler, *Isolationist Impulse*, p. 281.

[9] *Facts in Review*, October 19, 1939, pp. 5–6.

that he had learned from reliable non-German sources before the outbreak of hostilities that a regiment of Polish volunteers had been formed to murder and terrorize the Polish citizens of German blood in case of war. Thus, he said, "Germany . . . was determined to end the Polish reign of terror and to liquidate Versailles," and then he added, "Today, whatever role the future may assign to him, Hitler is first in war, first in peace, first in the hearts of his country-men."[10]

Three months later Viereck seemed less sure of the wisdom of Germany's aggression. He wrote to Oswald Garrison Villard, a noted pacifist and noninterventionist whom he grudgingly admired, that if the Japanese were considered to be "Prussians of the East," it now appeared "as if the Prussians are the Japs of the West," in that they certainly had adopted the custom of hara-kiri. He asked Villard what he made of it; Viereck confessed that he was confused. Villard, only a casual acquaintance of Viereck's, had little to offer. He replied that his impression after spending nearly four weeks in Germany was that the German people were overwhelmingly against Hitler and the war but were unable to do anything "because he has the revolvers."[11] Viereck did not explain why he felt that Germany was in the process of committing suicide.

Whatever misgivings he may have had about his course of conduct, Viereck managed to repress them. In April and October, 1940, he filed supplemental copies to his original registration as an agent of a foreign principal. On October 25, 1940, he admitted that in the preceding six months he had received payment of $3,000 each from his Munich newspaper employer and from the German Library of Information. He received an additional $7,650 for extra editorial and writing work. Another supplement was entered on March 17, 1941; this statement and its predecessor were notarized by Viereck's attorney. In the latter registration Viereck changed slightly his answer to item eleven—he now described himself as "author, editor, and publicist" instead of merely as an author and journalist. He also included a cablegram

[10] G. S. Viereck to Elmer Gertz, September 11, 1939, Gertz MSS.
[11] G. S. Viereck to Oswald G. Villard, December 21, 1939, and Oswald G. Villard to G. S. Viereck, December 28, 1939, Villard MSS.

he had sent to the publisher of the *Muenchner Neueste Nach-richten* on February 11, 1941, in which he told Wirsing that he had an American publisher for Wirsing's book, *One Hundred Families* (a diatribe again English international financiers) and asked to serve as his American representative on the handling of the book. He promised author Wirsing a 10 percent royalty and asked for $5,000 to $10,000 for advertising and distribution costs. Wirsing approved the plan on February 19.[12]

There is little doubt either that Viereck, a man of established literary reputation and considerable editing and writing ability, did perform notable service for the German government. The German Foreign Office regarded him as their "most valuable liaison agent" (*wertvollste Verbindungsmann*) in the United States, paid him accordingly, and tried to exploit his talents to the utmost.[13] American observers and critics also rated him highly as a propagandist. In October 1940, for example, *Fortune* magazine called him the most talented and one of the most effective Nazi propagandists in America. In 1941 the House Un-American Activities Committee likewise considered him to be one of the outstanding pro-Nazi propagandists in this country.[14] And in subsequent studies he was referred to as the "leading spokesman of U.S. Germandom,"[15] and the "head and brains"[16] of the German-sponsored espionage network. Among the intellectual rationalizers of fascism, it should perhaps be noted, Lawrence Dennis was clearly superior to Viereck. The latter, after all, did not explicitly advocate fascism for America nor try to construct a political theory for it. But as a journalist and propagandist, he could devise plausible excuses for German aggression and American neutralism.

[12] Registration statements in files of Criminal No. 68584, Archives of Federal District Court, District of Columbia; Supplement to Registration Statement by G. S. Viereck, March 17, 1941.

[13] Rogge, *Official German Report*, p. 130, 325–30.

[14] "The War of Nerves: U.S. Front," p. 143; U.S. Congress, Special Committee on Un-American Activities, *Report on Axis Front Movement in the United States, Appendix*, Pt. VII, 78th Cong., 1st Sess., 1941, pp. 39–41, 54.

[15] Gerson, *Hyphenate*, p. 101.

[16] Sayers and Kahn, *Sabotage!*, p. 167.

The German government valued Viereck not only for his fluency as a writer of propaganda but also as a supposed expert in the analysis and gauging of American public opinion. As noted previously, Viereck's contract with Giselher Wirsing was intended mainly as a cover for his basic job of supplying his old friend Hans Dieckhoff in Berlin with regular summaries and evaluations of American public opinion toward events in Europe. In 1943 Viereck justified this arrangement by calling Dieckhoff a man "who knew and loved the United States." Dieckhoff was considered to be the German Foreign Office's leading expert on American affairs; thus he was put in charge of the America Committee which was organized early in 1940 as a unit of the Foreign Office headquarters in Berlin. This committee had the specific task of trying to help prevent the reelection of Franklin Roosevelt in 1940 and 1944, but it also concerned itself with improving the effectiveness of German propaganda aimed at the United States.[17] To get his reports to Europe, Viereck ordinarily sent an envelope by mail to a maildrop in Lisbon, Portugal, with an inner envelope marked for Dieckhoff or Wirsing. He did not anticipate that the British censor on Bermuda would intercept and copy or retain this material. Portions of these reports were subsequently divulged in 1942 and 1943 when Viereck was placed on trial for violating the Foreign Agents Registration Act.

These "newsletters" offered judgments on a variety of matters. In a letter on April 10, 1940, he complained of Dorothy Thompson's presence in Italy, surmising that she would probably write of weaknesses in the Italian economy. Also, in his opinion, the activities of Clare Boothe Luce in Europe would "bear watching," since she was the author of that "poisonous play, 'Margin for Error' which is still running on Broadway." In another instance, he recommended to Dieckhoff some "excellent" material in the *Congressional Record* placed there by Congressmen Fish and Thorkelson.[18] In still another report he cited reactions in the American press and radio and in Congress to events in Europe, stressing those which indicated a "growing sentiment" for peace

[17] Rogge, *Official German Report*, pp. 47–48, 131–33; *Washington Post*, July 15, 1943, p. 10:1.
[18] *Washington Post*, July 14, 1943, p. 7B:4.

among Americans. He claimed in the same report that Catholic sentiment in the United States was growing stronger against war, but he added, "It is very unfortunate that at this very moment the bishops of greater Germany allegedly issued a pastoral letter assailing Nazi steps against the church in connection with the school problem."[19] The extent to which the German government made use of such advice, innocuous as it seems to have been, is impossible to determine, but there has been no evidence to show that the Nazi leadership ever intended to let American public opinion alter or divert its course.

In spite of evidence to the contrary, Viereck maintained that he was not a tool of the German government. In June, 1940, he told a reporter of the *New Yorker* magazine that he was a poet and journalist who was mixing in politics "in a small way," but he denied he was a propagandist. He added, "behind the scenes, I do all I can to better relations between Germany and the United States. I do not care to be more specific." The reporter noted that on the walls of his apartment he had portraits hanging of Kaiser Wilhelm II and other Hohenzollerns, Hitler, Goebbels, General von Mackensen, Sigmund Freud, and Albert Einstein. He admitted he was no longer on speaking terms with some of these friends or acquaintances.[20]

Perhaps one could measure his value as a publicist in part by the monetary compensation he received prior to June, 1941, when the federal government ordered all German consulates and their agencies—such as the German Library of Information—closed down. (He discontinued his work for the *Muenchner Neueste Nachrichten* in early September.) In January, 1941, he wrote to Dr. Matthias Schmitz, recently appointed head of the German Library of Information, and requested an increase in salary, to $2,500 per month. Viereck pointed to the fact that since his work began, *Facts in Review* had grown from four pages per week to sixteen and from a modest circulation to nearly 100,000 copies. He claimed that his work in revising and preparing material for

[19] *Washington Post*, July 15, 1943, p. 10:1.
[20] "The Talk of the Town," *New Yorker*, June 15, 1940, pp. 15–16.

it was now equivalent to four or five articles monthly. He added that he would continue to act as Schmitz's chief literary adviser on all books sponsored by the Library, noting that the proposed monthly salary would not be appreciably more than what he was receiving at present, "all things considered." His work, he said, was helping "to break down with the battering ram of truth the barriers of hate and misunderstanding which propagandists abetted by malice and ignorance attempt to rear between your country and my own, the United States." His request was approved, and the new contract was appended to a supplemental registration statement on April 25, 1941. At that time he indicated that his compensation by the German Library of Information for the preceding six months had amounted to $25,504, and that he had received $8,300 from his Munich employer in the same period, the latter amount including an advance on his salary until February, 1942, and reimbursement for expenses.[21]

In all, according to an investigation in 1942, Viereck had received, between September, 1939, and the summer of 1941, a total of from $70,000 to $80,000 in salary and expense payments. But this figure may even have been too low. In a postwar interview, Herbert von Strempel, who handled much of the money dispensed by the German embassy, indicated that the total funds allotted to Viereck may have amounted to $200,000 or more. Even if one accepts the smaller figure, it appears that Viereck was Germany's highest-paid publicist in America.[22]

Along with his work as a correspondent and editor of a German periodical, Viereck in 1940 and 1941 devoted considerable energy to his publishing firm, Flanders Hall. Part of his inspiration for buying control of this small firm in early 1940 was derived from the success he had enjoyed with the Fatherland Corporation and its Jackson Press in World War I. In January, 1942, Viereck recalled that, in the latter part of 1939 as he browsed through the

[21] Supplement to Registration Statement, by G. S. Viereck, April 25, 1941; Sayers and Kahn, *Sabotage!*, pp. 171–72.

[22] Rogge, *Official German Report*, pp. 130, 136, 184–86; *U.S. v. Jos. McWilliams, et al.*, Appendix to Appellant's Brief, District of Columbia, No. 9438, 1946, p. 51.

books and pamphlets carried by the German Library of Information, the thought came to him that "among the eighty percent of the American people who were opposed to war, and among the many groups whose co-racials were oppressed by Great Britain," there would be a substantial market in the United States for this material.[23]

Accordingly, between early 1940 and November, 1941, when the exposure of Viereck's role in the firm led the Hauck brothers to dissolve it, Flanders Hall published about twenty titles, most of them translations from German works made available by the German Information Office. In publishing these, Viereck claimed that he avoided racist, "unreasonable," or anti-American material, but he usually substituted aliases for their German authors and took pains to conceal their true source. Typically, their target was British imperialism, especially malpractices in such areas as Africa, Ireland, and India. One of them, *Doublecross in Palestine*, even tried to arouse the Jews against the British, but did not have many sales in Jewish circles. In addition, Viereck published Irish polemics like Shaemas O'Sheel's *Seven Periods of Irish History*, and in what was probably his most successful venture, he put out the pamphlet *Lord Lothian against Lord Lothian*, ostensibly authored by Senator Ernest Lundeen, although Viereck himself had actually prepared it as a speech for the senator. The pamphlet also contained a foreword by "James Burr Hamilton," an alias Viereck had once used, and which was being used now by O'Sheel.[24]

Most of these publishing activities were not included in Viereck's registration statements. They were, he claimed later, "purely personal matters." The only exception, already noted, was his registration of Flanders Hall as an agent for Giselher Wirsing's *One Hundred Families That Rule the Empire*. Apparently in this case Viereck was afraid that the law would be construed to apply, and for once he was attributing authorship directly to a German national. It might be observed in passing that the book

[23] Viereck, "Story of Flanders Hall," pp. 1–2, 9, Viereck MSS.
[24] Rogge, *Official German Report*, pp. 167–69, 308; Viereck, "Story of Flanders Hall," pp. 3–6; *New York Times*, November 18, 1941, p. 10:5.

failed to sell and proved to be a poor investment for the German Foreign Office.[25]

In view of the worsening relations between Germany and the United States and the popular suspicion toward non-American sources of pro-German propaganda, Viereck decided in the spring of 1941 that it would be better to concentrate thereafter on books written only by American citizens. By that time, too, he had secured the confidence of several isolationist congressmen through his personal lobbying and participation in the Make Europe Pay War Debts committee. Through the committee's secretary, Prescott Dennett, he subsequently obtained a manuscript, *We Must Save the Republic*, written by Representative Stephen A. Day of Illinois. Although Viereck said he had hoped to sell a million copies, the results were again disappointing. A second manuscript was obtained from Senator Rush D. Holt of West Virginia, whose father had been acquainted with Viereck during World War I and was a subscriber to *American Monthly*. Viereck had met the younger Holt in the late 1930's through Senator Ernest Lundeen. In early 1941 Viereck asked Dennett to help Holt complete two manuscripts, *Who's Who among the Warmongers* and *The British Propaganda Network*, so that Flanders Hall could publish them. Draft copies were also sent to Dieckhoff in Berlin— but, as Viereck was preparing to publish them, columnist Drew Pearson exposed Flanders Hall as a pro-Nazi operation, and Senator Holt withdrew his manuscripts.[26]

Compared to Flanders Hall, Viereck was considerably more successful on his fourth project—using the Make Europe Pay War Debts committee as a vehicle for his efforts to strengthen isolationist, anti-British, and pro-German sentiment in this country. As noted previously, this committee had attracted several legislators to its ranks, including Senators Ernest Lundeen and Rush Holt and Representatives Hamilton Fish and Stephen Day.

[25] Viereck, "Story of Flanders Hall," p. 10; Rogge, *Official German Report*, p. 133.
[26] *New York Times*, February 19, 1942, p. 20:6; Viereck, "Story of Flanders Hall," p. 11; Rogge, *Official German Report*, pp. 266–73.

These men comprised what O. John Rogge, a special assistant to the Attorney General from 1943 to 1946, called "Viereck's Capitol Hill Squad." Viereck claimed in January, 1942, that he had never actually met Congressman Day, but there is no denying he was close to the others, especially to Lundeen and Fish, and that he did try to use them for his own purposes.[27]

In the first half of 1940, for instance, he prepared four speeches for Lundeen, one of which was published as a booklet by Flanders Hall. Another of these speeches, called "Six Men and War," was delivered in the Senate in the summer of 1940 and then reprinted and distributed in 125,000 copies under Lundeen's congressional frank. The concluding words in this speech were "Europe for the Europeans; Asia for the Asiatics; America for the Americans"—a slogan that did worthy service for the isolationists. A third speech concerned German and American trade relations and was given by Lundeen at a banquet honoring the visiting Duke of Saxe-Coburg, and sponsored by the German-American Board of Trade in New York. Viereck obtained some of the data for this speech and for the one on "Lord Lothian against Lord Lothian" directly from the German embassy. Lundeen was scheduled to deliver the fourth speech, entitled "The German Element in America," at a meeting of the Steuben Society of America on September 14, 1940. However, on August 31 he was killed in a plane crash. Hamilton Fish, Jr., agreed to speak in his place.[28]

By this time Congressman Fish had allowed his militant anti-Communism to make him an apologist for the Nazis, whom he considered to be a major bulwark against Bolshevism. In particular, he tended to accept Nazi propaganda at face value. Agreeing to collaborate with Viereck and the Make Europe Pay War Debts committee, he allowed them to use his mailing list of about 100,000 names and his office facilities in mailing out copies of Lundeen's aforementioned speech in July, 1940. In addition, his secretary, George Hill, prepared for Viereck another list of more than 30,000 names previously gained from *Who's Who*. With additional names obtained from the fan mail of various other

[27] Ibid.
[28] *New York Times*, February 20, 1942, p. 11:4; Rogge, *Official German Report*, pp. 154, 158, 165, 266–67, 270.

congressmen, Viereck drew up a list of approximately 140,000 addresses for literature sponsored by the committee or by other sympathetic congressmen. Although Fish was a willing collaborator of Viereck's, there apparently were only two speeches of his, both demanding "No Convoys! No War!", which were reprinted in a large quantity (25,000 copies) and distributed under the auspices of the Make Europe Pay War Debts committee. He was also active in similar groups, particularly the National Committee to Keep America out of Foreign Wars.[29]

The four legislators already mentioned collaborated directly with Viereck. In addition, there were twenty other legislators who put into the *Congressional Record* articles and speeches recommended to them by Prescott Dennett or other individuals who were following Viereck's advice. According to a Justice Department report, Viereck had a hand in providing the material for at least thirty-seven articles which were entered in the *Congressional Record* by various legislators and then reprinted and distributed in quantities ranging from 5,000 to 125,000 each. It may be assumed that few if any of the twenty legislators referred to realized that Viereck had any hand in selecting or furnishing the "handouts" they received from Dennett, Hill, or others representing the Make Europe Pay War Debts committee. Dennett was to testify in July, 1943, that Viereck had purposely avoided joining any committees or taking a public role in their affairs. But he had remained active behind the scenes. For example, he had contributed about $5,000 to the work of the committee in 1940; most of this was used to publish speeches and a memorial card sent out following Senator Lundeen's sudden death.[30]

Viereck's first attempt to exploit the congressional frank as a convenient and inexpensive method for disseminating anti-interventionist literature was made in April, 1940, when he conferred with the secretary of Senator Gerald P. Nye on the possibility of ordering an astronomical six or seven million copies

[29] Ibid.
[30] Rogge, *Official German Report*, pp. 153–66; *Washington Post*, July 7, 1943, p. 11:1; *U.S. v. G. S. Viereck*, Criminal No. 71674, Summary of Testimony of Pvt. Prescott Dennett, Transcript of Proceedings (excerpt), July 1, 1943, D.C. District Court files.

of an anti-British speech Nye had delivered in April, 1939. Nye subsequently declined to deal with Viereck. However, Nye did consent later to Dennett's request for the reprinting of one of his speeches for the committee's use. In a more typical example of the way he operated, Viereck in June, 1940, merely took a copy of the *Washington Times-Herald* containing Karl von Wiegand's recent friendly interview with Hitler and gave it to Prescott Dennett with the suggestion that he find a congressman to insert it in the *Congressional Record*. Dennett found Representative Jacob Thorkelson of Montana willing to do this; adding remarks of his own to the interview, Thorkelson had the article reprinted as "The Danger of Invasion," and 5,000 copies were then reprinted and distributed under the congressional frank. On another occasion Viereck selected an article, "Giddy Minds and Foreign Quarrels" by Charles A. Beard, and gave it to Dennett, who in turn passed it on to George Hill. Hill then gave the article to the secretary of Senator D. Worth Clark, who persuaded the senator to insert it in the *Congressional Record*. It was subsequently reprinted (10,000 copies) at the expense of the Make Europe Pay War Debts committee. An innovation that the committee adopted at Viereck's suggestion in 1941 was the reprinting of six articles from the *Congressional Record* in the form of postcards.[31]

Of course, it would be incorrect to assume that all of the congressional isolationists had the same motives, or that they shared Viereck's friendly and optimistic view of Germany. Viereck did share with them the concept of "America First," which meant that the United States should serve its own interests first by refusing to come to the aid of even friendly powers outside the western hemisphere. This proposition in turn was supported by belief in the "Fortress America" idea, which held that, because of America's remoteness from Europe and Asia, this country could safely ignore changes in foreign balances of power as long as its defenses were adequate to prevent a naval invasion of this hemisphere. What most isolationist politicians and lobbyists did not share

[31] Rogge, *Official German Report*, pp. 155–57, 161, 165; also see *Washington Post*, July 7, 1943, p. 11: 1, concerning testimony of Gerald Movious and George Hill on Viereck's lobbying.

with Viereck was his special relationship to Germany—his kinship to the Hohenzollerns in particular—and his peculiar complexes which led him to glorify nationalistic German values. Nor did any of the isolationist congressmen have direct ties, as Viereck did, to German agencies in this country.

These ties, of course, made him vulnerable to later charges that he was really a German agent rather than a sincere "isolationist"—and in some respects he was. For example, he reported to the chargé d'affaires Hans Thomsen and to Hans Borchers, German consul-general in New York, on the progress being made to keep Congress neutral if not pro-German. Documents of the German Foreign Office, opened after the war, make it apparent that the embassy was involved in trying to exert influence, through obscure channels, on various isolationist groups and programs. In fact, Hans Thomsen on one occasion wrote his superiors that he was able "through a confidential agent to induce the isolationist Republican Thorkelson to have the Fuehrer interview inserted in the *Congressional Record.*" The "confidential agent" probably was Viereck. Thomsen tended to exaggerate in his reports to Berlin, claiming, for instance, in 1940 that he had "fifty Congressmen ready to explain pro-German views" at the Republican party convention.[32] Individualist that he was, Viereck probably took no orders from Thomsen—but at the same time he unquestionably aided the German cause while consciously convincing himself that he was doing what was best for America's interest in peace.

Viereck's stubborn loyalty to his cause came into conflict with a variety of external events in 1941, resulting ultimately in a confrontation with American authorities. In September, 1941, German submarines and aircraft attacked and sank or damaged several American ships. Consequently, the U.S. Navy extended its protective cover over most of the North Atlantic, and the President's "shoot on sight" order meant that the United States was at war with Germany, although an official declaration of such was

[32] See especially *Documents on German Foreign Policy*, Series D, Vol. VIII, Docs. 22, 129, 378, 641; Vol. IX, Docs. 31, 197, 492, 493; Vol. X, pp. 39–40.

still three months away. In this atmosphere, tolerance of pro-German publicists began to ebb; soon the agencies of justice started investigating the possibilities of taking legal action against them.

Accordingly, in September, 1941, a federal grand jury was impaneled in Washington to study evidence against Nazi agents in this country; it began its work with an investigation of the Flanders Hall publishing firm. In his syndicated column Drew Pearson had already drawn the public's attention to the fact that a speech written by Viereck for the late Senator Lundeen entitled "Lord Lothian against Lord Lothian" had appeared in almost identical form as a Flanders Hall book under the byline of James Burr Hamilton—one of Viereck's pen names. Pearson also noted that most of the Flanders Hall books had originally appeared in German or had been written by German nationals. Sigfrid and Adolph Hauck were subsequently subpoenaed by the jury, and their testimony undoubtedly implicated Viereck. The jury also acquired information from Mrs. Elizabeth Dilling, notorious anti-Semite and pro-fascist, who had sent the book on Lord Lothian free to all on her regular mailing list. With Viereck's role in the Flanders Hall operation at least partly established, on October 2 the jury called him to appear before it the next day. He was, in fact, the first registered agent of a German principal to be summoned. He immediately filed a petition in which he asserted that since newspaper accounts had characterized the inquiry as aimed largely toward his indictment, to testify as a witness in such a situation would subject him to self-incrimination and be an invasion of his constitutional rights. But his petition was overruled by the court and he appeared as directed.[33]

The grand jury was interested not only in Viereck's connections with the Flanders Hall publishing firm, but also with the Make Europe Pay War Debts committee, and with his use of the *Congressional Record* to disseminate propaganda. It sought evidence, too, of concealment in his other activities. It should be

[33] "Flanders Hall Investigated by Grand Jury," *Publisher's Weekly*, October 4, 1941, p. 1385; Drew Pearson, "Congressman's Nazi Connections," *Des Moines Register*, August 30, 1941, p. 4; *Washington Post*, October 3, 1941, p. 4:1; *New York Times*, October 3, 1941, p. 12:5.

noted that there was no law against being a propagandist. There were laws dealing with espionage, sedition, and sabotage; but with the possible exception of sedition, these crimes were patently inapplicable to Viereck. For example, there was no evidence that he attempted to secure classified government information or to sabotage any military operations. Thus the grand jury decided to examine Viereck's status under the Foreign Agents Registration Act. He had registered on several occasions, but had he fulfilled all the requirements of the act? Had he, for instance, given a comprehensive statement of the nature of his business as the registration form required? On this point in particular the grand jury decided the evidence of a violation was sufficient to warrant an indictment, which it promptly drew up.

The indictment carried five counts, one for each of the registration statements and supplements that he made, all alleging that he had willfully omitted material facts in describing the nature of his business. The jury obviously was not satisfied with his answer that he was acting as "author and journalist," although later investigation was to show that most other registrants had responded with similar generalizations. Count two, for instance, accused Viereck of failing to note in his supplemental statement of April 23, 1940, that during the period covered by the report he advised his foreign principals on political interests and public policy; that he disseminated material in books, periodicals, newspapers, and the *Congressional Record*; that he used false and fictitious names (especially on Flanders Hall books) to conceal from the American public the true names and identities of the writers; and that he advised Prescott Dennett and the Make Europe Pay War Debts committee, contributing money to defray its expenses for the purpose of molding public opinion on public policy.[34] These enumerations of his activities were essentially true. The legal issue, however, hinged primarily on whether such specificity was required by the act, whether all of the activities listed were relevant to the act of registration, and whether any alleged omissions were willful and thus felonious. A subsequent demurrer

[34] Indictment, *U.S.* v. *G. S. Viereck*, District Court of District of Columbia, September term, 1941, copy in Viereck MSS; *Washington Post*, October 9, 1941, p. 1:3.

by the defendant questioned the constitutionality of the statute, but this objection was rejected by the District Court.

Acting on the authority of this indictment, seven agents of the Justice Department called on Viereck at about 8:00 A.M. on October 8, 1941, in his residence at 305 Riverside Drive and placed him under arrest. Over his protests and those of his wife, and although not carrying a search warrant, these agents also searched through his home and office, taking with them various books, papers, and canceled checks. Impeccably clad in a brown suit and clutching his worn brief case, he was brought before U.S. Commissioner Isaac Platt in the New York Federal Building. William Power Maloney, who was assigned to the case as a special assistant to the attorney general, told the press that Viereck was the "top-ranking propagandist in this country" and "one of the most serious menaces" to it. Accordingly, his bail was first set at $20,000, but then reduced to $15,000 upon a petition by Viereck's attorneys, Daniel F. Cohalan, Jr., and Emil Morosini. Their client was finally released on bond at 5:00 P.M. and ordered to appear in Washington the next day to answer the indictment.[35]

Meanwhile, in a statement that he prepared during the day, he offered his customary defensive catharsis: that is, he professed his love for America, he charged his accusers with unworthy motives, and he ascribed his predicament to "war psychosis." He alleged that he was being persecuted because of his German blood and because he had resisted the interventionists who were intent on catapulting America into "Europe's war." He claimed, too, that if he had "paid homage to the British kings or the Red Master of the Kremlin" the government would not be interested in his finances or affairs. Finally, he saw his indictment as only one incident in "the perfidious plot to destroy the America we know and love." Soon thereafter, in a letter to long-time acquaint-

[35] Motion for Reargument of Defendant's Motion to Suppress Evidence and for Return of Same, Criminal No. 68584, January 22, 1942; Memo of Points and Authorities in Support of Motion to Suppress Evidence, Criminal No. 68584, January 22, 1942, Federal District Court, D.C., Archives; New York Times, October 9, 1941, pp. 1:1, 4.

ance and well-known civil rights lawyer Arthur Garfield Hays, he added "witch-hunt" to the sins of his accusers.[36]

The rhetoric of Viereck's statement when he was arrested was, of course, all too familiar. It was the distorted product of an idealized image of himself and the outside world which he could not seem to alter. It had become the standard defense mechanism for his ego—in fact, it represented the most consistent strand within his personality. He could not repudiate it without repudiating the basis of his own integrity. His Germanophilia did not, however, blind him entirely to reason or objective reality. When Arthur Garfield Hays expressed little sympathy for his predicament, Viereck replied, "I know that we all rationalize our instincts—you no less than I." Thus he admitted his subjection to long-formed but largely unconscious habits. He also felt constrained to emphasize that he was an individualist who accepted totalitarianism and collectivism only as temporary expedients in case of national emergencies. Germany, he asserted, "passed through such an emergency; we did not." Subjectively unable to apprehend the long-range threat of Nazi expansionism, he claimed that the image of America confronted by a dire emergency was "self-created."[37]

Although he considered his views to be more realistic than those of his opponents, Viereck actually was depicting the problem as a contest of "instincts," of ingrained habits of thought, which arranged reality in accordance with fixed mental stereotypes. He could not explain why his optimistic stereotype of Germany's intentions should be any more correct than the opposite view taken by the majority of Americans. Another ingredient of this argument was the Darwinian view that the nations most fit to survive would and should come out on top; thus Germany should be given a free hand in Europe to prove itself the fittest nation on that continent. At the same time, America should remain dominant in the western hemisphere and avoid any struggle

[36] *Washington Post*, October 9, 1941, p. 6:2; G. S. Viereck to Arthur Garfield Hays (copy), October 16, 1941, Viereck MSS.

[37] A. G. Hays to G. S. Viereck, October 14, 1941, Viereck MSS; G. S. Viereck to A. G. Hays (copy), October 16, 1941, Viereck MSS.

instigated from the outside unless it directly threatened her survival as a nation.

Another consistent feature in Viereck's reactions to his critics was his tendency to project his own feelings—that is, to identify in others the faults that often were most descriptive of himself. When he scored his detractors for being one-sided and obstinate in their prejudices, it was as if he were holding a mirror up to himself. This quality was dramatically displayed in November, 1941, in his response to Upton Sinclair's scathing attack launched against him in an open letter to *Nation* magazine. Sinclair described Viereck as a pompous liar and a hypocrite. He said Viereck was once a "real poet" but the "poet shudders with horror at what you have become."[38] Unable to repress his agitation, Viereck wrote a reply but apparently did not mail it. He evidently realized that additional notoriety at this critical point could only work against chances for a favorable outcome in his forthcoming trial. Yet his rhetoric was revealing. He excoriated Sinclair's "intolerable verbosity" and his "incurable mania for self-advertising." After giving vent to these words so descriptive of himself, he concluded in the spirit of a knight errant wounded by well-meaning but ignorant adversaries: "The roses and raptures of your radical rhetoric give no inkling that you would understand the instincts of a gentleman who refuses to sully his steel by crossing swords with a cad."[39]

In these last phrases Viereck displayed still another facet of his world view, namely his immature romanticism. Through his aesthetic mental filter he viewed life as a kind of jousting tournament where flashing knights did battle but no one really got hurt. Instead, both victor and vanquished gained some glory, and the spectators were kept amused. It was a view that excluded the apprehension of tragedy and despair and repelled any thought of self-deprecation. Even his vaunted gentility might be criticized as shallow, in view of the bellicosity of his pro-German nationalist rhetoric in the 1920's and his insensitivity to Nazi depredations

---

[38] *Nation*, November 29, 1941, p. 551.
[39] G. S. Viereck to Upton Sinclair, December 1, 1941, Viereck MSS.

in the 1930's. In brief, he was not about to repent, even in the face of outraged public opinion and threatened legal coercion.

In the meantime, on October 10, 1941, Viereck entered a plea of not guilty to the indictment. His arrest and arraignment received prominent attention in major city newspapers. In appearance he did not fit the image of the furtive and arrogant Prussian type. Short and slender, wearing heavy spectacles and a conservative suit, he resembled the stereotype of a college professor or other scholarly figure. The *Washington Post* offered the dubious compliment that he was the "acknowledged leader of pro-German thought in this country all his adult life." At another time and place, Veireck would probably have appreciated this kind of praise. Perhaps he still did, in his ambivalent way. One may surmise that he unequivocally disliked the October 10 remarks of prosecuting attorney William Maloney, who told reporters that Viereck was the "head and brains of an insidious propaganda machine, engaged in sabotaging the President's efforts to arouse the American people to their danger."[40] On second thought, though, he may have recognized in this imprudent statement overtones which served to reinforce his own view that his trial was politically motivated.

After he had pleaded not guilty, Viereck's attorneys were allowed time to file a demurrer, which they did on October 24, offering nine reasons why the charges should be withdrawn. They argued, in particular, that the alleged omissions on the registration statement did not constitute a violation of the statute, that material facts were not omitted in the registration statements, and that the statute failed to establish ascertainable standards of guilt or criminality and thus violated the Fifth and Sixth Amendments. Their demurrer was upheld for the first and fourth counts of the indictment but denied on the other three. In November a trial date of February 2, 1942, was set for his case. Meanwhile, on October 24, the federal grand jury in Washington indicted Congressman Fish's secretary George Hill on two counts of perjury,

[40] *Washington Post*, October 9, 1941, p. 6:1–2; October 11, 1941, p. 1:4.

one of them involving his testimony that he did not know Viereck.[41] A few weeks later Pearl Harbor was bombed, and soon America was officially at war with the Axis powers. These events made it even less probable that a jury could view with dispassion or detachment the activities of indicted pro-German publicists or apologists.

The circumstances of his arrest—the corps of agents used to apprehend him, the confiscation of personal property for use as evidence, the excoriating attitude of the government prosecutor, and the high bail bond—probably shocked Viereck into realizing that his chances of remaining out of jail were slim indeed. The prospect of imprisonment held no allure for him. As a part of his defense, he began searching for character witnesses, in spite of his attorneys' advice that such testimony would be irrelevant. He sent letters to a number of friends and acquaintances in which he represented himself as an innocent victim of the war spirit and in which he asked them to vouch for his good character. Some of those contacted were only barely acquainted with him but were valuable for their prestige. For instance, he wrote Joseph E. Davies, an assistant to the secretary of state and former ambassador to Russia. He knew Davies only from a discussion he had had with him several years earlier on the possibility of writing a series of articles on Russia. Davies reminded him that under questioning he would have to admit that he had heard doubts expressed about Viereck's loyalty and this fact may have caused him to decide not to collaborate with him on the proposed articles. Yet he assured Viereck that he had utmost confidence in his integrity and character.[42]

To a similar request Edgar Lee Masters—who also was only a casual acquaintance—replied that he did not think good character references would help because they did not relate to the legal issues. Channing Pollock, a friend of long standing, expressed a

[41] Demurrer by G. S. Viereck, Cohalan, and Morosini, October 24, 1941, Federal District Court, D.C., Archives; *New York Times*, October 25, 1941, p. 1:2; January 20, 1942, p. 21:5.

[42] Joseph E. Davies to G. S. Viereck, January 6, 1942, Viereck MSS; G. S. Viereck, *Men into Beasts* (New York: Fawcett Publications, 1952), p. 13.

similar view. Edwin Borchard, isolationist professor of international law at Yale, offered to sign an affidavit attesting to Viereck's good character and basic loyalty to the United States, but he did not care to testify. Viereck received a similar response from Padraic Colum, whom he had not seen for many years. Fulton Oursler told his onetime collaborator that his testimony would probably be damaging to him. Poultney Bigelow, aged world traveler, author, and Germanophile, was the only friend of Viereck's who unconditionally offered to testify in his behalf. Given these responses, Viereck finally acceded to his attorneys' advice not to use character witnesses.[43]

In mid-January, 1942, a major incident was precipitated when District Court Justice T. Alan Goldsborough attempted, under a new court rule, to secure jurisdiction over the case and to begin the trial about two weeks earlier than originally scheduled. The trial schedule had called for Justice F. Dickinson Letts to try the case. Believing Goldsborough to be biased against the government's position, the Justice Department on January 19 announced it would file an affidavit with the Circuit Court of Appeals, asking it to direct Goldsborough to step down. In the face of this prospective legal action and the obvious unpopularity of his position, Judge Goldsborough agreed to remove himself from the case after the charge of prejudice was withdrawn.[44] Predictably, Viereck's attorneys attempted to have Judge Letts disqualify himself on the grounds of being prejudiced against the defendant. When this failed, they tried for a change of venue, also denied.

Accordingly, Viereck's trial got underway on February 3, when jury selection began. It took time to obtain a panel of unbiased jurors, and it was not until February 16 that the first witness, Sigfrid Hauck, was called. The government's case was not especially difficult. Besides attesting to Viereck's financial and editorial interest in the Flanders Hall operation, government witnesses testified to his role in writing speeches for Senator Lun-

[43] Letters from these individuals may be found in Viereck MSS.
[44] *New York Times*, January 20, 1942, p. 21:5; January 21, 1942, p. 19:5; January 30, 1942, p. 11:3; March 4, 1942, p. 10:2.

deen, to his use of Congressman Fish and his secretary for distributing one of these speeches under Fish's frank, and to his assistance in setting up the Make Europe Pay War Debts committee. Especially damaging was the testimony given by the British censor on Bermuda, who offered in evidence a letter from Viereck to Hans Dieckhoff which had been intercepted by the British in 1941. The envelope to Dieckhoff, inside a larger envelope addressed to a mail drop in Lisbon, contained the manuscripts of two articles by Senator Rush Holt which Viereck was planning to have published by Flanders Hall. This evidence of Viereck's direct communication with an official of an unfriendly foreign power undoubtedly made a special impression upon the jury. Another prosecution witness testified that of the thirty-five portraits on the walls of Viereck's den, Hitler's was the largest. Chief prosecuting attorney William Maloney helped make Viereck appear even more deceptive and disloyal by quoting out of context statements from Viereck's book, *Spreading Germs of Hate*, that described the ways in which a propagandist must camouflage his motives and mode of operation in order to be successful.[45]

Instead of character witnesses Cohalan and Morosini sought to subpoena several federal officials and legislators whose testimony would contribute to the claim that their client had loyally offered his advice to the State Department, and that the congressional frank had also been used to mail out large quantities of interventionist literature. Among those ultimately served with subpoenas were former ambassador to Italy William Phillips, Senator Joseph Guffey, the Superintendent of Documents, and former State Department official Leonard H. Price. Phillips was the State Department official Viereck had talked to in 1933 regarding his impressions of the Nazi leadership. Viereck had also visited him at the American embassy in Rome on his last trip to Europe in 1939. Senator Guffey had allowed his frank to be used in mailing out a large quantity of interventionist literature via the

[45] *New York Times*, February 3, 1942, p. 14:4; February 17, 1942, p. 17:6; *Washington Post*, February 18, 1942, p. 1:6; February 19, 1942, pp. 1:4, 4:8; February 20, 1942, p. 1:1; February 26, 1942, pp. 1:3–4, 6:4. See also Rogge, *Official German Report*, p. 272.

Congressional Record. His testimony and that of the Superintendent of Documents would presumably show that the use of the congressional frank to disseminate partisan viewpoints was a common practice and should not be construed as a crime. Price would likely verify the contention of the defense that most of the registrations under the act carried the same kind of generic answers as those given by Viereck. The defendant himself, so it was decided, would not take the stand. Apparently his attorneys felt that he was likely to be too self-righteous, too conceited, and too glib to be believed by a jury.[46]

The defense's strategy failed in practice, largely as a result of adverse rulings from the bench. Viereck's counsellors tried first to establish their client's loyal motives and good faith by introducing his 1933 letter to President Roosevelt, in which Viereck offered to give him his estimate of the new Nazi leadership. Judge Letts, however, disallowed it as irrelevant. He also upheld the prosecution's objection to the defense's motion to question Senator Guffey and Ambassador Phillips, ruling that evidence concerning use of the congressional frank for anti-Nazi purposes would be irrelevant. The court likewise held that it would be improper for the defense to examine Leonard H. Price on how the State Department interpreted the Foreign Agents Registration Act. This problem of interpretation was considered a question for the court to decide.[47] Defense counselors hoped to show that their client's interpretation of the registration form corresponded to that of about 90 percent of all other registrants.[48] Completing the pattern, on March 3 Morosini tried to introduce into evidence a series of charts depicting over a period of time the number of reprints of congressmen's speeches; this, too, was blocked by a ruling from the bench. At this point, Morosini gave vent to his ire and accused Judge Letts of being biased in favor of the government and prejudiced against the defendant. He immediately

[46] *Washington Post*, February 17, 1942, p. 1:4; March 3, 1942, pp. 1:4, 4:2; March 4, 1942, pp. 1:3; Viereck, *Men into Beasts*, p. 13.

[47] Ibid.

[48] G. S. Viereck, Statement Concerning *U.S. v. G. S. Viereck*, in U.S. District Court, D.C., February 16, 1942–March 5, 1942, No. 8204, Viereck MSS.

rested the defense's case. The judge then decided to bar Morosini from the courtroom for the remainder of the trial. Still remaining as Viereck's counsel were Cohalan and Colonel O. R. McGuire; the latter, a well-known Washington lawyer and isolationist, had been retained in January to assist in Viereck's defense.[49]

Final arguments and summations began on March 4, and the case went to the jury the following day. The prosecution pictured Viereck as a man who had "shamed and defiled his American citizenship." The prosecuting attorneys implied that Viereck was motivated in large part by the ample monetary rewards he received. He was also depicted as a sly and devious operator who worked through and "used" people such as Dennett, Hill, and Fish in order to disguise or conceal his own role.[50] More germane to the charge was the contention that the defendant had deliberately concealed important facts which should have been revealed in his registration statement. Prosecutor Maloney closed with an intemperate and somewhat irrelevant appeal to the jury: "This is war, harsh, cruel, murderous war. . . . The American people are relying upon you ladies and gentlemen for their protection against this sort of a crime, just as much as they are relying upon the protection of the men who man the guns in Bataan Peninsula and everywhere else. They are relying upon you ladies and gentlemen for their protection. We are at war. We have a duty to perform here."[51]

The defense tried to sway the jury with the proposition that freedom of speech was on trial, that Viereck was only one of many isolationists who spoke out against interventionism prior to the bombing of Pearl Harbor, and that such mistakes should not impugn his patriotism. Probably no argument could offset the impression given at the trial that all the relevant evidence was against him. Viereck's chances were further compromised when

[49] New York Times, March 3, 1942, p. 13:1; January 30, 1942, p. 11:3; O. R. McGuire to G. S. Viereck, January 15, 1942; January 20, 1942; January 24, 1942; Viereck MSS.

[50] New York Times, March 5, 1942, p. 11:1.

[51] G. S. Viereck, Statement Concerning U.S. v. G. S. Viereck, in U.S. District Court, D.C., No. 8204, p. 11.

the judge instructed the jury prior to its deliberation that a proper construction of the Foreign Agents Registration Act would require that the registrant in his supplementary statements reveal all of his "political" activities for the previous six months, whether or not these acts were as an agent for the foreign principal.[52]

It probably came as no surprise to Viereck when the jury returned on March 5 after two hours of deliberation with a verdict of guilty on all three counts. He listened calmly as the verdict was read. Then the judge ordered him to jail pending determination of sentence. Two marshals took him by the arms. The shock of what was happening finally penetrated his defensive armor. One reporter heard him ask his escort, "May I say goodby to my wife?" in a voice "thin, high-pitched and wavering." Gretchen stood waiting, but the marshals side-stepped her. After straining against his guards, and reportedly "chattering in panicky syllables, 'my hat and coat—they are over there—my hat and coat—I want to get my things,' " her husband was led from the courtroom. Mrs. Viereck reportedly stepped back and sat down silently, "her eyes misty but her chin up." Having accomplished his duties, prosecutor Maloney felt free to comment to assembled reporters on those congressmen besides Hamilton Fish, Jr., who had abetted Viereck's pro-German aims. He named, in particular, Representative Stephen Day and Senator Rush Holt, whom, he said, "have smeared and besmirched themselves far beyond our poor powers to add or detract."[53]

On March 13 Viereck was brought back to the courtroom for sentencing. Prior to the judge's pronouncement, Viereck's attorneys pleaded for leniency, after which their client was allowed to present a statement. In it he claimed that the radio and press had helped generate an atmosphere of hostility toward him, and that the bombing of Pearl Harbor had made him one of its victims. He again alleged that his troubles began when he published

[52] *Washington Post*, March 5, 1942, p. 4:8; *New York Times*, March 5, 1942, p. 11:1; *Viereck v. U.S.*, U.S. Court of Appeals for D.C., September 21, 1942 (130 F. 2d 945), p. 950.
[53] *New York Times*, March 6, 1942, p. 1:5; *Washington Post*, March 6, 1942, pp. 1:1, 4:1, 4:3.

his first articles against Communism in 1929. He pointed out that he had requested the State Department to pass on his first registration statement and that he entrusted subsequent statements to his attorneys. He noted that the responses of most registrants were similar to his and that he was the only registrant to be indicted for violating the act. He complained that the provisions of the law were obscure. He claimed that he did not try to camouflage his work, and he defended his ghost-writing for Senator Lundeen by also mentioning that he had edited articles written by President Roosevelt for *Liberty* magazine. He denied that he was acting as a foreign agent in respect to his use of Flanders Hall, and he asserted that his relations with the firm were public knowledge almost from the start. The manuscript of Holt's book which was sent to Dieckhoff was actually intended to be forwarded on to Wirsing, his employer in Munich, he averred.[54]

In his concluding remarks, Viereck declared, "America is the only country to which I owe allegiance. But I am no hater of Germany. I deplore the cruel war between the land of my birth and the land of my choice. I did all I could to prevent the catastrophe." He hoped for eventual collaboration between the "greatest Germanic nations"—England, the United States, and Germany. In the meantime, he proclaimed: "I shall never foreswear my German ancestry, betray my convictions, or spit on the graves of my forefathers. Like Luther at Wittenberg and Woodrow Wilson in Washington: Here I Stand; I can do no Other."[55] Finally, in what amounted to an anti-climax, he noted that he was not a well man, and that he was concerned about the welfare of his wife should he be sent to prison. Yet whatever befell him, he told the court, he believed history would again vindicate his position.

In his reply, Maloney said he was "astonished by the diatribe" and accused Viereck of attempting to bring about a "scandalous comparison" between President Roosevelt and the late Senator Lundeen. Viereck, he said, had been "an enemy of our country for years past—an enemy with a gun in his hand and a knife at our

[54] G. S. Viereck, Statement Concerning *U.S. v. G. S. Viereck*, in U.S. District Court, D.C., No. 8204. Also see *New York Times*, March 14, 1942, p. 9:3.
[55] Ibid.

throat." And this statement was "the last sting of an adder before its head is crushed."[56]

Judge Letts remained unmoved either by defense counsel's pleas or by the defendant's oratory. He imposed the maximum sentence on each of the three counts and ordered the defendant to pay the costs of the trial. Specifically, Viereck was sentenced to serve eight months to two years on each count and was fined a total of $1,500. Court costs for which he was liable were expected to reach about $2,000.[57] Viereck was returned to his cell, but he was not yet ready to concede defeat. Determined to be vindicated, he asked his attorneys to proceed with an appeal.

Consequently, while Viereck remained in the "protective custody" of the District of Columbia, McGuire drew up and filed an appeal brief, claiming instances of forty errors in the conduct of the court and the prosecution. The brief stressed five alleged kinds of error. In the first place, it was argued, Judge Letts had acted improperly in refusing to admit various items of evidence and in telling the jury that the Foreign Agents Registration Act was designed to remedy "some of the ills" which the McCormack's committee had uncovered in its investigations. Second, there was improper conduct on the part of the prosecutor, particularly in his references to Viereck as a propagandist and in his inflammatory use of Viereck's book, *Spreading Germs of Hate*, which had been published many years prior to the period during which the alleged crimes had taken place. Third, there was the refusal to admit evidence showing that, in response to a law so indefinite that it was subsequently rewritten for greater clarity, approximately 500 of the 560 registrants on file had answered in a manner similar to that of the defendant. Fourth, there was the improper focus of the trial—the fact that the defendant had been charged with one crime and tried for another; that, indicted for willfully violating the Foreign Agents Registration Act, he had then been tried for the nonindictable offense of being a propagandist. Finally, there was the improper charge to the jury, de-

[56] *New York Times*, March 14, 1942, p. 9:3.
[57] Ibid.; Judgment and Commitment, *U.S. v. G. S. Viereck*, March 13, 1942, D.C. District Court files.

claring that the defendant should have reported all of his political activities whether or not they had been performed as an agent for a foreign principal.[58]

After examining the evidence, the Court of Appeals denied a retrial on September 21, 1942. In its opinion, the defendant's claim that he was indicted for one crime and tried for another—neither of which was a crime under the statute—was an objection "euphonious but not meritorious." It was also the court's opinion that the Foreign Agents Registration Act was definite enough to require more information than was given. In particular, the court asserted that propagandizing is a political activity definitely covered under the act. It denied that Viereck was tried for acting as a propagandist, but asserted he was tried for "failing to disclose some of his propagandistic work." On the main issue—whether the facts omitted by Viereck were required by the act and were material to compliance with the act—it agreed with the lower court's construction and judgment. On the other points raised by the defendant, ,the court either denied their validity or judged them to be of insufficient import to warrant a new trial.[59]

Although the appellate court's decision was rather long and detailed, it seemed to Viereck and McGuire that the basic issues and supporting points had still not been fully and impartially weighed. Viereck therefore prevailed upon McGuire to carry the appeal to the Supreme Court. The nation's highest court announced on November 16 that it would review Viereck's conviction, and on March 1, 1943, it arrived at a ruling. In a five-to-two decision, with Justices Black and Douglas dissenting and Jackson and Rutledge not participating, the Court ruled that there were two major errors in the conduct of the trial and that the verdict of the lower court should be overturned. First, the District Court judge had erred in declaring to the jury that "it is sufficient if you find that he engaged in the activities, whether on

[58] *U.S.* v. *G. S. Viereck*, Notice of Appeal, Criminal No. 68584, by O. R. McGuire; *G. S. Viereck* v. *U.S.*, Appellant's Brief in U.S. Court of Appeals for D.C., 1942, No. 8204, by O. R. McGuire, pp. 2, 12, 15, 22, 23–25, 34, 76, passim.
[59] *Viereck* v. *U.S.*, Court of Appeals, D.C., *Federal Reporter*, No. 130, 2d Series, pp. 945–64.

behalf of his foreign principal or on his own behalf." The Supreme Court ruled instead that the registrant need report only his business on behalf of the foreign principal. The second error was that in his closing remarks to the jury the prosecuting attorney "indulged in an appeal wholly irrelevant to any facts or issues in the case, the purpose and effect of which could only have been to arouse passion and prejudice." In their dissenting opinions, Justices Black and Douglas cited the general intent of the act to prevent secrecy and the right of the secretary of state to have complete information on the registrant's business.[60]

The reversal precipitated legal action to secure Viereck's release and provoked comment in Congress. While McGuire sought an immediate mandate for Viereck's release, Senator William Langer of South Dakota—a recalcitrant isolationist—proposed a Justice Department investigation into Viereck's prosecution and indicated that he would seek to have the government recompense Viereck for the expenses of his trials and for the time he had spent in jail. Senator Burton Wheeler added his approval of the Supreme Court's action; he was glad to note that the court had not been carried away by the "present war hysteria."[61] On March 5, 1943, Viereck was released from jail ("durance vile," in his words). In the meantime, however, Attorney General Francis Biddle announced the government's intention of retrying Viereck with the aim of proving that the very same acts proved in the first trial were committed by him as an agent of a foreign principal.[62]

Within three weeks of his release from jail, the government had a new six-count indictment on file against Viereck. After entering a plea of "decidedly not guilty," he was released by the District Court into the custody of his attorney under $5,000 bond. The new indictment differed from the previous one in that it specifically charged him with being an agent of the German For-

[60] O. R. McGuire to Mrs. G. S. Viereck, October 5, 1942, Viereck MSS; *New York Times*, November 17, 1942, p. 17:4; *Viereck v. U.S.*, 458 U.S. 1–9 (1943).

[61] *Congressional Record*, 78th Cong., 1st Sess., 1943, Part 2, p. 1461; Rogge, *Official German Report*, p. 440.

[62] *New York Times*, March 3, 1943, p. 4:5; March 5, 1943, p. 19:1; March 6, 1943, p. 15:6.

eign Office, with willfully and unlawfully omitting this fact from his registration statements, with using Flanders Hall to publish books originally supplied by the German Information Office in Berlin (an arm of the German Foreign Office), and with disguising the latter fact by the use of aliases.[63]

In preparation for his new trial, Viereck on April 22 took the pauper's oath, claiming that the costs of his previous trial and appeals had left him destitute. Viereck later said that he had spent $35,000 in costs and fines for the first trial and appeals. Actually, he had had additional assets, but sometime prior to his second indictment he turned them over to his wife, who eventually disposed of them in her own manner. Having declared himself a pauper, Viereck was assigned at court expense two attorneys —Leo A. Rover and John J. Wilson.[64]

The second trial got underway on June 21, with Sigfrid Hauck again testifying for the prosecution. However, the proceedings were suddenly halted two days later, and Judge Bolitha Laws declared a mistrial. It had been discovered that one of the jurors was acquainted with a Justice Department attorney. A new jury was then impaneled and the trial was restarted.[65]

In making its case this time the government called a long list of witnesses, each of whom could reveal something about Viereck's activities. For example, Otto Borsdorf, a former receptionist and messenger at the German consulate in New York, testified that he had delivered sealed messages to Viereck, and that the defendant had visited the consulate on an average of two or three times weekly. Prescott Dennett, then a private in the Army but under military detention, described Viereck's role in the origins of the Make Europe Pay War Debts committee. Harry Abramowitz, an acquaintance of Viereck's since 1927 and a long-time bookkeeper for him, said that in 1940 Viereck had received $500

[63] Indictment, *U.S. v. G. S. Viereck*, Criminal No. 71674, D.C. District Court files; *Washington Post*, March 24, 1943; p. 1:2; *New York Times*, March 24, 1943, p. 25:2; March 25, 1943, p. 23:7.

[64] *New York Times*, April 23, 1943, p. 7:2; Viereck, *Men into Beasts*, p. 105.

[65] *Washington Post*, June 22, 1943, p. 6:4; *New York Times*, June 24, 1943, p. 23:7.

per month from the German Library of Information, plus a lump sum of $22,871 that had been entered as "special editorial work on books, literary services, white book, professional services." George Hill, who had already served a term for perjury for denying any connections with Viereck, told of the latter's activities in getting speeches or articles planted in the *Congressional Record* and having them mailed out postage free. Other witnesses brought out the fact that material distributed by the German Information Office (*Informationstelle*) for propaganda purposes could also be found in books published by Flanders Hall. Finally, there was the evidence showing that Viereck's employment by Wirsing was mainly a cover for reporting to Hans Dieckhoff and the German Foreign Office. Included here as prosecution exhibits were the "newsletters" that Viereck had written and mailed in 1940 and 1941.[66]

Viereck was hard put to explain why his reports went to Dieckhoff, but he offered the excuse in later testimony that Dieckhoff's address was used as a possible means of evading British censorship.[67] As already noted, however, Viereck's employment by Wirsing was mainly a disguise for his reporting to Hans Dieckhoff. But in 1943 the evidence for such an arrangement was only circumstantial. It is not clear why Viereck felt it necessary to use Dieckhoff's name at all if Wirsing had agreed to be a go-between, but his decision to do so proved to be a mistake.

Defense counselors faced heavy odds in mounting effective arguments for their client. Since he had dealt with foreign principles whom he had not named in his registration statements, it seemed feasible only to argue that he did not *willfully* or knowingly evade the requirements of the Foreign Agents Registration Act, and that he was a respectable and patriotic citizen, at least in his basic motives, who fully intended to abide by the law. Taking a different approach from that used in the first trial, Viereck's

---

[66] *U.S. v. G. S. Viereck*, Criminal No. 71674, Summary of Testimony of Pvt. Prescott Dennett, Transcript of Proceedings, July 1, 1943, D.C. District Court files; *Washington Post*, July 7, 1943, p. 11:1; *New York Times*, June 26, 1943, p. 1B:8; June 27, 1943, p. 7M:1; June 29, 1943, p. 21:7; July 7, 1943, p. 17:1.
[67] *Washington Post*, July 14, 1943, p. 7B:4.

attorneys placed both Viereck and his wife on the stand. Gretchen, who took the stand on July 12, was described by one reporter as "slight" and "birdlike." She answered questions about their domestic setup and said her husband spent most of his evenings "hard at work." Both sons, she noted, were at that time in North Africa. Then her husband took the witness stand, and he was seen to "fidget nervously" as he asserted that he had never advocated Nazi doctrines for this country, although he recognized National Socialism's value to Germany as a means of restoring her importance and "self-respect." After Viereck warmed up to his subject he could hardly be restrained. He elaborated on all his activities, explaining and glossing his motives at each step. He became so voluble that his own counselors advised him to be less expansive. Viereck himself said a few years later that it may have been a mistake for him to take the stand. He remembered, "I was too glib, too sure of myself, too provocative. Juries don't like that sort of thing."[68]

Viereck's attorneys for their part attempted to defend their client as an American of high ideals who had merely been promoting a cause "dear to his heart—the cause of isolationism." They emphasized, too, that the *Muenchner Neueste Nachrichten* was not a Nazi party organ, and that his work on anti-British, anti-war books and his lobbying was done on his own. They discounted the contention that his connections with Flanders Hall involved him with the German Foreign Office. Most important, they said it was his desire to keep America out of a "bloody war" that led to his work as a lobbyist.[69]

Whatever favorable doubts the defense may have raised in the minds of the jury were probably dispelled in part by the devastating cross-examination that began on July 14. This interrogation disclosed that in the fall of 1939 Viereck had written to Dieckhoff that the German government should issue a group of official publications to counteract British propaganda in the United States, and that he suggested writings dealing with topics such as British policy in India and Palestine, and English slums.

[68] Ibid.; *Washington Post*, July 13, 1943, p. 5:1; Viereck, *Men into Beasts*, p. 114.

[69] *Washington Post*, July 13, 1943, p. 5:1.

The German Foreign Office subsequently sent pamphlets and books to the German Library of Information on these subjects; it was these texts that Viereck edited and translated for publication by Flanders Hall. Viereck had also suggested that Dieckhoff head a committee which would "send the right things" to "all English-speaking countries."[70] Defense counsellors were also confronted by testimony from Sigurd Schultz, former Berlin correspondent for the *Chicago Tribune*, who said that Viereck had created consternation among American correspondents at the Nazi rally in Nuremberg in 1938 with his vocal indorsement of German policy in Czechoslovakia. Moreover, the prosecution quoted damaging phrases from his book, *Spreading Germs of Hate*, and at one point Viereck rose halfway out of his chair to protest loudly against the prosecution's repeated use of these phrases. This, he declared, was an attempt to "trip him" into admitting that he "circumvented the law." In response to other charges, he could only keep reiterating that his activities as a publicist were inspired by "purely patriotic motives as an American citizen," and that he still endorsed the concept of "America for Americans and Europe for Europeans."[71]

The case finally went to the jury on July 16. The judge, in his charge to them, carefully avoided repeating the mistake in the previous trial by stating that the defendant was required to name only those activities performed in behalf of the foreign principals for whom he had registered. The other issue, of course, was whether Viereck had named all the foreign principals for whom he had worked. It was evidently difficult for the jury to agree on Viereck's guilt on all six counts. The jurors were out for nearly eight and one-half hours before they returned with what might have been a predictable guilty verdict on all counts. As the verdict was announced, Viereck appeared impassive, while his wife sat in "stricken silence, her eyes downcast." The judge ruled that the defendant must return forthwith to his jail cell.[72] Five months of

[70] *Washington Post*, July 14, 1943, p. 10:1, and July 15, 1943, p. 10:1; Rogge, *Official German Report*, p. 47.

[71] *Washington Post*, July 15, 1943, p. 10:1.

[72] *Washington Post*, July 17, 1943, p. 1:2; *New York Times*, July 17, 1943, p. 15:6.

strained freedom were over. Seemingly resigned to his fate, Viereck returned to his "second home" in the District of Columbia jail.

Sentencing was set for July 31, and on that date Viereck again availed himself of the opportunity to present a statement in his behalf. He thanked the judge for his fairness in conducting the trial, and then he repeated the old canards about being victimized by war psychosis and circumstantial evidence "buttressed by perjury" (which he had alleged of one witness) and deliberate exaggeration on the part of several witnesses. He complained of the year he had already spent in prison because of "judicial errors." Washington's farewell address, he reiterated, was the "fixed star" in his political firmament. He sounded more credible when he added, "If I had known that I forfeited my right to participate in American politics by my work for the Munich newspaper and Library of Information, I would not have accepted any such contracts, no matter how lucrative." He admitted that "emotionally" he had favored Germany "against any country except the United States," but America's interest, he said, had always been first with him. In defending his high salaries as a publicity agent, he claimed they were not out of line with his previous earnings and that the "abuse and literary boycotts" he faced working for an unpopular cause actually made him underpaid. He concluded by promising to continue the battle for his good name and for the "most precious of the Four Freedoms—Freedom of Speech," and by again expressing confidence that he would ultimately be justified by the high court of history.[73]

Judge Laws did not inflict the maximum sentence, which would have been twelve years in prison and a $6,000 fine. Instead, he sentenced Viereck to a prison term of one to five years, whereupon the defense attorneys filed another appeal to higher courts. Viereck also took the unusual liberty of writing a letter to Judge Laws, in which he continued to argue that his conviction was a miscarriage of justice. He reiterated his charge that the testimony of Sanford Griffith was untrue. Griffith had claimed he overheard

[73] G. S. Viereck, "Statement before Sentencing," July 31, 1943, Viereck MSS.

Viereck at a meeting of the Overseas Press Club, saying that the German government was prepared to "spend plenty of money" to get accurate analyses of American public opinion polls and that he could obtain and had obtained money from the German embassy. Viereck also alleged that a senator, whom he later identified as Gerald Nye, had volunteered to take the stand for him to refute some testimony given against him, but that for "sound technical reasons" his defense counselors did not avail themselves of the offer. Finally, he complained that the new sentence actually left him with three months more to serve than he had left of the first sentence. "Canaries," he said, "may thrive in cages, not songsters like myself," and to understand his feelings, the judge should read his poem "Bastille, D.C."[74]

The gist of Viereck's argument to the Court of Appeals was that his credibility as a witness had been improperly attacked. However, as one might suspect, the appeal was denied. It was then taken to the Supreme Court, which on March 27, 1944, announced its refusal to review the case.[75] All avenues for legal redress were exhausted. The best he could hope for was parole, commutation, or reprieve. He would subsequently try these avenues, but without success, partly because he had become involved in still another trial—the so-called sedition trial of 1944.

Even while Viereck was pursuing the reversal of his conviction in 1942 for violating the Foreign Agents Registration Act, he was indicted for violating yet another law. On July 21, 1942, the Washington, D.C., grand jury which had indicted him on the earlier charge now grouped him with twenty-seven others and formally accused them of violating the sedition and conspiracy sections of the Sedition Act of June 28, 1940, called the Smith Act. The indictment charged that these individuals had "conspired, combined, confederated and agreed together to commit acts prohibited by Section 9 of Title 18, U. S. Code (Smith Act)

[74] *New York Times*, August 1, 1943, p. 1:2; *Washington Post*, July 16, 1943, p. 9:1; G. S. Viereck to Bolitha Laws (copy), n.d., Viereck MSS.
[75] *U.S. v. Viereck*, No. 8578, U. S. Court of Appeals, D.C., 1944, *Federal Reporter*, 2d Series, Vol. 139, f. 2d, pp. 847–52; *New York Times*, January 11, 1944, p. 21:1; March 28, 1944, p. 9:1.

in that they with intent to interfere with, impair and influence the loyalty, morale and discipline of the military and naval forces of the United States would advise, counsel, urge and cause insubordination, disloyalty, mutiny and refusal of duty by members of the armed forces," and distributed written and printed matter to the same end. As to Viereck's part in this alleged conspiracy, the grand jury cited his role in organizing and using the Make Europe Pay War Debts committee and the Flanders Hall publishing firm as outlets for distributing "seditious" literature.[76]

With this case it would appear that the government—represented largely in the person of William Power Maloney, who had drawn up the indictment—was trying to fight the war at home with all weapons at its command, including dubious legal prosecutions. In fact, in trying to tie into a conspiracy this motley group of sometime Nazi or Japanese sympathizers, the government took on a challenge that it never successfully resolved. The evidence for prosecuting the indictment was so inadequate that the government brought no one to trial under it. Instead, a second indictment was drawn up on January 4, 1943, which retained the previous charges but traced the conspiracy back to January, 1933, and added five new defendants. Soon thereafter, the District Court sustained a demurrer and dismissed the first count of the second indictment, ruling that charges relating to overt acts occurring prior to December 8, 1941, would have to be eliminated.[77]

The second indictment also brought more protests from a few isolationist senators on Capitol Hill, who claimed that the sedition defendants were really under fire for having been isolationists. These critics included Senators Burton Wheeler, Gerald Nye, and Robert Taft, and Congressman Hamilton Fish, Jr., and Clare Hoffman. With some of their colleagues they questioned the legality of the continuous sittings of the grand jury and the nature of alleged evidence, and they complained of reported advance disclosure of testimony presented in the grand jury room. In the wake of these grumblings, the Justice Department replaced

[76] Indictment, *U.S. v. Winrod, et al.*, 1942, copy in Viereck MSS.
[77] Heinz Eulau, "Sedition Trials: 1944," *New Republic*, March 13, 1944, pp. 337–39; *Chicago Tribune*, October 12, 1942 (Graphic Sect.), pp. 5, 14.

prosecutor William P. Maloney with Oetje John Rogge in February, 1943.[78]

Meanwhile, Viereck and other defendants attempted to have the indictments invalidated on grounds of insufficient evidence and of the alleged unconstitutionality of the Smith Act on which they were based. Such efforts were to no avail. Nevertheless, the Justice Department still refrained from attempting to prosecute under the second indictment, and instead grand jury proceedings were reopened in October, 1943, resulting in the drawing up of a third indictment which excluded twelve names on the previous instrument adding eight new ones. Technically, all three indictments remained in force, but it was the third one which finally was made the basis of a trial that began on April 17, 1944. The new instrument included German-American Bund members for the first time—five of them—and it also named thirty-five organizations and forty-two publications as co-conspirators with the defendants.[79]

Viereck was transferred from the Atlanta federal prison to the District of Columbia jail in early 1944 to stand trial with the other twenty-nine defendants. The substance of the charge remained the same: that these individuals conspired to undermine the morale and discipline of the armed forces. The phrasing of the indictment differed from that of its predecessors, however, in that Rogge deemed it wise to emphasize criminal intent by describing the program of the Nazi party as aimed at destroying democracy (which included undermining the morale of America's armed forces), and then accusing the defendants of having "joined in this movement" and having actively cooperated with each other and with members and leaders of the Nazi party to accomplish the party's objectives in the United States. The suc-

[78] *New York Times,* February 7, 1943, p. 34:6; "Trial of the Viereckites," *New Republic,* January 4, 1943, p. 21.

[79] *U.S.* v. *Winrod, et al.,* Plea in Abatement by G. S. Viereck, January 25, 1943; *U.S.* v. *Winrod, et al.,* Demurrer by G. S. Viereck, February 5, 1943; *U.S.* v. *Joseph McWilliams, et al.,* Appendix to Appellant's Brief, U.S. Court of Appeals, D.C., No. 9438, p. 15; Maximilian St. George and Lawrence Dennis, *A Trial on Trial; The Great Sedition Trial of 1944* (Washington: National Civil Rights Committee, 1946), pp. 114–21, 181, 437–38.

ceeding statement in the indictment accused these individuals of directly violating sections one and three of the Smith Act since its enactment on June 28, 1940. Rogge explained several years later that his intention was to preserve the rights of the First Amendment by not charging the defendants with violating the "advocacy" provisions of the act. Instead, he used only those provisions outlawing conspiracies to cause military insubordination or to counsel the same by use of printed material, and he "narrowed" the application of those provisions by seeking to indict only those who in addition had "some form of Nazi connections."[80]

The sedition trial finally got underway in the last week of April, 1944. From the beginning it bore the earmarks of a circus. The thirty defendants were represented by twenty-two lawyers who saw fit from the start to disrupt the proceedings by "objecting, concurring, complaining," as one writer put it.[81] Another periodical referred to the defendants as a "grab bag" united only by "hatred and contempt of the Roosevelt administration, of Jews and Communists, and anyone else who disagreed with them." They argued, bickered, and wrangled with Rogge. When one made a motion it was sometimes repeated by the others in turn. One such motion was made to postpone the trial until depositions would be taken from Hitler, Goering, and Goebbels.[82] It is not known to what extent Viereck took part in such shenanigans, but it is probable that his courtroom courtesy was somewhat better than the average. A few years afterward, Viereck said, "We were not all crackpots, although there were some mavericks and soreheads among us."[83]

Beyond the character and manners of the defendants, there was the legal predicament of trying to prove a conspiracy by a group in which many individuals had not had personal contacts with the others accused of conspiring with them. Viereck himself claimed that he knew only two of the other defendants, and one of them he had not seen for thirty years. In a subsequent report

[80] Rogge, *Official German Report*, p. 174.
[81] *Time*, May 1, 1944, p. 17.
[82] *Newsweek*, May 1, 1944, p. 34.
[83] Viereck, *Men into Beasts*, p. 131.

on the trial, prosecutor Rogge mentioned only that Viereck had direct, personal conversations with Lawrence Dennis when both were involved with Friedrich Auhagen's American Fellowship Forum. In his opening statement to the jury on May 17, Rogge indicated that the charge of conspiracy would be based primarily on the connections of the defendants with officials of the German government and with leaders of the Nazi party in Germany.[84] Yet, if this accusation could be proved true of their activities after Germany and the United States had declared war on each other, the more proper charge would have been treason.

It is true that all of the defendants had published articles or books or made statements and established personal contacts which typed them as apologists (and most of them as outright advocates) of Nazi or fascist policies, at least until Pearl Harbor. To this extent they had been connected with a movement to destroy democratic institutions. But the government was unable to prove either that they had a common program or that they made deliberate efforts to counsel insubordination among American military personnel. It was inevitable, of course, that some of the literature "had turned up at army posts," as Rogge later phrased it, and this fact offered some basis for the prosecution's contentions.[85] Yet this fact was not in itself evidence of a conspiracy. The prosecution could also show that most of the defendants had "connections" with fascists in foreign countries outside Germany, but one may question whether an exchange of correspondence, a personal meeting, or the procurement of literature from such sources constitutes evidence of a conspiracy when objective proof of intent or of action is lacking.

Furthermore, the prospect of dispensing justice in a courtroom crowded with defiant defendants and defense lawyers grew dimmer as the weeks passed. By August 28, when a two-week adjournment was ordered for vacation, one of the defendants had died, and two had been granted motions of severance because of obstreperous conduct. Six defense lawyers and one defendant serving as his own counsel had been fined a total of $1,000 for

[84] Rogge, *Official German Report*, p. 182; St. George and Dennis, *Trial on Trial*, p. 125.
[85] Rogge, *Official German Report*, pp. 174, 430.

contempt of court. One lawyer had in fact been barred from the courtroom. Some of the defendants had to be persuaded by their counselors to stop wearing grotesque false faces and signs reading "I am a Spy."[86] One is tempted to contrast the liberties of these defendants with the drumhead proceedings going on about the same time in Germany in which the defendants—accused of complicity in the plot against Hitler—were being vilified and humiliated, deprived of their freedom and dignity, all at the behest of dictatorial and brutal Nazi judges. Yet there was reason for these sedition defendants to feel that they had been unjustly indicted and that American legal traditions were being violated. One tradition, that of a speedy trial, proved impossible to fulfill—and, in fact, seemed to be precluded by the large number being tried together.

Nevertheless, determined to carry out the mandate of the indictment, the prosecution continued to present its evidence as the trial plodded on in the fall of 1944. Proceedings came to an abrupt halt when Chief Justice Eicher, who had been presiding, died suddenly in November. As might be expected, only one of the twenty-six defendants agreed to the trial continuing with another judge. The result was the declaration of a mistrial. By that time there already had been about 500 mistrial motions made by defense counsel. A trial transcript of nearly 18,000 pages had been compiled, but only thirty-nine out of a possible hundred witnesses had been heard. Also, barely more than 1,000 of the 4,000 prospective exhibits had been entered into evidence. One can only imagine how long a retrial might have taken. In answer to motions for retrial or dismissal, the Justice Department on March 1, 1945, told the District Court that it did not oppose a speedy trial and suggested that a trial date be set. However, the court could not do so since it already had 480 criminal cases pending. At the same time, the government remained adamant that the case should be tried. Because of the crowded court calendar, no further trial action was taken in 1945.[87]

[86] *Time*, August 28, 1944, p. 15.
[87] *U.S.* v. *McWilliams, et al.,* U.S. Court of Appeals, D.C., *Federal Reporter*, No. 163, 2d Series, p. 697; *Newsweek*, December 11, 1944, p.

By early 1946 the District Court appeared ready to act on pending motions to dismiss the indictment. In the meantime, several appeals by Viereck for parole or clemency had been rejected, and his chances of obtaining parole were virtually nil as long as other indictments remained in force against him. In late February, 1946, Rogge informed the attorney general that certain Supreme Court decisions in 1944 and 1945 (*Hartzel* v. *U.S.*, *Keegan* v. *U.S.*, and *Baumgartner* v. *U.S.*), in which convictions had been reversed on violation of Smith Act and Selective Service Act provisions, led him to believe that the Supreme Court would act similarly on any conviction in the pending sedition trial. At the same time he expressed his belief that "international Fascism" was not dead. Despite his misgivings, he agreed at the attorney general's bidding to interrogate German officials and investigate records having a bearing on the sedition case. While this investigation was being conducted in the spring and summer of 1946, the District Court postponed motions for dismissal of the case.[88]

Finally, on September 17, the attorney general received the report on the European inquiry.[89] It furnished additional evidence relevant to the case, and Rogge was more convinced than ever that the fascist threat to democracy was far from over. Nevertheless, he repeated his recommendation that the government *nolle prosequi* all three sedition indictments "because it is difficult in this country under Supreme Court decisions to be guilty of sedition." On September 20 Rogge expressed the same opinion before the court, but the attorney general subsequently overruled his special assistant and replaced him with another prosecuting attorney, Theron Caudle. The government thereupon requested the court to set a trial date, but on December 2, 1946, the District Court ruled to dismiss the indictments. The Justice Department appealed this decision but lost on a two-to-one ruling by the Cir-

44; *U.S.* v. *McWilliams, et al.*, Appendix to Appellant's Brief, U.S. Court of Appeals, D.C., No. 9438, pp. 16–17.

[88] Rogge, *Official German Report*, pp. 407, 431–32; *U.S.* v. *McWilliams, et al.*, U.S. Court of Appeals for D.C., *Federal Reporter*, No. 163, 2d Series, p. 698.

[89] Report transcribed verbatim in Rogge, *Official German Report*, pp. 407–47.

cuit Court of Appeals laid down on June 30, 1947. The delays in retrying the case and the doubts expressed by Rogge on the probability of sustaining a conviction were instrumental in the court's ruling.[90] Thus came to an end what must have been the most drawn-out and bizarre indictment and aborted trial in American legal history.

The final dismissal of the sedition case came as an anticlimax for Viereck, who was given his freedom in May, 1947. To be sure, these indictments had hung over his head for several years and may have been instrumental in preventing parole on the sentence he was serving. However, the trial had not been the inconvenience for him that it had been for the other defendants, most of whom had to live on meager earnings while they resided in Washington during the proceedings. At least one defendant was known to have slept on park benches at night. In the absence of legal conviction, such inconvenience may have served its purpose as a substitute punishment. Nevertheless, for Viereck the trial meant an assignment to better quarters in the District of Columbia jail,[91] a move that gave him some relief from the previous routine. It could not, however, offset other setbacks and tragedies, especially the death of his younger son in battle while the sedition trial was in progress. Indeed, his five years in prison brought many trials and few triumphs.

Predictably, these events ruined Viereck's reputation beyond repair, and they even more obviously brought to a close his career as a pro-German propagandist. Never again could he play the role nor enjoy the respect that had made him a prominent, if sometimes notorious, figure in the years between 1914 and 1942.

[90] Ibid., p. 439; *U.S.* v. *McWilliams, et al., Federal Reporter*, No. 163, 2d Series, pp. 698–99.
[91] See Viereck, *Men into Beasts*, p. 137.

Viereck lived on until March, 1962, when he died of a cerebral hemorrhage. He was not able to effect a reconciliation with his wife, who had liquidated most of their remaining assets and turned the proceeds over to Jewish and Catholic charities.[1] Poorer but wiser from his prison experience, Viereck expressed regret, although with reservations, over his misjudgment of the Nazis.[2] Nonetheless, in the 1950's he could still speak of the "travesty of Nuremberg" and claim friendship with some individuals connected with extreme right-wing groups. But he himself avoided membership in any of these groups, and he criticized a couple of his acquaintances for flirting with anti-Semitism.[3] Some of his old Jewish friends like Ludwig Lewisohn and Elmer Gertz resumed friendly, if guarded, relations.

Viereck's main ambition was to resume a literary career. He succeeded in part. He wrote a novel and a book of memoirs based on his prison experience, as well as another novel reminiscent of the Wandering Jew theme.[4] His two novels fared poorly on the market, but his memoirs, sensationalized somewhat by the title *Men into Beasts*, went through two editions totaling about a half million copies. He also wrote a number of poems in prison but

[1] Interview, Niel M. Johnson with Elmer Gertz, March 12, 1966.

[2] Viereck, *Men into Beasts*, p. 60.

[3] G. S. Viereck to H. Keith Thompson, May 5, 1953, Viereck MSS; G. S. Viereck to Edward Fleckenstein, May 5, 1953, Gertz MSS.

[4] George S. Viereck, *All Things Human* (London: Duckworth, 1950); Viereck, *Men into Beasts*; George S. Viereck, *Gloria: A Novel* (London: Duckworth, 1952). The latter novel was printed in the United States as *The Nude in the Mirror* (New York: Woodford Press, 1953).

failed in attempts to get them published. He distributed at his own expense in 1955 an elegy, *The Bankrupt,* that expressed dismay over the development and use of the atomic bomb and over the alleged bankruptcy of Christianity and western civilization.[5] The poem was put on display at the Hiroshima memorial museum by a Japanese writer who had received a copy.[6]

In early 1959 his son Peter took him into his home in Hadley, Massachusetts. There was at least a partial reconciliation, as Peter recalls that his father confessed regret over his "Nazi interlude" and that he finally admitted the justice of Peter's thesis in his book on Nazism.[7] But it is doubtful he ever fully repented. He had maintained a steady refrain of self-justification in the decade after his release from prison, and he seemed unable by temperament or character to admit that he had committed any vile or wrongful deeds. There seemed to be no basic change from the attitude reflected in the following lines that he had written in 1930 when he finally discovered that President Wilson was not the deliberate malefactor he had thought him to be:

> Now, with unfolding eyes, we see
> The paradox of every fight,
> That both are wrong and both are right,
> That friend is foe, and foe is friend,
> And nothing matters in the end.[8]

It is appropriate at this point to summarize the main ideas presented in this study and draw conclusions from them. One of the major objectives has been to describe how Viereck interpreted Germany to America. According to Viereck's portrayal, Germany was a land that had earned a rightful place by 1914 as a dominant power in Europe and as an enviable model of national energy and pride. He pictured Germany as an innocent victim of Anglo-

[5] George S. Viereck, *The Bankrupt* (Chicago: Union Press, 1955), manuscript in Viereck MSS.

[6] Michihiko Hachiya to G. S. Viereck, September 23, 1955, Viereck MSS; Viereck, *The Bankrupt,* p. 1.

[7] Peter Viereck to Niel M. Johnson, June 21, 1967. Peter Viereck's *Metapolitics* (1941) condemned Nazism as a product of an irrational "steel romanticism."

[8] G. S. Viereck, *My Flesh and Blood* (New York: H. Liveright, 1931), p. 305.

French envy and vengefulness at the outset of World War I and held that military necessity justified her attack on Belgium and on merchant ships on the high seas. He passed off the war-atrocity stories as "lies" (many of them were) and claimed their circulation was enhanced by British control of most news from Europe and by the machinations of clever British propagandists in the United States. Germany, he noted, had no plans to threaten the security of the United States nor to violate the Monroe Doctrine —that is, until the Zimmerman telegram undercut this particular argument. Until March, 1917, Viereck presented an image of Germany quite like that offered by other pro-German publicists, including the bulk of the German-language press in America.

Viereck likewise followed most other pro-German editors in only slowly altering the German image after April, 1917. Indeed, it was not until the closing months of the war that he was able to criticize the German government for its "militarist" leadership and its rule by a "clique." But never did he join in the anti-German tirades that depicted the Kaiser as the "Beast of Berlin" and the German soldier as a "Hun." Nor did he change his rhetoric to extol the virtues of England or France.

Viereck's most vivid rhetoric was reserved for his descriptions of Germany caught in the crises of the early 1920's. Here he presented a picture of Germany falsely accused of war guilt and starved and ravaged by her occupying enemies, chiefly France. The result was a Germany committed to future revenge and expansion. But the reader is left with a feeling that this mood was only temporary, and Viereck did not exploit this theme of "irredentism" or the lust for lost territory again until 1933. Germany was also a country experimenting with republican government, which Viereck found acceptable but not necessarily final. He found virtue in the evidence of right-wing nationalist strength (as in the election of Marshal Paul Hindenburg to the presidency in 1926), and he presented evidence of pro-Kaiser feelings, but he did not show Germany afflicted with "Kaiserism," nor did he speculate on the probability of a return to power by the Hohenzollerns. His image of the Kaiser was that of a wise and kind elder statesman devoted to Germany's interests above his own. In brief, during the 1920's he projected Germany as a nation fired by resentment in the early 1920's but seemingly resigned to her fate by the latter half of the decade and no longer a disturbing force in Europe. It is perhaps a tribute to Viereck's "Americanism" that while he could register the intense feelings of German nationalism in the early 1920's he reflected a general American complacency about the viability and endurance of the German republic in the latter half of the decade. But obviously Americans should have paid more attention to his earlier clues about the strength of German "irredentism."

This irredentism came to the fore in the 1930's. The Nazi regime excited in Viereck those feelings that had lain dormant for several years, and he again accepted a role that he had adopted in 1914—that of paid publicist for a beleaguered ultranationalist German government. Viereck seemed convinced that Nazism was the old German nationalism in new garb. This feeling offered him a rationalization for promoting its policies, and his task was made easier by the fact that many Americans had come to accept the revisionist idea that German nationalism had not been a real threat to American security in 1917. In a sense this allowed for more "objectivity" in the American press, but again, as in 1915 with the sinking of the *Lusitania*, Germany's leaders and their apologists found it more and more difficult to allay American discomfort with obvious Nazi callousness—particularly toward German Jews and liberals. Viereck's favorite counterthemes were that the German revolution had been relatively bloodless as well as popular, that anti-Semitism was not an essential ingredient of Nazism, and that Hitler's regime had saved Germany from the threat of Bolshevik revolution. These arguments appear to have been common among American pro-Nazis, except that anti-Semitism was espoused by most of them.

As late as 1938 he was able to predict and justify in *Liberty* magazine Hitler's anticipated annexation of the Sudetenland as a rectification of the "errors" of Versailles. Although he criticized the Nazis for *Kristallnacht*, he implied that Hitler was a decent man who would respond to world opinion. But this episode, followed by the annexation of the non-German areas of Czechoslovakia in early 1939, induced *Liberty* to sever its ties with Viereck when he still refused to condemn Nazi policies or the work of native fascists in America. After September, 1939, his job was not so much that of putting a gloss on Germany's fallen image as it was that of supporting the isolationist movement to keep the United States out of a war against Germany. A part of this program was to blacken Britain's image as much as possible—a technique that was not very successful in light of increasing American sympathy for Great Britain in 1940.

In addition to his work as a publicist for pro-Germanism in America, Viereck undertook in 1915 to influence American political policy in a more direct manner. He took an active, though not outstanding, part in the embargo campaigns of 1915, and he joined other German-American leaders in a meeting with the chairman of the Senate's Foreign Relations Committee in 1916. He likewise used his journal to endorse a series of presidential candidates between 1912 and 1924, only one of whom (Harding) was successful in winning the office. In both the 1920's and 1930's he established personal contacts with a group of congressmen that shared his anti-British, pro-isolationist and pro-German views, exchanging articles and information with them. His major successes came in 1939 and 1940, when he assisted in setting up an isolationist committee and in making extensive use of the congressional frank to disseminate material of an anti-British, pro-isolationist nature. He was not successful, however, in his attempts to influence executive policies. He failed to persuade President Harding to appoint German-Americans to high office, and he did not succeed in gaining entree to President Franklin Roosevelt, whom he hoped to advise on European affairs.

Another problem to be dealt with is Viereck's dual loyalties. It has been contended that he felt special ties of allegiance to Germany but that his primary loyalty was to America. As early as 1909, in his report on his first return-trip to Germany, he made it clear that he preferred America to Europe, even to Germany, despite the latter's attractions. It is also pertinent to note that his literary models were English and American, not German. Moreover, unlike the militant pan-Germans before World War I, he did not promote anti-Semitic racial ideas, nor did he feel that Germany should intrude on American interests in the western hemisphere. Moreover, he showed little interest at that time in

Germany's attempts to extend her economic hegemony into southeastern Europe and the Middle East. He did not expressly call for German supremacy over England outside the European continent, but he probably would have willingly accepted Germany's hegemony in the eastern hemisphere while America dominated the western. Although pro-German, Viereck was not a pan-German; he could claim that he was always for "America First."

Next to the "America First" theme was that of "Fair Play" for Germany. With the use of this slogan, he implied that Germany had less chance of receiving a fair hearing in the American press or legislative halls than did Britain or France. Therefore, he could argue that he was doing something worthy and commendable—giving a hearing to a country that was not properly appreciated or understood by most Americans. Virtually all observers agree that on the eve of World War I popular sentiment favored England over Germany, although it is also conceded that most Americans did not think much about world affairs at all in that period. The majority of observers also agree that Germany at that time did not intend to challenge American dominance in the western hemisphere. Consequently, it was plausible to argue that Germany deserved a fair hearing and that a German victory in 1915 and 1916 would not have threatened American security.

What Viereck did not grapple with effectively was the question of how German ideals and values fit in with those of the United States. To his advantage there were present a growing distaste for puritanism in American life (something associated with the Anglo-Saxon legacy), an expansion of university education on the German model, a desire for more social-welfare legislation already pioneered by Germany, and a more positive role for the state in the nation's economy. Viereck pointed to these things as German contributions to western culture. Still, one can argue that these trends were logical responses to industrialism and not necessarily a legacy of Germanism. Moreover, Americans could hardly fail to recognize the resemblance between German Kaiserism and the Old World autocracy against which they had rebelled over a century earlier. The enthusiasm with which Americans wanted to "hang the Kaiser" in 1917–18 appears indicative of this. In short, Viereck did not appreciate the depth of the democratic mystique in America and the difficulty one could expect in convincing Americans that they had anything useful to learn about political ideals and practices from the German example. His political judgment was warped mainly by his personalist and elitist assumptions, as well as by his aesthetic disregard for the mechanisms of checks and balances of power.

Later Viereck would defend his pro-Germanism not only as just but also as "instinctual." He still claimed his deepest loyalty was to his "chosen mate," America, but he could not deny the instinctive feelings for his mother country. Through such aesthetic metaphors, he could continue to rationalize his support for a regime whose sins had become more flagrant. What he did not account for was the fact that many German-born Americans did not feel as he did; nor did he explain why Americans of non-German descent, such as Father Couglin or Joseph McWilliams, also felt constrained to defend German Nazism. Yet he was reaching closer to the truth when he began to put the emphasis on the instinctual rather than the logical, since the issue actually depended on the validity of his premises and definitions rather than the rationality of his method.

Also relevant to his defense of dual loyalties was his belief in the Freudian principles of the supremacy of unconsciously inspired emotions and of the ambivalence of the psyche. In accordance with the first principle, he could honestly believe that all men rationalize their emotions, that feeling—not rationality—is the *summum bonum*. This fit with his aesthetic scale of values and made it possible for him to accept unanalytically his emotional attachment to Germany. The idea of ambivalence as an inherent part of the human personality seemed to allow him to accept the contradictions of his position and the contrary feelings and doubts that he expressed—a rare occurrence until the eve of World War II.

What seemed not to occur to him was the possibility of genuine neutrality; for all his isolationism, he was never neutral in his sympathies. Unlike many American isolationists who could be anti-British without being pro-German, Viereck accepted these attitudes as two sides of one coin. He operated from the premise that to be pro-American one must also be pro-German and anti-British. Yet one needed only to be anti-British, as were the Irish-Americans, to have merited Viereck's attention and support. One may argue from hindsight that there was no genuinely neutral course which America could have followed in 1914–16 or 1939–41, because to embargo trade, for instance, would have been indirectly beneficial to Germany in both instances. Viereck seemed to recognize this, and his attempts to prevent American economic or military intervention in Europe were actually intended to weaken Britain and France.

Our final task is to assess the significance of Viereck's career as a publicist and apologist for German causes and to suggest an explanation for his motives and rationalizations. In judging his significance, one must attempt to measure his success as a propagandist. If one rates him by his ability to get his views presented to a wide public, then he appears to have been at least moderately successful. Particularly notable was the relatively large circulation he achieved in the early phases of World War I with his weekly journal. Similarly, in the mid-1920's, even though his most militant rhetoric did not find its way much beyond the small audience of his monthly journal, he was able to broach many of his views to a broad public through the Hearst newspaper chain. Again, after 1930, he obtained nationwide attention for his opinions by contributing regularly to the mass-circulated *Liberty* magazine. Moreover, he was successful in building up the circulation of *Facts in Review* and in writing and distributing material to thousands of Americans via the congressional franking privilege. In his use of this latter technique, he was the most successful of those who registered as agents of a German principal. And when one considers the estimates of him made by journalists, government officials, and historians—judgments that place him foremost among pro-German publicists and apologists—it becomes apparent that he was a talented writer and prominent partisan for the causes he espoused.

Yet, if one measures his success by the degree to which his views were accepted by the public and its leaders, he would have to be labeled a failure. As an early example, he failed to convince the American people that the German invasion of Belgium was justified, or that reports of German atrocities in that country were complete fabrications. Subsequently, he could not persuade them to forgive and forget the *Lusitania* disaster, nor, when subjected to submarine warfare, to refrain from entering the war. Still later, he was unable to win much sympathy for a Nazi regime run so obviously by an amoral, power-worshipping clique, nor could he keep America out of war in 1941, or make credible his wartime pose as a martyr. For a time, to be sure, as disillusionment with World War I set in and isolationist and anti-British sentiment swelled, he found himself in tune with American public opinion and was able to contribute something to revising the history of World War I and strengthening noninterventionist policies. But this was more by accident than design. Other figures and leaders, operating from different motives and with different value systems, did much more to create the isolationist mood; once developments abroad had changed that mood, Viereck and a hard core of like-minded individuals found themselves isolated and ineffective.

If Viereck was ineffective in changing American opinion, this was still not always apparent at the time, at least not to the German officials who expressed confidence in his ability by providing him with funds or salaries for projects that he himself had largely instigated. His launching and able guidance of *The Fatherland* in 1914 had done much to establish his reputation as an eloquent spokesman for pro-German policies, and on the basis of this and his later accomplishments he seems to have had little trouble "making deals" with the German tourist office in 1933 or with Foreign Office officials in 1939 and 1940, "deals" that by 1941 were providing him with a generous salary. There were, to be sure, some German officials who doubted that Germany was getting her money's worth. This was true, for example, of the German ambassador to the United States in 1916, and of Herbert von Strempel, the financial officer for the German embassy in the 1930's. The latter believed that Lawrence Dennis was the best American apologist for the Nazis.[9] But people like Heinrich Albert and Hans Dieckhoff believed strongly in Viereck's abilities,

[9] Rogge, *Official German Report*, pp. 130, 136, 184–86.

and they helped make him a key figure in Germany's propaganda efforts.

Although Dieckhoff believed that Viereck was valuable to Germany as an analyst of American public opinion, what the latter offered in this respect seemed to have little or no effect on German behavior. Answering a query in 1969, Giselher Wirsing asserted that he was "absolutely sure" that Viereck's ideas and proposals had "no impact whatsoever" on official German policy. The Americans, he suggested, had greatly exaggerated his importance to Germany.[10] He is probably correct. Hitler, who after all made the major decisions, seemed to operate from a rigid stereotype about the United States; like the Kaiser before him, he discounted the hazard of antagonizing the American public and its government. He apparently paid little heed to analysts of American public opinion.[11]

It seems safe to conclude, then, that Viereck's direct influence on public policy, either of the United States or of Germany, was very slight. He could be credited only with playing some part in fostering American noninterventionism, with occupying a prominent place among those writers and publicists who promoted this cause, and with articulating the pro-German case in the United States.

His inability to make an appreciable impact on political policy stemmed in part from the fact that the German-Americans did not constitute a single political entity. They in fact had not formed a unified political bloc since the Civil War era when, under the leadership of the '48ers, they solidly backed abolitionism and the cause of the Union.[12] In 1912 the majority of Viereck's readers favored the progressivism of Theodore Roosevelt, but none of the three candidates seemed to think it necessary or feasible to

[10] Giselher Wirsing to Niel M. Johnson, August 5, 1969.

[11] Hitler's distorted and fixed view of America is documented in Gerhard L. Weinberg, "Hitler's Image of the United States," *American Historical Review* LXIX (July, 1964): 1006–21, and in Hans L. Trefousse, "Failure of German Intelligence in the United States, 1935–1945," *Mississippi Valley Historical Review* XLII (June, 1955): 84–100.

[12] Joachim Remak, " 'Friends of the New Germany:' The Bund and German-American Relations," *Journal of Modern History* XXIX (March, 1957): 41.

make a special appeal to Americans of German descent. On other issues, German-American influence was inadequate to bring about an embargo in 1915, and a year later the German-American vote was split between the two chief candidates despite the anti-Wilson position of the German-American press. Viereck made a well-publicized attempt to swing his ethnic brethren behind Harding in 1920, but they and many other Americans seeking normalcy hardly needed such goading. Moreover, it was apparent that prestigious German-Americans like Charles Nagel did not want to become identified with "hyphen politics."

Nagel's reaction illustrated the unpopularity of any "-ism" except "Americanism" in the 1920's. This general antipathy to and failure of "hyphenism" was evident, too, in such phenomena as the immigration restrictions, the adoption of nationwide prohibition (against the wishes of most German-Americans), and the revival of the Ku Klux Klan. But probably equally important in blunting ethnic consciousness was the mood of commercialism; Viereck's comments about the "silk-stocking" element gave evidence that making money and enjoying the products of a burgeoning economy were preoccupations with middle-class German-Americans as they were for their compatriots.

The failure of La Follette in 1924 also represented a failure for pro-Germanism in that, even with the help of the Steuben Society, he was unable to generate a genuine threat to either major party. Still, La Follette's isolationism and revisionism became the popular attitude by the end of the decade. But the more friendly feeling toward Germany did not include any tendency for the public to demand the restoration of Germany's "lost" territories. Viereck's pro-Germanism went further—too far for most Americans—in its pro-nationalist and irredentist assumptions.

Pro-Germanism in America encountered other obstacles in the 1930's, beyond the repulsiveness of the Hitler regime. One was the German-American Bund, which was officially divorced from any German sponsorship, but which in the eyes of many was an arm of Germany's Nazi Party.[13] The Bundists promoted this impression by their penchant for wearing Nazi-like uniforms and

[13] Ibid.

for indulging in arrogant and storm-trooper type antics. Their behavior undoubtedly did more harm than good to the cause of
pro-Germanism in America, and Viereck was well-advised to
steer clear of them after 1934. Even the Steuben Society felt
constrained to repudiate the Bund.[14] Ambassador Dieckhoff,
recognizing the anti-Nazi orientation of the majority of German-
Americans, advised his superiors not to try to organize any movement among them lest the few that still remained friendly should
fall away. Associated as it was with Nazism, pro-Germanism became even less popular in the 1930's—a trend indicated in the fact
that thirty German-language newspapers and periodicals ceased
publication between 1933 and 1939 and circulation dropped off
by about 250,000 to a level barely over 1,000,000.[15]

Just as pro-Germanism was degraded by its association with
Nazism, so was the isolationist movement of 1939–41 damaged
by the support it received from such elements as the Bund and
other noisy native-fascist groups like the Christian Mobilizers.
According to Selig Adler, their vicious actions convinced many
people that Hitlerism posed a real threat to American internal
security as well as to peaceful international relations.[16] Crude and
unsophisticated, these groups proved easy targets for Americans
who believed that isolationism served as a convenient cover for
the work of disloyal pro-Germans. It is significant that Viereck
himself found it necessary to hide behind isolationist congressmen in 1940–41; such had not been the case in 1914–16. This
difference indicates what had happened to the respectability of
pro-Germanism in the meantime.

Finally, there is the psychological problem of classifying his
type of behavior. His approach differed in many ways from that of
other American supporters of fascism or Nazism. He was not, for
instance, an ideologist like Lawrence Dennis, nor a crude, un-
lettered bully like Fritz Kuhn of the German-American Bund.
Nor did he wish to import fascism into America. And he did not
fit the patterns usually associated with the Nazi personality. He
was certainly unusual, for example, in his kinship to the Hohen-

14 Ibid.
15 Ibid.
16 Adler, *Isolationist Impulse*, p. 294–95.

zollerns, his prominence as a romantic poet, his friendships with outstanding individuals of Jewish descent, his promotion of the Freudian view of man, his upper-middle-class manners, and his reputation as a well-traveled journalist and interviewer of great men. These features hardly constituted a Nazi "syndrome." Nor was Viereck the possessor of an "authoritarian personality," as described by psychologist T. W. Adorno and his associates. He was not "rigid and unimaginative," nor "herd minded," nor a "moral purist," nor subject as a child to harsh discipline by a domineering father.[17] Nor, as another stereotype of Nazism would have it, did he come from a lower-middle class fearful of being "proletarianized."

Since Viereck did not fit these patterns, one might conclude that he was bought. Yet this, too, lacks validity. One should remember that he could have remained well paid as a contributor to *Liberty* magazine and other journals, had he eschewed his favoritism for the Nazi movement. Moreover, his sympathy for the Nazis was evident before he had a chance to profit from it.

It is difficult, then, to place Viereck into a conventional category that might offer ready-made explanations for his behavior. One must deal with the fact that he possessed a peculiar constellaton of habits and values, which, taken in conjunction with each other, moved him along the path he took. There were the strong emotional attachments and tendencies toward romanticism that were formed during his childhood and youth. Reinforcing these was his confusion about ultimate ends and about ethical and moral values—a confusion that he shared with many of his contemporaries. Repeatedly expressing doubts about the existence of any permanent moral truths, he committed himself to the more evident aesthetic values of beauty and of Eros, and later, when challenged to face the "untrue ethic" of Nazism, he replied, "What is truth?" and then proceeded to take up again the mantle of propagandist, a role in which he knew he excelled.

It is also especially important to note the arrested emotional

[17] See T. W. Adorno et al., *The Authoritarian Personality* (New York: Harper, 1950), and Samuel R. Flowerman, "Portrait of the Authoritarian Man," *New York Times Magazine*, April 23, 1950, pp. 9, 28–30.

development reflected in his tendency toward narcissistic behavior. Capable at times of charming such men as Sigmund Freud, George Bernard Shaw, and Edward M. House, Viereck nevertheless displayed a consistent habit of glorying in his own reflection and defending at all costs a distorted, idealized, and romanticized image of himself and the world. It was apparent in his poetry and novels as well as his publicity work, and it made him largely impervious to either logic or moral arguments, especially since he felt that he was destined or compelled to act in this way. In the crisis of the 1930's he successfully resisted the pressures of people, including close friends like Paul Eldridge and Fulton Oursler, who tried to open his eyes and mind to the evils of Nazism.

In the latter respect, his behavior was particularly remarkable in the late 1930's and early 1940's. One can understand why his established reputation brought him again to Germany's defense in 1933, but it is much more difficult to comprehend his later insistence in defying American public opinion and risking the loss of friends by maintaining a rigid loyalty to the cause of an increasingly hated regime. It is here that the concept of narcissism seems especially helpful, since personalities of this type usually find it relatively easy to ignore the promptings of the superego, which might be thought of as the conscience or the moral norms of the social environment. It may be, too, that this explanation of Viereck's behavior offers some insight into the behavior of other notorious publicists, extremely partisan journalists, or political extremists. This possibility, at least, might bear some further exploration.

Books

Adler, Selig. *The Isolationist Impulse: Its Twentieth Century Reaction*. London: Abelard-Schuman, Ltd., 1957.

Adorno, T. W., et al. *The Authoritarian Personality*. New York: Harper, 1950.

Arndt, Karl J., and Olson, May E. *German-American Newspapers and Periodicals, 1732–1955*. Heidelberg: Quelle and Meyer, 1961.

Bailey, Thomas. *A Diplomatic History of the American People*. New York: Appleton-Century-Crofts, 1964.

Baker, Ray Stannard. *Woodrow Wilson: Life and Letters, Facing War, 1915–1917*. Garden City, N.Y.: Doubleday, Doran and Co., 1937.

Barnes, Harry Elmer. *The Genesis of the World War*. New York: Alfred A. Knopf, 1926.

Beale, Howard K. *Theodore Roosevelt and the Rise of America to World Power*. Baltimore: Johns Hopkins University Press, 1956.

Bernstorff, Johann H. *My Three Years in America*. New York: Charles Scribner's Sons, 1920.

Bischoff, Ralph F. *Nazi Conquest through German Culture*. Cambridge: Harvard University Press, 1942.

Brooks, Sidney. *America and Germany, 1918–1925*. New York: Macmillan, 1925.

Bruntz, George G. *Allied Propaganda and the Collapse of the German Empire in 1918*. Stanford: Stanford University Press, 1938.

Cargill, Oscar. *Intellectual America: Ideas on the March*. New York: Macmillan, 1941.

Carr, Robert K. *House Committee on Un-American Activities, 1945–1950*. Ithaca, N.Y.: Cornell University Press, 1952.

Child, Clifton J. *The German-Americans in Politics, 1914–1917*. Madison: University of Wisconsin Press, 1939.

Collier, Price. *Germany and the Germans from the American Point of View*. New York: Charles Scribner's Sons, 1914.

Compton, James V. *The Swastika and the Eagle: Hitler, the United States and the Origins of World War II*. Boston: Houghton Mifflin, 1967.

Davidson, Frank P., and Viereck, George S., Jr. *Before America Decides: Foresight in Foreign Affairs*. Cambridge: Harvard University Press, 1938.

Derounian, Arthur [also under pseud. John R. Carlson]. *Under Cover: My Four Years in the Nazi Underworld of America*. New York: E. P. Dutton, 1943.

Dodd, William E., and Dodd, Martha. *Ambassador Dodd's Diary, 1933–1938*. New York: Harcourt, Brace & Co., 1941.

Doob, Leonard W. *Propaganda: Its Psychology and Technique*. New York: Henry Holt and Co., 1935.

Dulles, Foster Rhea. *America's Rise to World Power, 1898–1954*. New York: Harper and Bros., 1955.

Farago, Ladislas. *German Psychological Warfare*. New York: Committee for National Morale, 1941.

Faust, Albert B. *The German Element in the United States*. Vol. II. Boston: Houghton Mifflin, 1909.

Fay, Sidney. *The Origins of the World War*. New York: Macmillan, 1929.

Fischer, Fritz. *Germany's Aims in the First World War*. New York: W. W. Norton, 1967.

Freud, Ernst, ed. *Letters of Sigmund Freud*. New York: McGraw-Hill, 1964.

Frye, Alton. *Nazi Germany and the American Hemisphere, 1933–1941*. New Haven: Yale University Press, 1967.

Germany Speaks. London: Butterworth, 1938.

Gerson, Louis L. *The Hyhenate in Recent American Politics and Diplomacy*. Lawrence: University of Kansas Press, 1964.

Hart, Albert B., and Ferleger, Herbert R., ed. *Theodore Roosevelt Cyclopedia*. New York: Roosevelt Memorial Association, 1941.

Hawgood, John A. *The Tragedy of German-America*. New York: G. P. Putnam's Sons, 1940.

Hoke, Henry. *Black Mail*. New York: Reader's Book Service, 1944.

Hughes, H. Stuart. *Consciousness and Society: The Reorientation of European Social Thought, 1890–1930*. New York: Random House, 1958.

Johnson, Walter. *The Battle against Isolation*. Chicago: University of Chicago Press, 1944.

Jonas, Manfred. *Isolationism in America*. Ithaca: Cornell University Press, 1966.

Jones, Ernest. *Sigmund Freud: Life and Work*. Vol. III: *The Last Phase, 1919-1939*. London: Hogarth Press, 1957.

Kürenberg, Joachim von. *The Kaiser: A Life of William II, Last Emperor of Germany*. Trans. H. T. Russell and Herta Hagen. New York: Simon and Schuster, 1955.

Lafore, Laurence. *The Long Fuse: An Interpretation of the Origins of World War I*. New York: J. B. Lippincott, 1965.

Landau, Henry. *The Enemy Within: The Inside Story of German Sabotage in America*. New York: G. P. Putnam's Sons, 1937.

Langer, William L., and Gleason, S. Everett. *The Undeclared War, 1940-1941*. New York: Harper and Bros., 1953.

Lasswell, Harold D. *Propaganda Technique in the World War*. New York: Alfred A. Knopf, 1927.

Lasswell, H. D., and Childs, Harwood L. *Propaganda and Dictatorship: A Collection of Papers*. Princeton: D. C. Poole, 1936.

Lasswell, Harold, et al. *Propaganda and Promotional Activities: An Annotated Bibliography*. Minneapolis: University of Minnesota Press, 1935.

Lavine, Harold. *Fifth Column in America*. New York: Doubleday, Doran and Co., 1940.

Lavine, Harold, and Wechsler, James. *War Propaganda and the United States*. New Haven: Yale University Press, 1940.

Lewisohn, Ludwig. *Expression in America*. New York: Harper and Bros., 1932.

Link, Arthur S. *Wilson: The Struggle for Neutrality, 1914-1915*. Princeton: Princeton University Press, 1960.

Lumley, Frederick E. *The Propaganda Menace*. New York: Century Company, 1933.

McAdoo, William G. *Crowded Years: The Reminiscences of William G. McAdoo*. Boston: Houghton Mifflin, 1931.

MacKay, Kenneth Campbell. *The Progressive Movement of 1924*. New York: Columbia University Press, 1947.

Mackenzie, Alexander J. *Propaganda Boom*. London: John Gifford, 1938.

Marx-Engels Werke. Berlin: Dietz Verlag, 1967.

May, Henry F. *The End of American Innocence*. Chicago: Quadrangle Books, 1964.

Mehring, Franz. *Geschichte der Deutschen Sozial-Demokratie*. Berlin: Dietz Verlag, 1960.

Mock, James R. *Censorship, 1917*. Princeton: Princeton University Press, 1941.

Mock, James R., and Larson, Cedric. *Words That Won the War: The Story of the Committee on Public Information, 1917–1919*. Princeton: Princeton University Press, 1939.

Morison, Elting. *The Letters of Theodore Roosevelt*. Cambridge: Harvard University Press, 1954.

O'Connor, Richard. *The German-Americans: An Informal History*. Boston: Little, Brown, 1968.

Ogden, August R. *The Dies Committee*. Washington: Catholic University of America Press, 1943.

Papen, Franz von. *Memoirs*. Trans. Brian Connell. New York: E. P. Dutton, 1953.

Peterson, Horace C. *Propaganda for War: The Campaign against American Neutrality, 1914–1917*. Norman: University of Oklahoma Press, 1939.

Peterson, Horace C., and Fite, Gilbert C. *Opponents of War, 1917–1918*. Madison: University of Wisconsin Press, 1957.

Ponsonby, Arthur. *Falsehood in Wartime*. London: George Allen and Unwin, 1928.

Pringle, Henry F. *Theodore Roosevelt: A Biography*. New York: Blue Ribbon Books, 1931.

Riess, Curt. *Total Espionage*. New York: G. P. Putnam's Sons, 1941.

Rogge, O. John. *The Official German Report*. New York: Thomas Yoseloff, 1961.

Roper, Elmo. *You and Your Leaders: Their Actions and Your Reactions, 1936–1956*. New York: William Morrow, 1957.

Roth, Guenther. *The Social Democrats in Imperial Germany*. Totowa, N.J.: Bedminster Press, 1963.

Rowan, Richard W. *Secret Agents against America*. New York: Doubleday, Doran and Co., 1939.

St. George, Maximilian, and Dennis, Lawrence. *A Trial on Trial: The Great Sedition Trial of 1944*. Washington: National Civil Rights Committee, 1946.

Sayers, Michael, and Kahn, Albert E. *Sabotage! The Secret War against America*. New York: Harper and Bros., 1942.

Squires, James D. *British Propaganda at Home and in the United States from 1914 to 1917*. Cambridge: Harvard University Press, 1935.

Stern, Fritz. *The Politics of Cultural Despair: A Study in the Rise of the Germanic Ideology*. Garden City, N.Y.: Doubleday, 1965.

Stout, Rex, ed. *The Illustrious Dunderheads*. New York: Alfred A. Knopf, 1942.

Strong, Donald. *Organized Anti-Semitism in America*. Washington: American Council on Public Affairs, 1941.

Symonds, John. *The Great Beast: The Life of Aleister Crowley*. London: Rider and Co., 1951.

Tauber, Kurt R. *Beyond Eagle and Swastika*. 2 vols. Middletown, Conn.: Wesleyan University Press, 1967.

Untermeyer, Louis. *The New Era in American Poetry*. New York: Henry Holt and Co., 1919.

Tansill, Charles. *Back Door to War: The Roosevelt Foreign Policy, 1933–1941*. Chicago: Henry Regnery Co., 1952.

Usher, Roland G. *Pan-Germanism*. New York: Houghton Mifflin Co., 1913.

Viereck, George S. *All Things Human*. London: Duckworth, 1950.

———. *As They Saw Us: Foch, Ludendorff and Other Leaders Write Our War History*. Garden City, N.Y.: Doubleday, Doran and Co., 1929.

———. *The Candle and the Flame: Poems*. New York: Moffatt, Yard and Co., 1912.

———. *Confessions of a Barbarian*. New York: Moffatt, Yard and Co., 1910.

———. *Debate between George S. Viereck and Cecil Chesterton*. New York: Fatherland Corporation, 1915.

———. *A Game at Love and Other Plays*. New York: Moffatt, Yard and Co., 1912. (First published, New York: Brentano, 1906.)

———. *Gedichte*. New York: Progressive Printing Co., 1904.

———. *Glimpses of the Great*. London: Duckworth, 1930.

———. *Gloria: A Novel*. London: Duckworth, 1952.

———. *The Haunted House and Other Poems*. Girard, Kans.: Haldemann-Julius Co., 1924.

———. *The House of the Vampire*. New York: Moffatt, Yard and Co., 1907.

———. *The Kaiser on Trial*. New York: Greystone Press, 1937.

———. *Men into Beasts*. New York: Fawcett Publications, 1952.

——. *My Flesh and Blood: A Lyric Autobiography with Indiscreet Annotations.* New York: H. Liveright, 1931.

——. *Nineveh and Other Poems.* New York: Moffatt, Yard and Co., 1907.

——. *The Nude in the Mirror.* New York: Woodford Press, 1953.

Corners, George F. [George S. Viereck]. *Rejuvenation: How Steinach Makes People Young.* New York: T. Seltzer, 1923.

Viereck, George S. *Roosevelt: A Study in Ambivalence.* New York: Jackson Press, 1919.

——. *The Seven against Man.* Scotch Plains, N.J.: Flanders Hall, 1941.

——. *Songs of Armageddon and Other Poems.* New York: M. Kennerly, 1916.

——. *Spreading Germs of Hate.* New York: H. Liveright, 1930.

——. *The Strangest Friendship in History: Woodrow Wilson and Colonel House.* New York: H. Liveright, 1932.

——. *The Temptation of Jonathan.* Boston: Christopher Publishing House, 1938.

——. *The Three Sphinxes, and Other Poems.* Girard, Kans.: Haldemann-Julius Co., 1924.

Viereck, George S., and Eldridge, Paul. *The Invincible Adam.* London: Duckworth, 1932.

——. *My First Two Thousand Years: Autobiography of the Wandering Jew.* New York: Macaulay Co., 1928.

——. *Prince Pax.* London: Duckworth, 1933.

——. *Salome, the Wandering Jewess: My First Two Thousand Years.* New York: Horace Liveright, 1930.

Viereck, Peter. *Metapolitics: From the Romantics to Hitler.* New York: Alfred A. Knopf, 1941.

Wagenknecht, Edward. *The Seven Worlds of Theodore Roosevelt.* New York: Longmans, Green, 1958.

Wilde, Oscar. *Intentions.* London: Unicorn Press, 1945. (First published, London: Osgood, McIlvaine and Co., 1891.)

William II. *My Memoirs: 1878–1918.* London: Cassell and Co., 1922.

Wimsatt, William K., Jr., and Brooks, Cleanth. *Literary Criticism: A Short History.* New York: Alfred A. Knopf (Vintage Books), 1967.

Wittke, Carl. *German-Americans and the World War.* Columbus: Ohio State Archeological and Historical Society, 1936.

——. *The German-Language Press in America.* Lexington: University of Kentucky Press, 1957.

Articles and Periodicals

[Abbot, Leonard]. "The Poetry of George S. Viereck: An Appreciation by Leonard Abbot," *Book News Monthly* XXVI (September, 1907): 31–34.

Adler, Selig. "The War Guilt Question and American Disillusionment, 1918–1928," *Journal of Modern History* XXIII (March, 1951): 10–23.

American Monthly. 1921–29.

"American Sympathies in the War," *Literary Digest* XLIX (November 14, 1914): 939–41, 974–78.

"American Outcry at German Jew-Baiting," *Literary Digest*, April 1, 1933, pp. 3–4, 28–29.

"The Anti-Nazi Boycott," *The World Tomorrow* XVI (September 28, 1933): 535.

"Chesterton-Viereck," *New Republic*, January 23, 1915, pp. 7–8.

Dernburg, Bernhard. "The Ties that Bind America and Germany," *World's Work* XXIX (December, 1914): 186–89.

Der Deutsche Vorkämpfer. 1907–10.

"Do the German-Americans Dictate Our Foreign Policy?" *Review of Reviews* XLI (March, 1910): 349–50.

Eldridge, Paul. "Of Nazi-ism in the United States," *Panorama*, February, 1934, pp. 6–7.

Eulau, Heinz. "Sedition Trials: 1944," *New Republic*, March 13, 1944, pp. 337–39.

"Ex-Kaiser's Friend again in Political Hot Water," *Newsweek*, August 15, 1938, p. 11.

The Fatherland. 1914–17.

Fay, Sidney. "New Light on the Origins of the World War, I., Berlin and Vienna, to July 29," *American Historical Review* XXV (July, 1920): 616–39.

"Flanders Hall Investigated by Grand Jury," *Publisher's Weekly*, October 4, 1941, p. 1385.

Flowerman, S. H. "Portrait of the Authoritarian Man," *New York Times Magazine*, April 23, 1950, p. 9.

German Library of Information. *Facts in Review.* August, 1939–June, 1941.

Gertz, Elmer. "A Bizarre Fellowship," *The Chicago Jewish Forum* III (Winter, 1944–45): 97.

Haldemann-Julius Monthly. 1925.

Hamilton, Clayton. "George Sylvester Viereck's Verse and Prose," *The Bookman*, June, 1907, pp. 426–27.

Heyn, Edward. "The War Spirit in Germany," *Harper's Weekly* LV (October 7, 1911): 17.

House, Edward. "Is England Forming an Alliance with Japan?" *Liberty*, December 22, 1934, pp. 5–6.

The International. 1912–16.

"Israel to Boycott Germany," *Literary Digest*, September 1, 1934, p. 20.

Jonas, Manfred. "Pro-Axis Sentiment and American Isolationism," *The Historian* XXIX (February, 1967): 221–37.

Kimball, W. F. "Dieckhoff and America: A German's View of German-American Relations," *The Historian* XXVII (February, 1965): 218–43.

Liberty magazine. 1927–39.

Lutz, Ralph H. "Studies of World War Propaganda, 1914–1933," *Journal of Modern History* V (1933): 496–516.

McMillen, Neil R. "Pro-Nazi Sentiment in the United States, March, 1933–March, 1934," *Southern Quarterly*, October, 1963, pp. 48–70.

Muensterberg, Hugo. "The Germans at School," *Popular Science Monthly* LXXIX (December, 1911): 602–14.

———. "The American College for Germany," *Science* XXVI (September 20, 1907): 361–68.

Monroe, Harriet. "The Viereck Incident," *Poetry* XIII (February, 1919): 265–67.

New York American newspaper. August, 1923; June–November, 1926; July, 1927; September–December, 1929; 1930–32.

New York Evening Post. 1915.

New York Times. 1909, 1914–62.

New York World. 1915.

Notman, Otis [Madeleine Doty]. "Viereck, Hohenzollern?" *New York Times-Saturday Review of Literature*, June 29, 1907, p. 413.

O'Sheel, Shaemas. "The Return of George Sylvester Viereck," *The World*, April 13, 1930.

Parker, Gilbert. "The United States and the War," *Harper's Magazine* CXXXVI (March, 1918): 521–31.

Review of Reviews XXXI (June, 1905): 768.

Rundschau Zweier Welten. 1911–12.

"Spotlight on Viereck," *Newsweek*, September 29, 1941, p. 17.

"Talk of the Town," *New Yorker*, June 15, 1940, pp. 15–16.

"To George Viereck (Personal)," [Open letter from Upton Sinclair], *Nation*, November 29, 1941, p. 551.

"Trial of the Viereckites," *New Republic*, January 4, 1943, p. 21.

"Viereck Kisses the Rod," *Nation*, April 25, 1934, p. 460.

Viereck, George S. "Bernard Shaw's Paean on Bolshevism," *New York American*, July 17, 1927, p. E-1.

————. "Einstein Sees Economic Reorganization Needed to Revive Prosperity in Germany," *New York American*, January 4, 1931, p. E-2.

————. "Forging Swords into Dumbells," [Interview with President von Hindenburg], *Liberty*, May 5, 1928, pp. 7–9.

[Viereck, George S.]. "Freud's First Interview on Psychoanalysis," *New York American*, August 19, 1923, p. ME-3.

————. "George Bernard Shaw in a Colloquy with George Sylvester Viereck: A Final Statement of Faith," *Liberty*, August 1, 1936, pp. 18–19.

————. "German-American to His Adopted Country," [Poem], *Current Opinion* LXI (July, 1916): 56.

————. "Germany Revisited," *Freude und Arbeit*, February, 1939, pp. 97–99.

————. "Germany Revisited," *The Independent*, September, 1956, p. 8.

————. "Hitler the German Explosive," *American Monthly* XV (October, 1923): 235–38.

————. "How Freud Unveils the Subconscious Mind," *New York American*, August 26, 1923, p. LII-6.

————. "Iron Chancellor," [Poem], *Literary Digest* XL (April 17, 1915): 888, and *Current Opinion* LVIII (May, 1915): 357.

————. "Is Oscar Wilde Living or Dead?" *Critic* XLVII (July, 1905): 86–88.

————. "It Can Happen Again," *Liberty*, April 17, 1937, pp. 29–32.

————. Letter to Editor, *Independent* LXIX (August 11, 1910): 305.

————. "The Loeb-Leopold Case and Psycho-Analysis," *Haldemann-Julius Monthly*, February, 1925, pp. 151–59.

————. "Master Spy Tells Almost All," *American Mercury* LXXXV (December, 1957): 137–40.

————. "Modern Germany—Mad?" *Arena* XXXVII (May, 1907): 566–70.

————. "Mussolini Knew ... Twelve Years Ago," *Social Justice*, May 9, 1938, p. 7.

————. "Other Side of the Moon," *Current Literature* XL (June, 1906): 675–78.

————. "Prisoners of Utopia," *Saturday Evening Post*, December 14, 1929, pp. 22–23, 175–81.

————. "Pyatiletka," *Saturday Evening Post*, January 18, 1930, pp. 17, 83–85, 89.

————. "Reason Alone Can Cure Ills of Social Organism: Shaw," *New York American*, June 13, 1926, pp. 1, 11.

————. "Russia Marks Time," *Saturday Evening Post*, November 30, 1929, pp. 14–15, 94.

————. "Surveying Life at Seventy," [Interview with Sigmund Freud], *American Monthly*, October, 1927, p. 10.

————. "Thomas Mann Says: Psychoanalysis Is the New Gospel of Emancipation," *New York American*, December 8, 1929, p. L-I-1.

————. "War Propaganda," *Saturday Evening Post*, June 15, June 22, June 29, July 27, and August 17, 1929.

————. "We Can Beat Dictators at Their Own Game," *Nation's Business* XXVI (April, 1938): 16–21, 66–68.

————. "The Web of the Red Spider," *Liberty*, June 17, June 24, July 1, and July 8, 1933.

Wickets, Donald F. [G. S. Viereck]. "What the Dies Committee Overlooked," *Liberty*, December 24 and December 31, 1938, January 7 and January 14, 1939.

Viereck, George S. "What Life Means to the Kaiser," *Liberty*, October 15, 1927, pp. 79, 81–82.

————. "What Will Hitler Do Next?" *Liberty*, May 14, 1938, pp. 4–5.

————. "When I Take Charge: Hitler Shows His Hand," *Liberty*, July 9, 1932, pp. 4–7.

Wickets, Donald F. [G. S. Viereck]. "Will the Catholic Church Be Hitler's Waterloo?" *Liberty*, February 4, 1939, pp. 6–7.

Viereck, George S., and House, Edward M. "Seas Must Be Free, Says Colonel E. M. House," *New York American*, December 29, 1929, p. E-1.

Viereck's magazine. 1917–21.

"The War of Nerves: U.S. Front," *Fortune* XXII (October, 1940): 47–51.

Washington Post. 1941–43.

"What Hitler's Rule Means to the World," *Literary Digest*, April 8, 1933, pp. 1–2.

Wickware, Francis S. "What We Think about Foreign Affairs," *Harper's* CLXXIX (September, 1939), 397–406.

Wittenberg, Ernest. "The Thrifty Spy on the Sixth Avenue El," *American Heritage* XVII (December, 1965): 60–64.

Government Documents

George Sylvester Viereck v. U.S.A. 458 U.S. 1–9 (1943).

Congressional Record. Vols. LVII, Pt. 2; LXI, Pt. 6; LXV, Pts. 3, 5, and 11; LXXXIII and Appendix; LXXXIV–LXXXVI; LXXXIX, Pt. 2.

U.S. House of Representatives. Special Committee on Un-American Activities. *Hearings, Investigation of Nazi Propaganda Activities and Investigation of Certain Other Propaganda Activities.* 73d Cong., 2d Sess., 1934.

U.S. House of Representatives. Special Committee on Un-American Activities. *Hearings, Investigations of Un-American Propaganda Activities in the United States.* 77th Cong., 1st Sess., 1940.

U.S. House of Representatives. Special Committee on Un-American Activities. *Hearings, Investigations of Un-American Propaganda Activities in the United States.* Appendix, Pt. III, 76th Cong., 3d Sess., 1940.

U.S. House of Representatives. Special Committee on Un-American Activities. *Preliminary Digest and Report on the Un-American Activities of Various Nazi Organizations and Individuals in the U.S., Including Diplomatic Consular Agents of the German Government.* Appendix, Pt. II, 76th Cong., 3d Sess., 1940.

U.S. House of Representatives. Special Committee on Un-American Activities. *Report on Axis Front Movement in the United States.* Appendix, Pt. VII, 1941.

U.S. Senate. Subcommittee of the Committee on Judiciary. *Hearings on the National German-American Alliance.* 65th Cong., 2d Sess., 1918.

U.S. Senate. Subcommittee on the Judiciary. *Hearings on Brewing and Liquor Interests and German and Bolshevik Propaganda.* Sen. Doc. 62, 66th Cong., 1st Sess., 1919.

U.S. State Department. *Documents on German Foreign Policy, 1918–1945.* Series C, Vols. III and IV; Series D, Vols. VIII, IX, XI, and XII.

U.S. *Statutes at Large.* Vol. LII, Ch. 327.

U.S. v. *Joseph McWilliams, et al.* District Court, D.C. Appendix to Appellant's Brief, No. 9438, 1946.

U.S. v. *McWilliams, et al.* 163 F. 2d 697 (1946).

Viereck, Louis. "German Instruction in American Schools," *Report of [U.S.] Commissioner of Education*, 1901. Vol. I, pp. 531–708.

Viereck v. *U.S.* 130 F. 2d 945 (1942).

Viereck v. *U.S.* 139 F. 2d 847 (1944).

Other Sources

Archives of Federal District Court, Washington, D.C., Criminal Case Nos. 68584 and 71674.

Garrison Manuscripts. Harvard University, Houghton Library. Letters between Oswald Garrison Villard and G. S. Viereck from 1919 to 1945.

Gertz, Elmer. "The Stormy Petrel: Being the Life, Writings and Motives of George Sylvester Viereck." Unpublished holograph MS, 1936. (Typescript version was retitled "Odyssey of a Barbarian.")

Gertz Manuscripts. Manuscripts Division, Library of Congress.

Hamilton, Florence. "The Man with the Hoe: The Poet and the Problem, The Intellectual Biography of Edwin Markham." Unpublished MS, 1937.

Viereck, George S. "More Lives Than One." Unpublished, undated autobiography. (Peter Viereck Personal Files.)

————. Scrapbook. New York City Public Library.

Viereck Manuscripts. Special Collections Department, State University of Iowa Library.

Viereck Manuscripts. Harvard University Library. Letters from Kaiser Wilhelm II to G. S. Viereck between May, 1923, and January, 1929.

George S. Viereck Papers, Edward M. House Collection, Yale University Library.

Woodberry Manuscripts. Harvard University Library. Eight letters between George E. Woodberry and G. S. Viereck from 1907 to 1913.